RED
→ RED
→ W WITHDRAWN
→ Red.

VENETIAN MASTERS

Copyright © Bidisha, 2008

All rights reserved.

Summersdale Publishers Ltd
46 West Street
Chichester
West Sussex
PO19 1RP
UK

www.summersdale.com

Printed and bound in Great Britain

ISBN: 1-84024-634-0
ISBN 13: 978-1-84024-634-6

VENETIAN MASTERS

Under the Skin of the City of Love

Chapter One

On the bus from Treviso Airport to Venice I can see square, shuttered, chalkily tinted villas behind long paths and spiked gates. Everything's dry and sunny. At a crossing I spot a young man on a bicycle, a brown-haired angel beamed down from Planet Chic: dark brown slim trousers, a slightly lighter brown fitted jacket, an olive green shirt buttoned up to the top, charcoal grey waistcoat, leather satchel. Slim, lovely face and abundant dark, wavy hair, straight out of a cigar advert. I'm visiting Venice for the first time, staying at a palazzo owned by the family of my best friend, Stefania.

I arrive at the bus station at Piazzale Roma, get off and immediately feel the May heat. The sun's fat in the sky and dripping like syrup. I don't log much except the grimy smell of exhaust fumes, the number of buses and the sun shining off them. This is the western corner of Venice, attached to the big spiral car park at Tronchetto, the motorway and the single route to the mainland. I make for the green-topped shelter where I'm meant to meet Stefania's childhood friend Ginevra – Stefania's at a meeting in Rome today. An older couple in their sixties, turtle-like, in glowing chocolate brown furs (never let the climate stop you wearing your money), kid gloves and dark shades, pointedly don't get out of my way when I try to stagger past with my huge sausage-shaped sports bag. They stand like the king and queen in a deck of cards, holding hands across the pathway.

Eventually Ginevra and I spot each other. She comes forward and asks me mildly how the journey was and if I want anything. Ginevra's very pretty, big-handed and tall and slender, caramel-coloured long hair with a fringe, tortoiseshell-framed glasses and pale, dry skin. Marvel at the elegance: her clothes match her colouring perfectly, fawn cord trousers, caramel fitted leather jacket, green silk scarf. I give Ginevra my rucksack and take the sausage bag myself. We're due to drop everything off at Stefania's apartment in Cannaregio, in the north of the city.

'Here it is not so beautiful,' says Ginevra regretfully, in English, in her light, cultured, descending voice.

'It's very beautiful,' I say shortly. 'The light. But I know that's a cliché.'

'But I do not see you looking so astonished...'

'No, but I am. I can't believe I'm here, at last.'

'This area is very touristic,' says Ginevra slightingly. 'All the prices are times four than the prices for Venetians. Including for other Italian tourists. When I order I must be sure that the shopkeepers hear my Venetian accent. Then they pretend that they are doing you a special deal and you are not to tell anyone about your discount... We can go by vaporetto – water bus – or we can go by walking, what you prefer?'

'Let's walk. I'm not tired.'

What is there around me? A lot of young people (none with acne), large, flat, stony buildings, skinny streets, easy shallow bridges, paving, marble, bright tilting water, a sweet salt-smell everywhere.

'We keep right? To the right? That is very Venetian,' Ginevra says as we walk. She guides me away from a large white bridge that's too crowded. 'In Venice you must know the secondary streets, or there are too many people.'

We turn aside and follow a thin, shadowy passageway, emerging into a small, empty square with silent brown buildings on all sides. We cross it and go down another alley, and onwards.

'Stefania lives in one of the most beautiful palaces in Venice, on the Canal Grande,' Ginevra says, 'and below her live her parents, and next door lives the brother of her mother – her uncle.'

'I like that system, of extended families.'

'Yes, in this situation you can have privacy when you want and you can have company when you want.'

Stefania's parents are called Lucrezia Ritter and Gregorio Barone. I met them a couple of times in London and they're both extremely elegant. Lucrezia's a political theory professor (currently at a conference in Turin) and Gregorio professes about the history of medicine.

We arrive at a small, cool square where the houses, like the flagstones below, are a smart grey. The main doors have metal grilles, brass buzzers and engraved brass name plaques – these families aren't going anywhere in a hurry. Ginevra lets me in and we take a breather before climbing the marble stairs. The bottom floor, level with the waters of the Canal Grande – which we sense and which glows outside the glass doors on the other side – is kept dark and used as a storeroom.

The hallway's a blinding white, the marble stairs are sharp and high. We pass two heavy white doors and go on up to an airy landing with a skylight. We unlock two double-width, double-height oak doors, and then I see Stefania's apartment for the first time: large, empty, classic, with terracotta floors and shuttered windows all along, sparse expensive furniture, everything heavy, everything beautiful.

'Stefania's *rich*,' I say bluntly, in surprise.

'She is a modest woman,' says Ginevra with a smile. 'You should see the furniture that they have in the... store? The up-room? The attic. Every piece is ancient.'

'How much is a decent apartment here, to buy?' I ask, looking around.

'About four hundred thousand euros at the least, and then you pay for it to be restored. Venice is one of the most expensive cities in Italy. And restoration costs a lot because you can only use Venetian men who understand these buildings.'

She leads me into the living room, which is furnished with a white daybed, a small desk, an ugly red armchair and bookcases full of philosophy and film theory books.

'Now I will show you the most beautiful – see – look?' says Ginevra.

'View?'

'Yes, the most beautiful view. We *open* – we open the shutters.'

So we do, and I gaze out limply. Behold the Canal Grande for the first time: a slow curve lit with milky silver-blue daylight over smoke-blue glinting water, with slices of pale pink, pale yellow and buff-coloured palaces on the other side and the statue-encrusted church of San Eustachio on the opposite bank – seagulls on saints' heads.

'Stefania's father told me to reserve a place at a restaurant for tonight, for the three of us. Or if you are too tired?' Ginevra asks.

'No, I'd love to have dinner – that's *exactly* what I'd like to do. But I feel bad about you going to all this effort. If you have something to do?'

'No, no. Please. It is no effort. And, you know, I recently graduate –'

'Congratulations!'

'Thank you. So I am now on my vacation.'

As she relaxes, Ginevra's English becomes perfect. It's the early evening and we decide to go for a walk before dinner, passing through clattering streets full of shops, cafes and people, then alleys barely the width of my shoulders. I make my first social distinctions: Venetians skirt noiselessly past each other with a look of contempt in the corner of their eyes; tourists stumble and apologise, clutching soggy maps and reeking of anxiety. The American families are huge – sporty huge or fat huge, but all huge. The English families are tense, very tense. The high incidence of good-looking things puts me into a bit of a stupor. Everywhere I turn there's something lovely and forgotten, the curve of a railing, a scroll of white stone around a doorway, the crisp font of engraved names. Even the pattern of mould around the slimy wellheads looks good.

'Be careful of the dog shit,' says Ginevra suddenly, taking me by the collar and steering me around a smeared paving stone. 'It is everywhere in Venice. You are supposed to pick it up but some old people do not bother. And there are a lot of old people in Venice. And they all have dogs.'

'Do you have one yourself?'

She shakes her head: 'I have observed Stefania's dog for many years now. Nero. You will meet him. But I do not like it when they... do the bidet?'

'When they lick their balls?' I say bluntly. 'Me neither. I can never ignore it, I can't look away and I'm afraid I can *never* pretend that it's cute.'

We cross the famous Rialto Bridge, going up the middle between all the shops, which are tiny alcoves stuffed full like treasure chests, selling watches, jewels, leather, cashmere. People crowd the edges, staring down mesmerised. Here in the centre of the city, pinned over the Canal Grande, everything seems to be half bright air, half jewelled water – and all money. We go to the fish market, the *pescheria*, in the oldest part of town: wet shadows, sour, addictive fish smells, sluiced water, columns white and grey.

'This is the ancient heart of Venice,' says Ginevra. 'This building is number one,' she stamps on the ground, 'the first one that was here. The oldest palaces in Venice all have names, and they are known by their names.'

'You should write a history of Venice, Ginevra.'

'No, I can't, I am not like you and Stefania,' she demurs. 'Everything takes a long time for me. I took eight years to study for my first degree. This is the system in Italy, you can choose when you take your exams. We are the oldest students in Europe. I have never had a job.'

'But you were studying! And twenty-six is very young.'

'You are never too young to look for a job.'

'What did you graduate in?'

'European languages,' she says, with a look to mean 'and how useful was that?'

'Ah! You're a linguist, that's the best skill of all. Because you speak English beautifully... no, but you do... for God's sake,'

I say above her protests, 'you know all the difficult forms but you're dropping the easy ones.'

'When I meet – met – you at the station I could not remember the contrary of cold.'

'Opposite. Hot. The human mind is an amazing thing! You knew how to say "dog shit" but you forgot how to say "cold". What kind of job would you like to do?'

'Well, I love *books*,' she says with an expression of sudden rapture. 'But there are no – houses?'

'Publishing houses?'

'Yes. In Venice. Venice has no businesses like that. Only shops. Everything else is brought in.'

'So move. You could go to Rome or Milan. Or Paris, or London.'

'But they are too far. And there is an economic consideration. And I am shy... I do not think I have the power to make a good career, I always think and think and then I... lose jobs?'

'You let opportunities pass you by?'

'Yes, I am always too slow. I let opportunities pass.'

It's getting dark by now, a soft blue. The streets are very empty. We get up and go back over Rialto Bridge, which now has a strange glowing appearance, the stone seeming to spring up and hover between the banks.

'You notice there are very few people, because a lot of people come to work in Venice but they live outside. So these people you see,' Ginevra nods at a passing group, 'are Venetians.'

'And the ones who live outside live where?'

'In Mestre. And this is a place we must visit. A lot of cars, a lot of supermarkets, cement... I am being sarcastic.'

Ginevra, Gregorio (Stefania's father) and I are set to have dinner at La Zucca – The Pumpkin – a warm restaurant decorated all over with wooden slats like a ski cabin, with paintings, photos, sketches, pastels and the odd gouache of pumpkins on the walls. Gregorio greets me enthusiastically. He's short, square, always in a good mood and very dapper. He has a hoarse voice and bright blue eyes just like Stefania's, a bald head, a happy, gnome-like, interested face and expressive bushy eyebrows. He speaks excellent English.

We settle down and order. Talk turns to Ginevra's university dissertation, which won a Ca' Foscari Humanities Award at her graduation. She wrote a critical study of an obscure French man of letters:

'He wrote four travel books about Italy. Very few people have read them but they are very interesting because they represent a technical change in travel literature. It is between the Romantic journey of the young man on the grand tour and the technological inventions of the nineteenth century, the rise of the capitalist.'

'You should publish it,' I say immediately, and Gregorio nods.

'*Maybe*... my tutor was very enthusiastic. He told me to send it to the Centre for Cultural Research.'

'No, no. Be commercial,' I say.

'But it is academic writing. It has references to other books. I could publish a paper...' she replies doubtfully.

'Only three people in the world will read it,' says Gregorio severely, waving his hand as if to say piffle, small fry.

'You can explain all the references,' I tell Ginevra, 'make it more accessible. You can call it "Wine and Women in Italy",' at which Gregorio laughs loudly and claps me on the back, crying, 'Yes! Yes! "Wine and Women in Italy"!'

With a fairy-light pumpkin flan (the speciality of the place), a rabbit leg and a tiramisu in me I feel full of generosity and civility towards Venice. We wait for the bill, which Gregorio takes care of. Ah, the joy of dining with friends' parents. The waitress is a little dopey and we comment on it.

'If you do not like being a waitress you do not have to be a waitress. The doctor did not order you to be one,' says Ginevra to me in a low voice, and I laugh so accurately that the poor girl looks up and knows instantly what we've been saying.

After dinner we walk back through cool, dark Venice. Everything is stony, hard, black and echoing. Gregorio's full of conversation and throws me bite-sized history-drops, saying proudly, 'Ah! This is an interesting square. You see here the Arab influence, the Renaissance Florentine influence, and the Venetian. Beautiful Venice!'

As we walk I notice people, nearly everyone we pass, glancing at us, not shiftily but with a firm top-to-toe assessment as though we're prize poodles at a dog show. We pass a few chic clothes shops on the way back to Stefania's house. I'm struck by the perfection of the things, the pared-down cut and drape of cloth, the clever colours and soft leather.

'The new clothing shops are growing in this street like mushrooms,' says Ginevra next to me, 'but aren't the styles a little too perfect? A bit bourgeois.'

'What are we if not bourgeois?' I reply dryly.

'But we do not need to dress like we are the Parisian wives of rich men.'

I laugh and we walk on slowly. We get to the grey metal-smelling square and say goodbye to her. She lives about fifteen minutes' walk away, in the other half of Venice, across the Canal Grande. Gregorio unlocks the clanging metal door, leads me back up the marble stairs and shows me his and Lucrezia's apartment. Trying not to let my mouth drop open I log an enormous white space with marble floors, a glittering chandelier, a row of oversized vases, burnt orange and deep blue, a modernist lamp like a shard of metal, a fifteen-foot-long glass table with reclaimed church pews, an ancient chest and gold-framed faded mirror, rooms coming off the main space and long doors at the end, and through them the glimmer of white balcony walls.

'Come, come, I will show you the seaside,' says Gregorio, opening the balcony doors. We step out, right over the Canal Grande: ink water with neon white chips of light floating on it, a low-slung sickle moon. Silence, creaking.

We say goodnight and I go up to Stefania's apartment, where a rush of last-minute energy makes me unpack neatly and completely. Eventually I shower and go to bed, bathed in pale light. There's no sound at all, except for the water. Perfect sleep.

My best friend Stefania arrives from Rome early the next day and is in the kitchen making coffee by the time I wake up. Stefania and I met in 2001 when we were studying for our MScs together in London. I was loitering by the buffet table at the getting-to-know-you function on the first day when a beautiful stocky girl came up and started talking to me. After our dissertations were handed in she went back to Italy to produce films. Over the last year or so her rough blonde hair's grown down to her waist and with her full red cheeks, snub nose, dry gold skin and turquoise eyes she looks like a clever cartoon lion. We eat breakfast gazing through the kitchen window at the endless chinks of tiled peaked roofs. The sunlight's a joyful pinky-yellow.

Over the next ten days we establish a routine: coffee at a different sugary-smelling *pasticceria* (dainty cake 'n' coffee place), standing at the counter while all around me slim, tall, *soigné* natives choose from the dozens of bite-size delicacies on display. Then we meet Ginevra for a day of sights and walks followed by an aperitif at an *osteria*. I'm woken every morning by the sound of water and of boats going by, boatmen's cries, pearlescent light. As a general rule, Ginevra and Stefania speak to me in English, as do her parents; everything else happens in Italian. There is a certain poised Venetian way of doing things, I notice, and when we're in our group of three girls we are treated with unremitting gallantry, efficiency and clarity by everyone we encounter. Shopping and eating are to be done lightly, casually, not greedily; conversation is lively but not sleazy; vulgarity is frowned upon, moderation rewarded. Coffee is to be drunk during the day, good wine at night. And one must always be well dressed, otherwise social ostracism will follow. We have our own cafe, Caffè Rosso in Campo Santa Margherita, and our own bar/eats place, La Cantina on the Strada Nova. I can order a cup of coffee and understand about half of what I'm hearing, until someone addresses me directly.

For the first few days everything looks the same: the bridges, the alleys and sunny dusty squares, the shops all selling things for the body, if not shoes and clothes then bags, scarves, brooches, underwear, gloves. Dickens described Venice as being coiled, wound, turned in on itself like a spring. Not true. In fact, everything is spliced and stacked upright and then sprinkled with roof tiles. The map makes it all look like soft curve, a yin-yang melting in the sea, but once you're on the streets, squashed in amongst the houses and turning left and right randomly, you're like a mouse in a box of old books. The buildings only get taller, squarer, darker, flatter and more identical. To get away from this in between museum visits, I linger on benches by the two coasts or along the banks of the Canal Grande. Record the differences: water that sounds like laughter, water that sounds like keys or chains or shingle, water that sounds like a gunshot, water like an echo. I can never tell what things are here, bells or engines or voices, children or birds, water or machines, the noises reflect and change. The sound of a boat's engine is one single note deep in the water and sounds like a chair scraping across the floor.

One morning Stefania and Ginevra take me down to San Polo in the middle of Venice, on the other side of Rialto Bridge (what I think of as the other half of the biscuit), where the streets are narrower, churchy, crooked and dank and secretive. The stalls of Rialto market are garish with cheap clothes and 'Venezia'-logo sweatshirts, imported leather wallets and fruit stalls offering slices of watermelon, tubs of strawberries and segments of coconut for drooping visitors. We see a group of kids and parents walking out from a school – and this is a notable thing, the visibility and respect given to family life, resulting directly in the boisterous, charming, unafraid children themselves. Not right now though: one little girl of about six breaks away from the group, crying and sobbing. She wails something to her mother, who follows with a languorous, tolerant smile. Stef grins and says to me, 'She say, why you always give attention to the guests and never to *me*?'

A few skinny streets take us to a workshop, sooty and small, in which handmade leather novelty shoes are set out like ever more elaborate cakes in the window. There are plain gold eighteenth-century style slippers, long clown shoes with bobbles at the heels, coy side-buttoned Victorian boots, spats in pink and black. In the background is a young woman with frizzy dark hair, working a piece of fuchsia leather through a black iron sewing machine. Her face is peaceful and she wears a slight smile.

'She's the one who makes them all,' says Ginevra as we peer in. 'There's a story about her. When she was young she woke up one morning after a dream and said, "I need to make shoes...

I am *going* to make shoes." And she went to that workshop and said to the man, "Here I am. I want to learn." And he said, you know, "Oh, now, you are too young, you are a girl, go away and think about it, maybe do something else, get married, this isn't for you..." Anyway, she did a course, the famous course on how to make shoes – this was the best course in Italy. And three years later she came back, went to the workshop, knocked on the door and said to the man, "I did this course. Now train me." She wouldn't leave until he took her. Now she owns the business.'

Cheered as I am by this tale I don't say that if it had been a seventeen-year-old boy, fuelled by a dream and full of energy, who had come knocking, the man would have hauled him in, shaken him rapturously by the shoulders, kissed him on both cheeks, praised him for his initiative, introduced him to his father, his uncle and all his brothers and set him immediately to work, all without the famous three-year cobbling course.

We go to Campo Santa Margherita, the liveliest square in Venice, lined with bars and cafes, crossed with tourists, older people, kids, elegant families, tradesmen and builders pushing rattling wooden carts full of debris. There's a takeaway pizza place, Pizza Al Volo, a tobacconist/postcard/stamp place, a cheap shop selling a bit of everything from school exercise books to socks and plugs. Very dry ancient trees in the centre. Seagulls swoop hungrily around the fish stalls, which are being hosed down for the day. A priest in his fifties walks past looking harassed.

'I always wonder if priests really need to wear their costumes when they're just walking around town,' I say to Ginevra. 'Maybe they just do it...'

'To get women's attention?'

'Ha! No! I was going to say, to get a free coffee or something.'

'I went to a Catholic school and the priests were always old and – *ugh*,' she says while Stef nods in scowling agreement. 'They used to say, "What do you have to confess? Do not worry, come here and whisper it in my ear, whisper it to me," and I used to say, "Why don't we use the little box – "'

'The confessional,' I say.

'Yes, "Why don't we use the confessional?" and they used to say, "No, it's OK, just quickly say it to me, we do not need the confessional."'

'"Come and sit on my knee..."'

'Exactly. They may be priests but they are still... men.'

I nod. The various old priests and Benedictine (black robes) and Franciscan (brown robes) monks I've seen here do not appear to glow with goodness and love – or even, for that matter, health and vitality. They have a defensive, shifty way of walking, not quite breaking into a run, as though they want to get away from the bailiffs or a friend whom they owe a favour.

Venice also hosts some solo oddballs. There's the drunken red seafaring man in his fifties who chats in dialect and sells dragged-up bric-a-brac from his boat, which is moored in one of the canals near the Guggenheim. He stands in the boat with one foot up on the stone rim of the canal, displaying re-gilded photo frames and rusted pocket knives, his eyes watering rheumily in the heat. And then there's the chap who owns the antiques shop opposite Arca pizzeria. He's about thirty-five, six foot four, very skinny and pasty, dressed in a burgundy velvet jacket, green velvet trousers, a flowing white scarf, a black velvet waistcoat and a white lawn shirt, none of which really sit right. Long, extremely self-conscious, boneless face. His hair's cut in a ladies' bob with a fringe. He's like an antique exhibit himself, roosting deep inside his shop, turning an ivory pendant over and over in his hand and practising his English in an exquisite voice:

'If you don't like this one perhaps I can find you something more suitable.'

'Strange man,' I remark once we're out of the shop.

'But he is not normal,' says Stef darkly. 'He once come, came up to me to begin a conversation in a bar one night, and he said to me – this is supposed to be a normal conversation – "Oh, I am attracted by your eyes, they are so magnetic, they are calling me." Even though he is obviously gay. And I always see him dressed in this Oscar Wilde way, sometimes with a flower –'

She gesticulates.

'In his lapel?' I say.

'No, a sunflower with a long...'

'Stem?'

'Yes. In his hand.'

We cross the little canal from Campo Santa Margherita over into Campo San Barnaba, then walk to Accademia past the Toletta bookshops – novels, art, design and architecture books, all themselves wonderfully designed and piled high in the window. And inside the shops? Completely empty. Not a single customer. Thinking about it, I've seen very few people reading in Venice. Something about the city seems to draw one away from intellectual labour of any kind. It seems wrong to shun the view in order to stare at a printed page instead.

'It's shaming,' I say to Ginevra as we look in. 'Look how many books there are in translation. And you can see they've spent time making them look good. In England we don't have that. Very few foreign writers are read in translation.'

Ginevra nods and gives the lonely, misunderstood sigh of the long-term bookworm. Before we move on I notice something depressing. In the Italian literature section there are about forty books on display, stacked tight along the glass. Not one by a woman. And that morning, when I was reading the newspaper Stef's parents get, there were no women journalists, no women on the list of staff writers and no women mentioned in any article. Every news photograph was of a smiling man in a suit surrounded by other smiling men in suits. I wonder at the gallantry I've witnessed over the past few days − wonder if it's merely the surface reward for women's actual exclusion.

From the San Polo half of the city, the famed and actually quite hideous wooden bridge at Accademia (imagine a matchstick bridge made of very *large* matches) can be got to via a series of sharp turns and canal-crossings. We go down a narrow alley alongside a eurotrash art dealership, then get spat out at the base of the bridge, with the Galleria dell'Accademia on our right and some overpriced cafes on the left. The tourist places are identifiable by their garish canopies, too-slick staff and printed menus, the way the little bowls of crisps are ready and waiting on the tables. And the joke prices.

Stef, Ginevra and I climb the bridge and dawdle at the top. The sky and the water are the same colour, silver-speckled like an antique mirror, very soft to the eye. I watch the water push against the sides of the Canal Grande and feel morbidly hypnotised by it.

I meet plenty of Stef's acquaintances, all of whom are creative, chirpy, energetic, open-minded people just like her, and noticeably friendly towards me. The flow of my new friendships is stunted, however, by Stef continually having to turn to me and translate the conversation, which after all her labour often turns out to be something I wouldn't have been interested in hearing after all:

'No, sorry, just to translate into English: her sister boyfriend live, lives in Germany, and he is coming to visit next month and they are planning to take a trip by car to Florence or maybe Tuscany, so we are discussing about that.'

'Ah!' I nod and incline my face towards the conversation.

'Excuse me,' Stef will then say to me apologetically, in between bouts of translating the most boring parts of the proceedings, 'I have to speak Italian because I want to tell a story in a funny way.'

'Please!' I say. 'Tell the interesting bit in Italian.'

She buys me a *sprizz,* a signature drink here; despite my protests she's paid for nearly everything during these ten days. A *sprizz* is an orange-coloured translucent drink served with an olive and everyone, Stef tells me, has it in the early evening.

'You like it?' she asks. They're all looking at me kindly. We're in a bar, sitting outside while dusk falls.

'Um...' I give an imbecilic titter, 'sorry to be no fun but I'm afraid it tastes exactly like a very famous English cough medicine, so I do like it, but I can't drink it because it reminds me of that.'

We notice that the waiter, a pale boy with long dark hair and an angular face, dark eyes and pursed mouth like an Elizabeth Peyton portrait, is very beautiful and very self-conscious.

'You know he is Russian? Not an Italian boy,' says Stef. 'And he is a bit too much, no? We do not need a little performance every time we order a coffee.'

She asks me what I make of Venetians so far. I tell her that Londoners are more polite; there's a greater respect for space, perhaps out of a fear of being murdered otherwise. For example, a Venetian lady of seventy-odd standing squarely in the centre of the vaporetto wouldn't look at and wouldn't budge an inch (literally) for a young Chinese couple who had an enormous case to balance between them. She stood with her plump feet parted in their patent leather court shoes, her rigorously painted, almost lacquered, face fixed consciously to the view. They gave her looks of amazement which slid right off.

'You must remember that this is a small town and the people who live here have a small town mentality. They don't like outsiders, especially tourists,' says Stefania.

'On the plus side, I don't think there's anything in this city that isn't beautiful,' I say, 'except possibly the graffiti in that new quarter near the coast.'

'Eh, but you know most of it is done by, like, ten-year-old boys who think to be in New York. They are a little bit frustrate with living in a place like Venice... The bill has come,' says Stef morosely, 'so now we have to have the usual argument.'

'For God's sake, let me get this.'

'No. You are my guest.'

'So what? You're paying a high enough price by letting me invade your space for ten days.'

'It is only five euros.'

'Exactly! So let me pay it.'

'No, no, seriously Bidisha.'

'*Seriously*. That's what I'm saying... OK, that's it. I'm going to let you pay for everything and in ten years' time I'll buy you a car.'

Ginevra, Stefania and I dawdle back towards Stef's house. Her parents have invited me for dinner. It'll be the first time I see Lucrezia, Stef's mother, since I arrived. From San Polo we walk over the big white bridge outside the train station and follow the tourist trail, the Lista di Spagna, straight to Stef's house. This is garish Venice, only for the gullible: trashy shops, overpriced cafes, Internet points, flea-bitten hotels. It's the only direct route from the station straight to Rialto Bridge, so everyone takes it. There's no need to rush, we merely flow with the crowd, comfortable in the knowledge that all of us are going home to our dinners.

'So nice to have no cars. I don't miss them,' I say.

'You know what they say about driving in Rome?' says Stef. '"Scream and go."'

'Where are you going now?' I ask Ginevra.

'I will accompany you home and then go to my home for dinner.'

'Doesn't that mean you have to come all the way up, then go all the way back down?'

'I don't mind. I would rather be the servant than the master,' she jokes.

'Stef, I was wondering where all the poor people are,' I say after a few moments. 'There seems to be not much of a class system.'

'Yes, it is true that there are no poor people.' She breaks into Italian: 'Or at least no poor people in the way the British would understand them. We are not a vulgar society.' Back into English: 'The social divisions are very deep but very hidden.'

'And you?'

A delicate pause.

'It is true that on my mum side there is the old, old family, so we have beautiful houses, a lot of art.'

'They're the aristocracy?'

'Yes... no,' she says awkwardly.

'The intelligentsia?'

'Yes. Maybe something like this,' she agrees, but I think she's being modest.

As the three of us are waiting to let a glut of people pass the neck of a particularly narrow street I spot some iron rings high against a wall. They were once used to tether horses although Ginevra says cautiously, 'I think it is a seventeenth-century Venetian urban myth that people used to use horses here. How would you get them up and down all the bridges? Where would they exercise? And the walkways are too narrow, the horses would knock each other into the canal. Boats and walking were always better.'

We look along the canal and see a long black empty gondola passing silently at the corner, the gold scroll at the end like a raised dragon claw. The tubby gondolier's in his black and white convict top and round hat and – like the rascally chap who rowed Aschenbach in *Death in Venice* – doesn't look particularly Italian. I've only been in the *traghetti*, the gondolas that cross the Canal Grande for forty cents, standing up, feeling that I'm being conveyed in a cupped hand over rolls of tailor's velvet.

'You ever been on one?' I ask Stef as the gondola passes.

She frowns in disdain: 'Those things are not for Venetians.'

'Gondolas are sixty euros per ride,' says Ginevra, 'and the songs they are singing are Neapolitan. Nothing to do with Venice.'

'So it's a big trick?'

'Unfortunately, yes. I am sorry.'

That night there's a splendid dinner at Stefania's parents' place: slender bone plates, silver cutlery, cloth napkins, bloody wine, butter-baked beans, tenderest foal in a wintry, warming sauce, cheeses, breads, the Charbonnel et Walker chocolates I brought as a gift.

And what to make of Lucrezia Ritter, mother of Stef? She has very short curly grey hair like wire wool, a stringy powdered-white figure, a thin-skinned, fine, square face, very taut, almost frostbitten, with a canny, rather hard twinkle in her blue eyes.

All in all she gives an impression of discernment and Siberian dryness, pale as she is, like a piece of wood that's been bleached and salted on a cliff. She speaks excellent English with a stilted, almost Germanic accent, in her rasping and crumbling voice. Still, a vision of a happy marriage: at one point in the (Italian) conversation Gregorio laughs, charmed, and cups Lucrezia's head tenderly. Lucrezia notices me noticing them and blushes at the tips of her cheekbones, ice-pink on white.

Afterwards Stefania and I take the dog for a walk to help ourselves digest dinner. Introducing Nero the dog, king of the family: black all over, a medium-sized long-nosed mutt that Stefania found dumped in a bin in Milan. Despite living in the lap of luxury (literally – during dinner he sits with his nose on Gregorio's knee and his eyes blissfully closed), he still has the spikiness of a street dog. He barks shrilly, jumps on me a few times and that's it.

Gregorio sees us downstairs and gives me directions to the train station for the benefit of my general knowledge.

'You see that bridge?'

'Ah yes.'

'Don't go anywhere near it. Go in the opposite direction. There is no bridge on your route to the train station. If you see any bridges, run away!'

'I'd like to do a marathon here. Be good for the legs, all those bridges.'

'Ah! You know there is actually a marathon in Venice called the Up and Down the Bridges Marathon? The route is very difficult.'

We end the conversation there because Nero's stationed at the door pointing rigidly towards the street like a weathervane.

The holiday passes with sublime calm as I learn how to do everything graciously, firmly, stylishly, assertively. I know the cliché of the warm, vigorous, civilised Italians, but their warmth comes not from random generosity but from the happy observation of etiquette, the dependably long maintenance of families and institutions and the sanguine expectation that nothing will change. One must look good, behave well and understand one's position in society (me: young, accomplished female friend of old, well-established family's clever only daughter).

One afternoon I'm writing in the living room when I hear voices on the landing outside.

'I'll introduce you to my friend,' I hear Stef say in Italian.

I have just enough time to close my notebook and stand up when a tall, very young, thin, beautiful, honey-coloured, sandy-haired, pink-cheeked, blue-eyed cherubic boy comes in smiling simply, candidly...

'Oh, *hi*,' I say, sounding confident and – I'm sure – very pleased.

'Hi,' he says in sweet toffee English, and smiles back. Baggy jeans, tiny T. Full lips. Is it possible that he is... literally glowing with purity?

We shake hands, there's no vibe. When he's gone, Stefania tells me that he's called Renato, he's sixteen, nearly seventeen, one of her two cousins.

'I think maybe he is a little bit gay because last time I saw him he told me he could not decide whether to study biology or fashion design. And when we would visit him, when he was seven or eight, he would go away and come back with lipstick on...'

'Wearing ladies' clothes and singing a little song?'

'Yes. I hope if he is gay, he goes away. It can be hard in Venice.'

'He is so beautiful,' I sigh.

On my last full day we're thirsting for a view of the sea so we go down to the southernmost edge of the city, Zattere, and walk the long marble-lipped ledge watching the water shimmer in the sun like a hologram. Opposite us is the island of Giudecca with its three evenly-spaced white churches and low skyline. At the end of the walk there's a large wooden platform out over the sea, used as a landing stage for boats. Stef and I lie on the platform for a couple of hours, feeling the sea surge a few feet below us.

Eventually we drag ourselves up and drop in to see Stef's uncle, who's an industrial designer. The office is sleek, large and open-plan with architectural and design drawings up on the walls and models on display tables. Nobody appears to be that busy; even when they're working hard at their desks they still give the impression that they're having a coffee in a bar. The uncle is tall, cordial, blue-suited and pale, maybe sixty or so, with well-brushed white hair and a pointed nose. There are introductions to smooth, polite, blue-suited men all around the office.

'My English friend and I are just visiting my uncle,' Stefania explains to them in Italian.

'Oh, from school?' asks one solicitously.

'No! We are twenty-five and twenty-six years old,' says Stef in surprise.

'You're English?' a man asks me in Italian.

'Yes,' I reply.

'Nice to meet you,' he says in mincingly good English.

'Nice to meet *you*.' Nice, they have been taught, is a very English word.

'Do you suffer to be seasick?'

'Er. No...'

And that is how we find ourselves on a two-hour-long freezing cold boat trip around the industrial part of the lagoon with thirty boisterous thirteen-year-olds on a school trip. Actually, it's interesting – 'I like this industrial panorama,' as Stef says to me – looking at the grey factories and sheds and the metal chimneys coughing out warm black fog. Oddly enough there are no pictures of it in my Venice guidebook. This is the first time I've seen the waters of Venice look anything other than sparklingly pastel; this stuff is thick, sluggish, dingy matter, lurching upwards to an unnaturally dark sky.

After we're released from the boat Stef's uncle takes us to a *cichetteria*, a snack bar, and buys us a drink and some bites to eat. I have water, plus two damn good salty anchovy-and-pickled-onion things called *acciughe*, and look around while Stef and her uncle have a family conversation. Venice maintains a sharp distinction between its tourist side and its real self, the latter being more brisk and less obsequious. These snack bars are for Venetians only; one has to build up a flowing rapport with the chap behind the counter, who knows his wines inside out, and know what the snack delicacies are without asking or pointing. No time allowed for tourist prevarication, pidgin stuttering or watery I'm-not-from-here smiles. Businessmen remain standing, eat, drink and go, their tan briefcases flying casually behind them, everything civilised and formal-cordial, as long as everyone follows the rules.

It occurs to me that Venice is a Jane Austen novel brought to life: there's the elegance which masks a mercenary situation, the genuinely nice social niceties, the proper rhythm of everyday interactions, the respect accorded to one's elders, the pleasurable customs that preserve the status quo, the (I'm beginning to suspect) total powerlessness of women offset against their 'accomplishment', beauty, vivacity and charm. The Austenian theme is compounded when Ginevra joins us and we set off in pursuit of writing paper for our respective journals. Il Prato on the Calle delle Ostreghe between Accademia and San Marco offers printed papers of faded mint blue, strong china blue, salmon pink, saffron yellow and faded rust red covering vanity boxes, pen cases, photo frames; embossed writing cards with a single initial in regal blue or blood red; sealing wax in gold or red; quill pens and glass pens; endless rows of notebooks, loose sheets for wrapping or framing... Ginevra and I debate the importance of notebook size (to quote Goldilocks: not too big, not too small) and the superiority of the blank leaf to the lined. As I put my items on the counter the woman says that she likes my rings. I grin and take them off... a daring gesture, I realise, from the shocked looks around me. She tries them on and gets a little fluttery, which culminates gloriously in her giving me a considerable discount.

For my last night Stefania's parents have booked us a table at Mistra, a famous fish restaurant in the rich loft-living part of Giudecca. We persuade Ginevra to come, although she digs her heels in:

'Wait, wait... I need to think about this... no, of course I didn't have any plans for this evening, that's not the point... I don't like surprises... OK, I'll come.'

We take the vaporetto over to Giudecca just as it's getting dark. I look out at the low grey sky and miles of soul-stilling water pierced with boat-tethers like broken pencils. Giudecca's interesting – larger, richer, more modern and more general than Venice main, with warehouses and rich Americans' playpens. The restaurant's in a huge space with full height windows on all sides, but homely wooden tables and chairs. There are a few parties dining.

We sit down, Lucrezia and Gregorio at each end of the table, us three 'children' along the length. All the ordering has been taken care of by the (of course) long-time pal chef; we are merely to wait and be indulged. We're served delicate anchovies, herring, fresh salmon, cod in a tart sour sauce, bright-coloured grilled vegetables, a smidge of caviar, light home-made pasta lying fluffily on the plate (English pasta, I am told crossly by everyone, is like eating glue), all excellent, finished with a little dessert to sweeten the mouth, and just enough wine.

For some reason we begin talking about sexual harassment in the academic profession, agreed by all to be widespread, unacknowledged, deeply entrenched and far-reaching.

'In forty years of being an academic,' says Gregorio, who doesn't like any topic to become too serious, 'I have witnessed many affairs between professors and students, but true love? *Amore vero*? Never! Well maybe once. But I have witnessed thirty or forty cases – at least – of harassment, and in every case the tutor went to the student when she wanted to complain, and he said, "What? It wasn't anything. You have made a little mistake," or he said, "Oh come now, why do you want to go and do that, when you are just at the end of your degree, at this crucial time?" They discouraged her. But I do remember one time when a colleague of mine had one student, a very beautiful girl, very beautiful, but a poor student, and one day she said to him, "What is the mark for my essay?" And he said to me afterwards, "The mark is 'F' – but with an ass like that? An 'A'! Surely an 'A'!"'

Somehow in the midst of all this it becomes clear that there is a troublemaker in the not particularly full restaurant. Yes, an English troublemaker, I'm afraid, sent here by God to prove everyone's point. He shouts 'Oh yes!' gleefully at the top of his drunken voice when the new, large, young, very shy waiter breaks a glass. The waiter is meaty-faced and puffy-lipped, silent, mortified and very un-Italian. When he was serving us at the beginning, Stefania's parents asked where he was from.

'Moldavia,' he replied.

'Ah! Moldavia! I met a Moldavian woman once!' exclaimed Gregorio. 'Her name was Katrina – Karina – Karolina – I can't remember it. Name some Moldavian names beginning with "K".'

'I don't know,' said the shy waiter, blushing like a round bright light.

'Cara – Chiara – no... I can't remember it...'

'If you do remember,' said the waiter coolly, 'be sure to call me.'

'Ouch!' I said as he left.

The drunken Englishman comes forward now, dancing around to the piped-in tango music: short, thick, pale, a stocky stockbroker, posh, red-faced, with his soggy shirt falling out of his trousers. The chef bustles out of the kitchen in alarm but keeps his distance, watching with a terrified smile and leaning exhaustedly against the counter (where the blushing Moldavian waiter is polishing some knives) with his hand pasted to his forehead. The Englishman holds a shouted conversation with his companion, a dark-haired, very slim, pleasant-looking useless type sitting concavely in his seat and trying to disappear into the wall but still answering his friend and laughing at his jokes.

Suddenly the man goes over to the upright piano by the door, whips up the cover and starts playing saloon-bar tunes as hard as he can. By this time Stefania's parents have paid up and are getting ready to leave. We begin to drift unwillingly towards the door. Lucrezia and I accidentally catch the man's eye.

'We're not going to sing any songs about *Germans*,' he cries.

'But I am not German,' says Lucrezia very quietly and with a calm, mocking smile.

'Oh! Where are you from?' he shouts, still playing as loud as he can.

'Guess,' she replies in an icy, smiling whisper.

The drunk man ignores Lucrezia and begins to play a 'Chopsticks'-type tune. The restaurant's other guests are stunned Venetians unable to think of anything to say – unable, I imagine, even to put a name to what they are beholding.

'Where are you from then?' shouts the drunken man again with a leer, not looking at Lucrezia, and still playing the piano.

'Where do you think?' says Lucrezia silkily. She's toying with him like a black widow spider contemplating an after-dinner bite. 'Here we are...' She opens her arms and indicates the region. 'So use your power of deduction.'

'I don't know!' he says jeeringly and carries on playing.

'Guess,' she says.

'Guess,' I say.

'Guess, guess,' we say together.

'Guess-Guess, where's that?' he shouts merrily and begins to play a well-known romantic piano-practice tune, but he makes up his own words and shouts them at the top of his voice: '*You can sit on my face...*'

And yet nobody punishes him. A man behaves in a bestial, vulgar, offensive way and everyone steps forward and brushes it under the carpet. There is nothing to indicate to the man that what he is doing is wrong. He will return home thinking he's had a marvellous evening.

In top Venetian diplomatic style the chef walks us gently out, smiling, sighing and shrugging dolefully with the tiniest movements. I mention something to Gregorio and he is sympathetically shocked but, with the best intentions, tells me to put it out of my mind. Lucrezia has become glacial and opaque. Ginevra and Stef were in the bathroom and didn't witness it.

We walk silently back to the vaporetto stop. It's chilly and I pull my shawl around myself. Eventually I blurt out to Gregorio, who happens to be walking near me, 'I'm sorry, I'm still angry. I hate bullies.'

'Forget about it, forget it,' he says kindly, patting me on the back.

'One thug subjugates an entire restaurant and no one says anything, but if I accidentally dropped my fork, everyone would look.'

'Forget it, dear, put it from your mind...'

I do, forcibly, and on the ride home after dinner I sit by myself, get out my camera and start playing with it.

'Bidisha!' Gregorio calls out suddenly. 'We are ready!'

I look up: he and Lucrezia are embraced on the seat opposite me, looking expectantly at the camera. I laugh and take two pictures of them, one beaming with their heads close together, one with them both slumped over pretending to be asleep.

I had assumed that the evening was over but Stefania's cravenly hedonistic parents suggest that we all have one last drink at the famous, beautiful (and famously beautifully steep) Florian's cafe in Piazza San Marco. By now it's dark and Venice is sandwiched between two folds of equally blue sky and water. St Mark's Square is full of people, gold lights, street vendors selling too-perfect roses, music and the repeating shadows of arched windows, cloisters and columns. St Mark's itself is a humped shadow at the end of the square, big and bulbous like a Buddha statue.

Stefania's parents, it is no revelation to discover, know the people who run Florian's. We are ushered past the tourist tables outside and given prime seats in the bar, next to the cafe's mirrored and painted trinket-box rooms, with their carved spindly tables and velvet seats. We sit in a huddle amid the bottles, the textiles, the gilt, the money and the marble and watch two scruffily-dressed travellers (Australian? Middle-American?) sitting drinking beer across three bar-stools, their muddy rambling boots up for all to see.

'Classy,' hisses Lucrezia to Gregorio in Italian, indicating them. 'Why are they taking up the whole bar?'

Marino the bartender is the kind of person you couldn't imagine working anywhere else. He's also the kind of person, I might add, who is married with kids but obviously gay. He's tall and cadaverous but meticulously well-kept: trimmed hair, short combed moustache, moisturised long face, manicure, a single well-chosen pinkie ring, wearing a uniform of white jacket, white shirt, white cravat and slim black trousers. There are two small flags hanging among all the glasses behind the bar, both embroidered with an M. One's for Marino and the other's for the other main guy here (and Marino's secret life-partner I'm sure), Marco. I put this issue to Stefania and she replies with a joke secretive-official face, 'There are no gay people in Venice.'

Marino suggests that I try the Bellini – this is generally considered to be an excellent idea – so Bellinis all round, served with ultra-thin biscuits on a silver tray. Outside, a large orchestra merrily saws away in competition with the other orchestras around the piazza, especially the one from Caffè Quadri directly opposite. Gregorio tells me that Italian musicians are too expensive so the cafes hire orchestras from Eastern Europe on cheap contracts. They come here on the minimum wage even though they all have PhDs in musicology.

As a thank you to Gregorio and Lucrezia, Ginevra, Stef and I insist on taking care of the (astronomical) bill. They give in with a defeated cry of, 'All right, all right! We are old. The young people will pay.' Afterwards we meander northwards and Stefania shows me the luxury shopping streets around San Marco, every label represented, no prices on display, just mannequins in cashmere. The streets are still full of tourists, an interesting mix: families, art buffs, backpackers, dreamers, knots of young people, visibly rich chic couples out to spend money.

We cross the crowded Campo San Bartolomeo at the bottom of Rialto Bridge – yet more cafes, bars, pizza-slice places, some cheaper clothes shops, although nothing in Venice is really cheap – and take the straight route to Stefania's house from there. Back to the narrow streets, the perpetual restoration-work and builders' placards, closed *pasticcerie*. By now I've learnt to identify Stefania's turning by the traditional chaps' tailoring shop on the corner. Whenever we pass it in the mornings I stare in lustfully before the dark glares of the owner send me away. I gather he likes to keep the atmosphere XY-chromosome only, as in the good old days. It's a shame, because I like the combination of sensuality in the colours (one outfit can encompass an entire spectrum from off-white to sunshine yellow to strong ochre) and precision in the cut.

Just outside this shop we bump into fine young cousin Renato and his parents, out for a walk. A pleasant group chat follows. Stefania's uncle turns to me kindly and asks me something in Italian. I stare back like a sheep.

'She doesn't understand one single bit of what you just said,' says Renato to his father, again in Italian, but painfully I understand it. Everyone absorbs the insult and we all take a moment to rearrange our faces.

'I understand you enjoy the docks today?' says Stef's uncle haltingly in English.

'Ah! Yes. They were very interesting,' I reply politely, and leave a little silence.

The next morning passes quickly. Stefania and Ginevra take me back to Piazzale Roma and put me on the bus. Then we have the usual fight because Stefania's gone and bought the ticket while I'm checking the timetable, then won't take any money for it.

'That's not fair. For God's sake, *please* take the money.'

'Why?' she replies belligerently. 'It is your last day, let me pay for this.'

'In case you hadn't noticed, you paid all the previous days as well. And if it was something romantic like a little cake I wouldn't say anything but this is just a bloody bus ticket.'

'Exactly Bidisha. It's just a bus ticket, so who cares?'

'*I* care because you keep paying for everything. You horrible girls.'

I kiss them goodbye and get on the bus.

'Venice is always waiting for you,' says Stefania.

Chapter Two

Over the next seven weeks I find myself reminiscing about Venice via a series of leisurely hallucinations, possibly scored by Mahler, in which glittering water, bridges, cakes, cheese, clothes and good-looking locals all mix together in one enticing whole. This is not the same as missing an exciting experience – quite the opposite, because Venice is not 'exciting' in the base sense. It represents a solace and stillness which still resonate, even though I know they're the direct product of the city's conservatism, commercialism and stasis. Venice is the antithesis of London, where I've lived all my life and know so well now that all major Western cities – New York, Paris, Berlin – don't seem that different from it. I wish to learn a different way of life, in which the things I've prized until now (glitz and fortune being two obvious examples) are shown up in all their nothingness and any Brit brittleness is replaced by some of my Italian friends' serenity and good humour. But all of that is to justify what *is* after all quite a base attraction: Venice is beautiful, addictively so, and when you've seen it once you want more. There might be a point, I suppose, by which you've had so much that you feel sick, but I can't imagine it. I decide to get some money together and relocate to Venice for a few months, starting at the beginning of July.

Ginevra's on holiday in Sardinia and Gregorio and Lucrezia are away at conferences but the reunion with Stefania is as joyous as expected. She's working on a film project in Padova, forty minutes away by train, so I find myself happily alone on the first day. It's well into the eighties, too hot to go out without spontaneously igniting, so I sit on the balcony. Across the Canal Grande I can see the quick-stepping Venetians, all tanned dark, never sweating in the heat. Also never in shorts, caps or sandals. I like the gondola posts that stick up out of the water, some plain brown whittled logs, some candy-striped in spiralling red and white. I identify the various boats that pass: large, long trade boats containing leathery men and crates of produce; the fibreglass pleasure-boats of privileged couples; water taxis containing wealthy visitors and their luggage; vaporetti crammed with people, many of them standing filming the buildings as they pass, too interested in playing with their cameras to look at the real thing. There are noticeably more tourists about, compared to April. Swooping over the Canal Grande are cawing seagulls and hundreds of tiny squeaking bladelike birds, almost bats, that shoot past the window in clusters. On one vaporetto that passes I see a big man, oily and tanned with a massive stomach, holding a tiny brown dog the size, colour and texture of a leather wallet. The dog's so pooped by the heat that its tongue sticks out floppily like a bright pink clothes label.

Once the sun's gone down a bit I go for a walk. I enter an unremarkable *pasticceria* in a touristy stretch between Stefania's place and the train station, just by the fruit and vegetable stalls, to find an argument fully underway. At first I almost think it's being staged because, despite the rapid exchanges, flailing arms, raised voices, denunciations, denials and counterclaims, I get the distinct impression that everyone is secretly enjoying themselves, since when not shouting they're all leaning rather casually against the counter. Eventually I figure out that a guy, Italian, has asked to use the bathroom and been turned away because there isn't one. The manager of the *pasticceria* is blocking him and has one arm almost around him (but not touching him) in an effort to guide him out through the door. The rest of the staff are tossing in comments with hopeful glee like children throwing coins into a fountain. The other customers are sipping their espressos, nibbling their *pastine* (cakettes) and enjoying the show. I creep inside.

'Is this what it's come to?' wails the man, his hands cupped beneath his chin in disgust and beseechment. 'I come in here and partake of your custom, I pay my two euros, I say I want to do a wee-wee – and you refuse me?'

'Sir! Do not take on so, it's not a personal slight. We have no facilities for that kind of thing, merely a back room for the staff.'

'Oh, how can you say that so shamelessly to my face when all I've done is ask you for a favour?'

And on it continues, each side playing its part with unbending gusto and goodwill, and not shouting as such, more as if they're projecting their voices out of consideration for the audience. The man, however, does go on, and with classic conservatism – the conviction that no matter how beautifully he pleads, he is not going to be permitted entry to the hallowed staff commode – he's allowed to reach only a certain pitch, volume and velocity before the hand of God silences him forever. The hand of God is in this case a junior waitress – tallish, waxily pale, with colourless short hair and smudged glasses – who strides out of the back room, stands erect behind the till, puts one fist on her hip with the elbow jutting and uses the other hand to point unswervingly out through the door. Ordering him from on high in supple tones she says:

'*Signore*, no more of this. If you take a mere two steps from our door, you will see on your left a most serviceable public toilet which will suit your... every requirement.'

The act is passed with such certainty that it's as if the entire room has been blasted with light. Every person in it falls silent, then glances at each other. Then there's a burst of admiring laughter. The man, recognising his superior, has nothing more to say, goes blank, falls silent too and doesn't exit so much as dissolve into invisibility. Broadly smiling, rapt, the audience turns once more to the waitress as though expecting a second act. The other staff members are letting out giggles and claps and the woman, who'd been standing resolute as Boudicca, lets down her chin, unhitches her fist from her hip and gives a self-deprecating laugh. The atmosphere breaks, the other staff begin to tease her and she laughs again and turns to serve me (I'd been lingering, as ever, by the cakes). We look at each other and laugh further, me in admiring tribute, her in self-effacement.

'I'm sorry,' she says, 'when someone's going on like that I just *have* to say something!'

Next comes the day of the apartments, orchestrated by Stefania. I limply offer myself up to her superior organisational hand, since the best way to find an apartment in Venice is through personal contacts. The alternative is to be ripped off soundly like the American moguls who suck up the old palaces during the art, music, architecture and film festivals.

The first estate agent we meet is a vivacious woman called Marietta, who has dark skin, frazzled auburn hair and light brown eyes, a raucously laughing sexy squirrel. Unfortunately the apartment she shows us is too big, too beautiful and too well-furnished for me, like a rich person's Cornwall cottage, with a patchwork quilt on the high bed, a coffee table full of design magazines and a wide terrace running along the side of the building. The landlady's a tepid woman in her fifties, a tall well-dressed jelly in black linen, coral lipstick, dry blonde bob (two visits to the salon per week, I calculate, for a wash and set), who looks me up and down with a small smile before offering me the honour of paying her rent, which is more than 1,100 euros a month.

'She is just like all these rich old ladies in Venice who own, like, ten flats that she rent out. They have never worked,' says Stef disdainfully afterwards.

I like the second estate agent, Tiziana, whom we meet in the residential square outside her house. Stef rings the bell while I sag in the sun next to a shop that sells decorative things made of wood: a fake crumpled jacket, made of wood; a delicate orchid, made of wood; or how about a pair of discarded ladies' stockings, made of wood? Indeed: it's the type of joke you only need to get once. Tiziana comes out and glides forward with her long arms held out, her smile stretching over us like a parasol. She has a flat, intelligent face with milky blue eyes and floppy blonde hair with a smart fringe. She looks like a mermaid: citrus yellow vest and green peasant skirt, gold flip-flops on her tanned feet. She takes us to our second apartment of the day, exchanging family gossip with Stefania in her slow, deep, clear voice.

The second apartment we see is, Tiziana had warned us, 'spartan'. But even the Spartans, I imagine, liked their floors level and preferred their doors to close evenly in the frame. What we get is a piece of warped driftwood over a random hole, followed by a sharp unintended slope. There's a little fridge, a little table, a little seat, a kitchen range concealed behind cupboard doors, a bath with a rubber shower-attachment on the taps, a cell bedroom with a naked mattress on a plain bed frame. No linen, no plates, no knives, no doors between rooms. This apartment is little more than a cupboard that's been converted to make money for people who are already rich and there's something miserly and shameless about it. They've bought the meanest version of everything, the one plastic chair, the rubber hose of the shower, even a door made for another frame. Eight hundred and fifty euros a month.

The last flat is in a loud, busy, central area directly opposite Santa Maria Gloriosa dei Frari, a big brown barn of a church in San Polo. Visitors and Venetians are crossing or lounging in the huge square in front of it. I spot a busker playing the mandolin, bright sunlight, a couple of tourist cafes with one or two tables outside. The *sottoportego*, the low wooden arch that leads to the *campiello*, the mini-square, is at the base of a wide white bridge that's cutely humped like cake icing.

'Why do the tourists think it's OK to sit on the steps of a bridge?' Stefania asks no one in particular in Italian while Tiziana grunts disparagingly in agreement. 'Would you sit on the pavement in the middle of London?'

What infuriates me is that I can understand all of this without even trying, but when I want to say something or someone asks me a question, all the syllables get clogged in my mouth and I wind up spitting them out one by one like orange pips. We go to the *campiello* and I like it immediately. It's tiny, with brown paving stones, a newspaper hut, a wellhead with an iron grille over its mouth and an antiques shop, an art supplies shop called Artemisia and a bookshop along the sides. High above them are the salmon pink walls and brown shutters of surrounding apartments and the black and gold fortifications of a rich person's house concealed behind alarms, gates, brass, spikes, gargoyles and a carved stone shield with a family crest. I can't see what the *campiello*'s called because the painted wall sign has worn away. Along the side of the square there's a narrow alleyway ending flat in the green-slimed water (definitely not the place for a moonlight ramble).

Tiziana hammers on the first door, number 2571. A girl with a characterful voice answers cautiously from behind it and won't let us in until we've given her our respective life-histories and vowed that we're not murderers, whereupon she throws open the door and greets us all with cries and hugs. Me, Tiziana and Stef all find ourselves gigglingly charmed by this pixie girl, who's wearing, by the way, the smallest bra top and hotpants I've ever seen in my life. She's living there with three other girls, all students. The place suits me perfectly: a windowless stone kitchen with a hob and a central chipboard island, some stools, a windowless stone bathroom with a stand-up shower. Together about seven foot by nine. A narrow almost vertical staircase with open slat steps leads to a single room with a veneer floor, a single bed tucked into the corner, cheap wardrobe and not-ugly sofa bed. Two oblong shuttered windows look onto the *campiello*. It's cheap for Venice, 800 euros a month including bills, and everything's included;

sheets, duvets, pots and pans, mop, even spare lightbulbs and bin bags.

We step outside after being waved off tearfully by the girl, who promises to leave me all her cleaning solutions, some food and coffee and whatever shampoos and soaps I want.

'This is the one. It's perfect. Thank you Stef. Thanks Tiziana,' I say jubilantly.

I hear birds singing loudly with gorgeous formlessness above me and look up: on the second floor windowsill of 'my' building someone has set out three large birdcages surrounded by hanging baskets of piercing red and pink flowers. I feel a burst of happiness to see and hear them.

Tiziana gives a low-key smile and leaves us to work out the details, telling Stef to call her later.

'I will show you the way to Campo Santa Margherita,' says Stefania to me. 'You have chosen the best place to live, everything is five minutes by foot.'

'Thanks for everything you've done for me. I should have said that before.'

'You are not an easy person to help,' says Stef sweetly. 'But do you see, if you do not take my help everything becomes more complicate.'

'Complicated. Yes. I'm realising that now,' I say humbly.

We have a closer look at what is to be my neighbourhood, dominated by the gargantuan brown shape of Frari church, which dwarfs the smaller church and curve-porched *scuola* of San Rocco next to it. It's very pretty, a little close and echoing, a lot of young people, livelier and less commercial than the old-family space and wealth of where Stefania lives. Outside San Rocco a woman and a girl of about five are sitting eating ice cream and looking at a map. They're talking in American English and Spanish.

'You're funny, Mommy!' I hear the girl say animatedly.

'You're funny too,' the woman replies lovingly.

The kid doesn't like all the drab grey pigeons who're pecking about. She gets up and begins trying to shoo them away, her arms spread wide.

'Look, Mommy,' she says in dismay.

'Don't climb on the wall.'

'Can't you catch 'em, or kill 'em or – or turn 'em around somehow?'

Stefania and I go on and turn left in front of the *pasticceria*, Tonolo, passing the sunflower-carrying Oscar Wilde guy's antiques shop. He's inside, staring out. We pass the church of San Pantaleone, which looks like it was made using strips of untreated plywood. Another bridge, then into the already familiar-looking Campo St M. Some boy students come out of the scruffy winos' bar at the neck of the campo.

'How's your cousin? Renato?' I ask Stefania, reminded by them of him.

'Ah! He will soon be leaving for one year to go to America. The good thing is, if he goes, because he is so young he will become completely bilingual.'

And, goes her additional glance, he'll be able to explore his sexuality more freely if he's away from Venice.

We have to break off there, because we're being enthusiastically harassed by a guy begging for money. He's dark and slender, Moorish looking, in a blue workers' cap and shirt, holding a sign. Stefania gives him all her change, which is about fifty cents. He looks at it in distaste:

'Don't you have anything bigger? I can't buy anything with this. Look at it, it's nothing. What d'you expect me to do with fifty cents? Bread starts at one euro.'

'You can't be serious,' says Stef, 'I gave you all I have. And it's all you're going to get so leave us alone.'

He stands even closer to our table, nudging it with his thigh, and continues to rail at her:

'I'm so hungry, I come and ask you for help and I get *this*. This isn't good for much.'

'Why don't you sell your hat?' I mutter in English.

He turns to me and holds out his hand.

'Amazing,' says Stef in frustration.

I begin to rustle minimally for my wallet. Neither of us has brought much money along.

'No, Bidisha, you don't have to,' says Stef.

The guy continues haranguing us. I eventually give him fifty cents and he goes away. 'And now do you really think he's going to go and buy a sandwich?' I finish sadly.

That evening we celebrate the successful apartment hunt with dinner at an Italian-Arabic place with Mara and Bianca, some architect/designer friends of Stef's. At the next table is a family party of about twenty people, from an eighty-year-old grandmother to a three-month-old baby and everything in between, plus one small dog, Lorenzo, to whom we are all introduced. The restaurant is authentic, modest and tourist-free with tables set along the canal, velvet blue night-heat, no breeze, silent moving water. Mara's high-spirited and has quirky monochrome features, a buck-toothed grin, rectangular glasses and short dark hair. Bianca is equally lively and extremely beautiful with sad liquid blue Virgin eyes, almost English-faced until I see her profile, which is flat and long with a strong broken nose straight out of a Renaissance Doge's portrait.

The talk at our table is about how in summer everyone opens their windows so that it's possible, given how cramped Venice is, to hear everything everyone else is doing. Mara says to me in English:

'My boyfriend is half from Switzerland, so sometimes in the night I am disposed to allow him to read me some stories in the German language. One night, we were doing this, and from upstairs came a noise.' She nods meaningfully. 'And we listened for a while. I said to Dario, "We are thirty years old, we are lying in bed reading German. They are forty-five..." And it was two times.'

Bianca makes a dismissive noise and says to us laconically, 'But for two minutes each time?'

She offers a similar story about her own elderly neighbours, who do it 'like two little buffaloes'. Her grunting, snorting and woofing have us choking with laughter, which attracts the friendly attention of the family next to us. The baby is brought over on the grandfather's shoulder, danced on the table, swung around, held up and shown to the audience like an auction exhibit.

On the way home I keep staring at the moon, which is a solid bright orange and red, low in the sky, scorched neon with not a trace of white. Back at Stef's place we stand in the courtyard and go through a standard show of persuading Mara and Bianca to come up for a nightcap while they go through a show of hesitating, not wanting to impinge, considering it and hanging back modestly. Once the appropriate length of time has elapsed all four of us go upstairs. We open the balcony doors and sit out drinking port with ice, looking over the Canal Grande, a silent mobile blackness bobbing with lights.

'Oh, you know the beautiful Russian boy?' says Mara. 'The waiter? He now works at this very nice place, Postali. One day he was there, look very tired, so I said, "Oh, you look very exhausted." And he said, "Ah no, you see, I have a lot of things to think about." And I said, "Ah! What things?" And he said, "I am thinking about cigarettes, the different makes of cigarettes."'

Stef, Mara, Bianca and I all stare at each other in disappointment.

'OK, bye-bye, beautiful boy,' says Stef finally.

'Yes, we thought the cupboard was beautiful. We opened the cupboard. We saw what was inside. Now we don't want the cupboard any more,' I say.

'Did you know,' Stef tells me, 'there is a movement in Venice. It begin maybe about one year and a half ago, boys from rich families go to live on the street with dogs, beg for money.'

'But why?'

'For no reason. For apathy. There is no sociological purpose,' she says bluntly. 'They are not anti-capitalists. They ask me for money and I say, "Why? We have the same age. You can work."'

'You do not have some handicap,' Mara adds, 'that prevents you from working.'

'And you look and you see they are wearing Diesel jeans, new trainers and carrying a mobile,' says Stef.

'What do they say when you tell them off?' I ask.

She does an impression: a surly, slovenly shrug, too fagged even to reply.

When the port has been drunk Stef and I see Mara and Bianca off, then go for a turn around the neighbourhood. On the way back we discover a huge black suitcase with an airport tag on the handle, sitting abandoned in the middle of a side street. We walk around it thinking terrorism. The buildings above are shuttered and dark and there aren't any hotels nearby.

'Should I call someone?' says Stefania.

'Maybe. In nine cases out of ten it's just someone who left it here while they take their other luggage upstairs. But the tenth time out of ten... we could be saving the world.'

By chance we see a private security guard walking down the street. He's in a beige uniform with lots of belts, buckles and guard accessories and has a very pale Russian-type face with no tan, full curly lips and a thick nose. He sees us, scowls and pretends to be in a rush, brushing past in a high-shouldered way.

'Excuse me, sir,' says Stefania, calling him back firmly, 'do you know who that bag belongs to?'

'I don't know,' he shoots back immediately, without looking at Stefania or at the bag.

'Did you see anyone walking past in the last fifteen minutes who could've left –'

'I don't know.'

'What do you advise us to do?'

'I don't *know*,' he screams, clearly to mean 'I don't care and go to hell.'

He walks away, his chin high, while his scream still echoes around the streets. We stand staring after him.

'Why he did not stop?' says Stefania frustratedly. 'I am a woman!'

'I don't think he was quite the chivalric type, Stef. I think he probably tended in quite the opposite direction.'

In the end we call the local police and they're so happy to have something to do that they promise, amidst sounds of cheering and celebration, to race to the scene and waltz away with the fascinating mystery bag.

My apartment isn't going to be ready for another week so I stay on at the palazzo, sleeping on the antique boat-bed in the study. It's harsh outside, almost too bright to see between midday and four, and Venice smells of hot salted stone. From the balcony I see the millions of visitors across the Canal Grande beaten into submission by two in the afternoon, drooping next to the water, flopped on the steps. The water makes everything look like jolly good pantomime fun, even the transportation of a prisoner, which resembles a procession from a Visconti film: the white prison police boat, the guards in sombre blue uniforms, the convict in his bright orange spot-the-fiend jumpsuit. The ambulance which follows is a matching orange.

I go for a walk and spot a stunning woman in her mid-thirties, model-tall, red stilettos, endless legs, white linen mini skirt, black jacket, standing babytalking to a tiny terrier that's sitting thumping its tail on the pavement and looking up at her lasciviously, along with the other five hundred men in the vicinity. Also seen on Rialto Bridge: a sweet kid in a pushchair drops her toy and reaches over to get it. A much older but immaculately handbagged and black-clad signora sees it fall in her path and simply steps over it, looking neither at it nor the child. To make doubly sure she isn't contaminated she lifts her knees and handbag high out of the way of the toy and marches on, but can't resist smiling in grim pleasure.

I go into the Billa supermarket near Stef's house and buy various healthy things, feeling very native. At the checkout a slender boy with a snub nose, full lips, candid dusky eyes and long wavy dark-honey hair walks towards me, smiling lightly, unsure whether I recognise him or not. He's holding an enormous watermelon and is with his mother, who's faded and friendly in a sundress.

'Ciao Renato,' I say nonchalantly.

'Hello,' he says in his lovely gentle-voiced English. 'Are you staying at Stefania's flat?'

'No, her parents are away and I've got theirs. Nice melon.'

He laughs.

'Look. It is...' he checks the label, 'eight kilograms.'

'It's beautiful,' I marvel.

We shuffle along the queue. The woman in front mistakes me, gratifyingly, for an Italian, and asks if I could look after her trolley while she goes to fetch something she's forgotten. I have great pleasure in taking hold of her trolley with gentle possessiveness and waving her away with a magnanimous flip of the fingertips.

'Look at me,' I say to Renato, 'I'm a true Venetian now. To the extent that other Venetians trust me with their shopping.'

He laughs again. I am *so* charming.

'Stefania tells me you're going to America soon,' I say.

'Yes, for one year. I will go to finish school.'

'Are you nervous?'

He lets out a long, quavering breath: 'Everyone is asking me that. I'm nervous and not nervous.'

'Nervous in a good way.'

'Yes!'

'Well, I think it's an excellent idea. You'll be totally fluent. Although you speak perfectly now, you know.'

Renato's mother says something to him, then to me, and indicates the queue.

'We should push the lady's trolley forward to close the gap,' he says.

'*Should* we?' I say with what I realise later must be grotesque playfulness.

'Yes!' he replies. 'She will thank you for it.'

He switches his enormous watermelon to the other arm.

'You could kill someone with that,' I say.

'From the window...'

'Yes, just drop it on their head.'

He cradles it while I lay my hand against it.

'I am pregnant,' he says.

'Yes,' I say officially, 'I think you're just about nine months now.'

'Good afternoon!' says the guy at the checkout when it's my turn.

'Good afternoon!' I trill back. I ask for two plastic bags (five cents each), turn out not to need one and sell it to Renato and his mother. Later it does occur to me that I ought not to have sold it and should have merely given it. We walk off together, quiet and leisurely, back 'home', me dawdling behind in my flip-flops, him suffering because of the drag of the melon, which swings like a cannonball at the bottom of his bag.

'I'll say goodbye now,' I say Englishly at Stefania's parents' door.

'OK. Have a good dinner.'

'And you.'

Ciaos all round. I make a huge horse-meat salad for lunch, then sit out on the balcony all night. The sky's not flat at all but dome-like, a concentrated navy blue at the top, a washed pearly blue at the edges. Between eight and nine the sky goes from this to deep grey-violet and the lights on the Canal Grande come up, gold and silver orbs. I light a yellow citronella candle to keep the mosquitoes away. The midges looked like knots of thread. By midnight-thirty the canal is dark and quiet and conversations on the other side echo around.

When we were queuing in Billa today Renato asked me, 'Why are you in Venice for three whole months?'

'Four. I have to do some writing,' I said shortly. The truth is that I have to finish a novel which is so bad that whenever I read it, I find myself falling into a deep sleep, which lasts as many hours as the chapters I've read. So stopping at chapter five sends me to sleep for five hours and so on.

'So you seek inspiration?' Renato asked.

'Inspiration and serenity.'

'Venice is good place for that. But it's too hot. Have you been to the beach yet?'

'No. Hell no. No beach. Too many people, too much...'

'No, but it is not like that. Not many people. Sand, sea. Natural.'

'Maybe. The other thing is that I'm afraid of water,' I admitted.

'So that is the reason! Do not worry, in seventeen years I have not seen anyone fall into the water here.'

'Seventeen years is not a long time,' I said sternly.

'You might be the first person I see falling,' he teased me, laughing.

This conversation, banal though it was, and obscured by the sad heat-haze of my admiration, was nonetheless so innocent, so spontaneous and so devoid of any kind of agenda that it left its glow for the rest of the evening. It could never happen that way in London, I believe: to bump into a young boy and fall naturally into a conversation that is neither loaded nor trivial, neither flirtatious nor unnaturally prim, neither flattering nor self-promoting but easy in all ways, enjoyed merely for itself.

But then again, that's an Austen-like social point, isn't it? One must always be civil to the first cousin of one's closest friend, whose family's hospitality you're enjoying.

Stef comes in that evening after a long meeting about a film budget and we take Nero out as the sun sets. Many of the dogs of Venice are fascinated by him, the tall, dark, mongrel stranger. Nero himself is intrigued by some and totally ignores others. Stefania tells me the story of how her family took him on holiday one year. He attracted the attention of the neighbour's dog, whom 'he just used like a sexual toy'. Indeed Nero would crawl home every evening visibly exhausted by a full day of rutting. Inevitably, given this 'romance', to give it its euphemism, the two human families became friends and the other dog became pregnant. A year later Stefania and her parents made the journey to visit the puppies, each one of whom 'had the face of Nero and the body of the other dog'.

On the Strada Nova, Nero's gently leapt on and kissed by a snowy-white fawn-tipped collie, very lively and intelligent-looking, who puts a paw on his head and darts around him. The owners of the white dog are a friendly couple: a silent, smiling, porno-handsome wiry blonde guy in skintight black T-shirt and jeans and a stunning woman, tall, with a beautiful toned body, in a bright yellow cropped cycling top and trousers, fried blonde hair, foxlike face and sparkling aqua eyes. Showstoppers, both of them. Maybe they make aerobics videos together. The woman's very genial and I gather that the friendship between Nero and the snowy dog is an ongoing thing. On the way home, though, Nero has to be protected from the famous 'monster dog' of the area (Stef's phrase), a mixed bulldog/bloodhound/Rottweiler colossus that spots him from 300 metres away, stiffens from ears to tail and starts up with an almost human grunting bark, its eyes like the barrel-holes of a shotgun.

'You know, I walked though Rialto market today and I thought how easy it'd be to let my entire life go that way,' I say to Stef once we've escaped. 'I've been here four days and I haven't read a newspaper or watched the news once.'

'Yes, Venice is sometimes a bubble,' she ruminates. 'You can see it in people who have lived all their lives here, they are completely removed from the rest of the world.'

Chapter Three

The reality of moving properly to Venice sinks in when Stefania and I go to see Tiziana, the estate agent, to finalise my apartment details. We take Nero with us – he presses close to the shadows on one side of the street. Tiziana's house is on three sun-catching levels with honey-coloured floorboards, well-chosen antiques and a roof terrace scented with gardenia and rich with trailing plants and fruit trees. We sit down and get to business while Nero leaps about, watched by Coco, Tiziana's huge, ancient, knackered German shepherd, who follows us around with barely concealed fatigue, panting with every step and looking at us balefully from inside her coat. Nero sees this and begins to strut proudly.

'Nero always get excited when he is here,' says Stef to me, 'because he thinks, "Oh, Coco's invited me for a party! Coco is hosting me!"'

Tiziana and Stef talk about my flat amongst themselves and I understand most of what they're saying until Tiziana addresses me directly: 'Something something something something?'

A silence. I gape at her, then at Stef.

'Are you moving in on Monday?' Stef translates.

'She doesn't understand *anything*?' says Tiziana in Italian, looking dumbfounded – and I understand *that*. I suppose the flipside of Tiziana's openness is that she doesn't hide her negative feelings either.

I see Stef making a diplomatic response. I go very deep inside myself and sit there like a taciturn gnome on a riverbank. I am beckoned over, hand the deposit and one month's rent to Tiziana, who writes out a receipt and explains everything in halting but good-accented English. I nod, blink emphatically and do everything I'm supposed to, all from within a hot bubble of embarrassment. At the end she says to me in Italian, 'Have you understood?' I say yes but she doesn't look convinced.

The talk progresses and Tiziana tells a funny story, looking at both me and Stef, of which I understand not one word. Long after the laughter has finished she translates it: she has a centre-left newspaper delivered to her door every morning, but she also goes out especially to buy another very left-wing paper which would shock, astound and disgust the other people in the building if they saw it. She mimes their reaction: pancake-faced, mouth and eyes open, body flattened out against the wall because of the blast of insurgent red sentiment emanating from the paper.

We all leave together, including the two dogs, down the grand marble stairs, past the tapestry-design marble walls. Stefania tactfully goes on ahead.

'Thank you for everything,' I say to Tiziana in Italian.

'Don't be silly,' she says nicely, touching me on the arm.

'I can understand more than I can say.'

'Of course you can. It's always hard at the beginning.'

'You have to have an ear for languages,' I say slowly in English, touching my earlobe.

'Yes,' she replies emphatically, also in English. 'For example, Americans. They cannot learn languages at all.'

She sees us off in Campo Santo Stefano and Stef and I walk home. The sun's high and all the Italians have tucked themselves away for lunch. The only people still out — but there are multitudes — are visitors.

'Tiziana is nice, isn't she?' Stefania says as she unlocks her parents' door.

'I'll make lunch. Yes, she's very nice, I like her a lot.'

'But an estate agent...'

'I'm surprised. Estate agents are disgusting people in England. Everyone hates them.'

'Ah yes, it is the same here, they are disgusting people. But there are estate agents and there are estate agents.'

'True.'

Meaning that Tiziana is an elite agent, for elite society, in which we're all peachily cordial friends. We go into the kitchen and I begin making lunch.

'Tiziana runs the business with another friend of hers. But don't you think she deserve more? At the end of the day it is a shit job,' Stef says.

'She seems to like it,' I demur. 'She's good at what she does. You can tell from her house that she's a cultured person.' I shrug. 'Maybe she's found the kind of life that suits her. And she's still very young. She could change her career if she wanted to.'

'Young? No!'

'What is she? Forty?'

'What! Are you crazy? She has – she is at least fifty-five. She had a husband, who had a business and a lot of money. Then the husband lose, lost the business – and she lost the husband. And at the age of forty she have to start everything from the beginning. She doesn't like to have a partner because she always has a lot of work, and she is a grandmother.'

'No! She looks so young,' I say, not quite believing Stef. 'And she's so beautiful.'

'Eh, Bidisha,' she grunts, 'she does not look that young. In my opinion. If you compare with our mothers...'

I bite back the temptation to say truthfully, '*Your* mum looks like she's about a hundred and eight.'

That night Tiziana's invited us to an arty party at the very grand Metropole Hotel down on the Riva degli Schiavoni, overlooking the sea. Before getting ready we go for a run together in residential Cannaregio, tracing the waterfront and the long parallel canals at the northern edge of the city. On the Fondamenta Nuove we look at the rolls of glowing turquoise water, the permanent diamond mist and the waiting cemetery-island opposite. I look across the cloudy blue water to the cemetery that's moving, floating like a painted heaven on the horizon. There are tall, thick firs and the glow of greenery behind the brick walls.

'First time in my life I wished I was inside a cemetery,' I joke to Stef as we pound straight down the middle of an outdoor restaurant. The waiters are so nimble that they glide out of our way like figure skaters, trays aloft. The hospital's at the end of the *fondamenta* and I feel guilty for jogging so proudly when there are people in wheelchairs parked outside waiting for the ambulance boats.

After some blissful tepid showers we get ready for the big night. There is to be no coarseness, no drunkenness, no excess of any kind – not even an excess of joy. That would be unseemly. On the way out we bump into Stefania's uncle but tell him we're in a rush because we have to attend a cocktail party.

'Oh! Well then!' he jokes, bowing and edging away. 'A cocktail party! Who am I to keep you? Merely a humble businessman, a flunkey with no conversation. If you please, where is it, your party?'

'The Metropole, of course,' replies Stefania.

'Ah! The Metropole, of course, of course. I understand perfectly. Please, go. Go to your elegant party.'

We walk down to St Mark's surrounded by people coming home to dinner, going out for drinks, groups of young friends enjoying themselves – and no chance of being mugged by a seven-year-old. Stefania tells me that her uncle speaks excellent French, as do a lot of people of his age (and, Stef doesn't need to say, class).

'Before the Anglo-Saxon invasion French was the common language to study. So if you are ever stuck...'

'Got it.'

It's humid outside and within ten minutes we both feel as though we're sleepwalking. Slowly I'm beginning to recognise things: which end of the Strada Nova leads to the station and which to Rialto and San Marco; the two sides of Rialto Bridge; the direction of Accademia from Rialto; a constellation of designer shops (Frette, Prada, Ferragamo, Gucci); certain turnings.

'Stef, why didn't Ginevra come out tonight? She's back from her holiday.'

'She say we can call her any time and she will come out, but not to concert, not to party, not to bar and not to cocktail.'

'Oh great. Let's invite her over and we can all sit 'round making origami birds and doing puzzles. What's she doing these days? If she graduated in April...'

'Nothing.'

'Literally? You mean she gets up in the morning and does what? Reads a book?'

'Checks stuff on the Internet. I say to her, if you want to get into – press? *Stampa*? *Editoriale*? I have a friend in Milan, we can go to meet her and take a coffee, just for some advice, what to do, what to avoid. She says no.'

'But *why*?'

'I don't know.' Stef adds dramatically, 'I live with the nightmare that she will kill herself. I will receive a phone call in the middle of the night: Ginevra has killed herself.'

'She doesn't seem depressed to me,' I object.

'But she always answer the phone, "*Pronto-o-oh...*" in this heavy, depressed voice. And she really has an ironical mind, a good sense of humour, a great culture.'

'Maybe she's just lazy?' I hazard. 'Laziness can seem like depression to the non-lazy.'

'My mum calls her Big Lazy Ginevra,' Stefania admits.

'Ha! To her face or behind her back?'

'Only behind her back.'

We're joined en route by Mara. I'm introduced to her parents, two virtually identical short, plump, plain, friendly, honest-looking people, and I see the class difference between them and Stefania's family. Stef has told me that Mara is ashamed of her parents because they're uneducated and own a shop; she's the first of her family to have studied past school. The five of us complain about the heat and Mara's dad, taking out a folded cotton handkerchief and pressing it to his neck, mentions the oppressiveness of the sirocco. I have a flash of Aschenbach then and remember, as though *Death in Venice* really happened, the smell of the canals and the disinfectant. In reality the rumoured cholera outbreak was in Palermo.

The Metropole, Stefania tells me, is a hotel for rich Americans but has a social club patronised by rich Venetians. We walk through the ice-cold lobby admiring the dark wood and pink marble decor. A sumptuous older lady comes out as we're going in and every waiter, sub-waiter, busboy, porter, receptionist and maid pops up their head to wish her a good evening – must be a platinum card customer. We go through to an outdoor restaurant overhung with white jasmine, white lilies and gardenias and lit with gold and white candles. At the end is a paved garden with round stone benches, a white octagonal marquee, a jazz band (coffee jazz, not gonzo-bonko jazz), fizzy prosecco in tumblers and the best-dressed, most nicely-behaved crowd of middle-aged people I've ever seen. The men, as one, are dark-haired, tanned, in featherweight linen shirts with brown leather belts and sandals, chinos or chino shorts or linen suits, all so tawnily neutral that it makes me thirsty just looking at them. And the women are spectacular. Not only are they chic, they're genuinely beautiful, every single one, and all are conversing with cordial confidence. As well as men, women and children, there are also dogs at the party. A Dalmatian passes by with a certain dignity.

'Bianca has a dog like that,' Mara tells me. 'He is very unfit. He is so fat they thought he was pregnant, but he is not. Now he is so big he looks like a cow.'

'Mara is feeling frustration for other men,' Stef says to me suddenly from my other side.

'Yes, I have some problems with Dario,' remarks Mara.

'Be strong,' I counsel.

'But it is hard,' says Mara. 'Finding a good boyfriend is like finding a good pair of jeans. You have to try on one hundred and twenty seven pairs before you get the right one.'

'We are not a bed-and-breakfast service,' says Stef.

Mara's previous boyfriend, Stef tells me, was a well-known historian, a clever, thoughtful, learned man who enjoyed giving his opinion about things (when invited) in newspapers. He introduced Mara to a world of dinner parties and other bright gents, who liked to get together and talk about justice, equality, liberty and the like. Indeed they spilled many words on the subject. Within six months of them meeting, Mara's boyfriend was (a) cheating on Mara and (b) using her as a childminder to look after his son.

'It is difficult to find the right man for *you*,' says Stef to me. 'I think the perfect one will be very old, very rich −'

'Oh, and impotent too, please −'

'But kind, that support you in your business, with a lot of money. And that die quite soon.'

'Then my happiness will be sealed,' I solemnly predict.

Luckily the arrival of Tiziana moves us off this topic.

'Thanks for this beautiful party,' I say in Italian. I learnt that today.

She slumps back in amazement: 'But you say it perfectly.'

'Yes, I'm an authentic Venetian girl now,' I say merrily.

Stef bumps into an old friend (male) who's on crutches.

'What happened to your foot?' she asks him.

'I broke it on Moses' stone!' he jokes.

'And the great love? How's that?'

'Ah yes, the great love. The great love lasted a year and that was that.' He laughs and shrugs sadly before moving on.

'See?' says Stef to me immediately. 'He is a nice boy.'

'And you want me to do what, get him when he's lame and depressed?'

Afterwards there's a free experimental music concert in the Telecom Italia building, formerly a cloister. We file into the courtyard and admire the walls of the tall sand-coloured building around us, four floors high, the sill of each arched black window flickering with citronella candles. There are two or three hundred people sitting around, leaning against the pillars or cooling the soles of their feet on the marble. The music consists of a recorded commentary of some guy mumbling to himself on a train, accompanied by four lumpy Buddhist-retreat-visiting (probably) people in hessian/beads/ankh/sandals coming up to the mic and sawing a piece of string with a violin bow, gently and then violently crinkling some tinfoil, spilling some lentils across a tin tray and so on. I look around the hall. Many people are yawning but oddly none are laughing. Mara leans over:

'The music is experimental,' she admits, 'but the spoken part is very interesting and very funny.'

'I wanted to see this,' says Stef once we're outside afterwards, in a tone of telling me off, 'because the composer is very well known. He is an old man, so he is not just some boy who make meaningless noise. He has done some stuff that is really interesting and I think important.'

We also have tickets that night for a modern dance performance in watery, empty, pallid Arsenale, the only place in Venice that feels truly spacious: fortresses, wide pale stone on broad walkways, hulking, sparse, pointed bridges. The venue's the Corderie dell'Arsenale, part of the old ship-building complex where they once made naval rope. It's full of high, rough, dark stone, round pillars and perspiring, gorgeously costumed Venetians.

And what is a Venetian cultural audience like? All grown up, and amazingly ill behaved. They sit complacently, coughing and tapping their feet, chatter throughout, look around and keep getting up and sitting down again, dawdling and conversing. There's no stage and the performance space is marked out by a large area of black mats. Crossing this terrain is an otherworldly-looking pale woman all in black, stepping deliberately from one side to the other. Her body's like a single length of cord. The audience is not impressed as they watch her go back and forth. They begin whispering naughtily:

'I'm scared.'

'She goes that way and then she goes *that* way.'

'Where are the other dancers?'

'Oh no, not again.'

'I think I can detect a pattern here.'

'I can't tell what *those* people are doing. They're part of the dance... oh, no, they're looking for seats.'

'*Mamma*, where are we going for dinner?'

On our way out afterwards I see my favourite bridge in Venice. It's between the two stretches of the Riva di Ca' di Dio and the Riva San Biagio. I think of it as the bridge made of sugar, utterly plain, pure floating white, hung from the sky, an alien object with nothing behind it but the sea, which at nine-thirty that night is like cobalt blue paint, the sky a single shade lighter, meeting in a long and subtle line.

Back up by Rialto, close to the *pescheria*, we go to an *osteria* with a pretty spread of tables outside, the Canal Grande close by, no railings. I notice a woman watching me. She's in her early fifties, very fresh, with no make-up on and a pale, composed face with clean, white bobbed hair, a pressed blue and white men's shirt, canvas trousers and espadrilles. She's leaning just inside the doorway holding a small tumbler of red wine. I sense the still, almost starched atmosphere around her as we pass.

Lo and behold, the waitress is another old friend of Stef and Mara's and charges us only three euros in total – for three tall flutes of prosecco, cheese and bread. We've just said goodbye when the older lady who was watching me comes forward and lays her steady, civilised gaze on me.

'Excuse me,' she says in Italian, 'I just wanted to say, the dress you're wearing is very beautiful.'

'Thank you,' I reply graciously. It's my favourite dress. In fact it's my only dress: plain buff-coloured silk, knee-length and long-sleeved, with a fine gold edge. My mum had it made for me.

'Such a beautiful colour and line and on you, with your bearing, it's lovely. Is it from Venice?' asks the woman.

'No, it was made in India,' says Stefania for me, watching the woman in her pleasant, inscrutable way.

'Ah! Tailor-made. Yes, that is obvious. I used to own a similar dress. Pale pink with a gold border.'

We drift away cordially. Stefania and I find ourselves walking next to each other smiling slyly.

'That was a very nice lady,' says Stef.

'Yup.'

'A kind of bohemian lady.'

'Oh yes.'

'Very friendly.'

'Very friendly and elegant. An art teacher doing a grand tour,' I suggest.

'Ah, no, but she was Venetian. I could tell from her accent. But definitely an art teacher.'

'Definitely,' I say, starting to laugh.

'And maybe a lesbian,' says Stefania bluntly.

'Yes, maybe a lesbian!'

Venice may officially have no gay scene... in which case there are an awful lot of people here who simmer with 'unofficial' longings.

On a Venetian night out, one must stroll casually from venue to venue, taking a sip of prosecco here, a bite of bread or meatball (*una polpetta* – lovely plump word) there, enjoying the balmy atmosphere and the sheer sauntering joy of being alive. The civilised nature of life here means that people start going out at night at the age of fourteen or so and continue until well into their nineties.

We wind up at Postali, the Parisian-style bar round the corner from my new flat, on the Rio Marin. Inside there's another friend of Stef's, a woman with a strange handshake: she seizes my hand really hard, lifts it up a few inches and then loosens all her fingers completely like a crane, and my hand drops out. She has a slimy possessive boyfriend, his arms wrapped right around her, holding her fast to the seat. We're all introduced but he doesn't want to know.

The beautiful stupid Russian boy is working behind the bar and Mara, who perishes of drought without male attention, goes to chat him up. The ensuing conversation, recorded verbatim, goes like this:

'It's the first time I've worked here for the entire week,' he says. 'Usually I only work occasionally.'

'No, that can't be true,' says Mara charmingly.

'No. It is,' he says, puzzled.

'But every time I come here, you're here.'

'Ah,' he replies, and his puzzlement deepens.

'So maybe it is – destiny?' prompts Mara.

'I don't know,' he says, and he's being sincere: he really doesn't know.

Mara retreats from this and drops into her chair with a sigh.

'He's not interested,' she says with something like relief. 'And he's stupid.'

'But Mara. We knew this,' says Stef.

Afterwards we go to see my flat and stand in the *campiello* looking up at the window. I breathe deeply.

'I'm just checking that it doesn't smell of algae like some parts of Venice. If it does I'll just have to keep reminding myself that it's perfectly natural. Or pretend it's something else,' I say.

'Ah! The beautiful perfume of violets!' Mara proclaims. 'How delicate the fragrance is!'

The next morning I head to the beach with Stefania and her boyfriend Bruno. It's a sunny, windy, hot day and Venice is crowded with overweight children from all over the world. I hear a particularly rotund American boy of eight or so saying in a high voice, 'Dad? Can we take a break? I need to catch my breath.'

'Sure,' says Dad, 'let's take a break and you can catch your breath.'

I mean, it's only ten in the morning, the kid's eight years old, what's he been doing all week, toiling up the Dolomites? As well as the tourists there are lots of older people doing their daily shopping on the Strada Nova. The vegetable stalls are open, kids are running around their grandparents' knees. Children have quite a degree of freedom in Venice as there's no chance of them getting hit by a car.

Stefania and I are standing by a shop looking at nothing in particular when Nero snaps at a fluffy, thimble-sized dog who bounces away and flies up into its owner's arms, squeaking lustily like a children's toy. The owner and his wife immediately clutch the dog up and begin breathing hard in panic, turning the dog over and over, squeezing it and searching hysterically through its fur for signs of damage. Stef and I look at each other blandly. Nero is unbothered and slumps to the ground.

'I'm very sorry, I wasn't watching him properly,' says Stefania to the man. 'Is there any blood?'

'No! What were you thinking? Your dog should be muzzled.'

'But my dog didn't attack yours, it was only a snap. If you're sure your dog's OK... I do apologise, I hope nothing's wrong with it. But what can you do? They're dogs. That's their way.'

But what the man really wants is a fight. He's boiled-faced, fat, with a straining gut in a T-shirt and pleated polyester trousers. His wife is silent, over-tanned, tall and bulbous-bodied with raw red lipstick, tropical-print leggings and gold-appliquéd T-shirt. The dog's the tiny excitable neurotic type that you can strangle one-handed.

'That is *not* their way,' hisses the man at Stefania. 'Your dog is a threat, he should be put down.'

'But why? As you can see, he didn't even touch your dog. When he was a puppy he endured a lot of aggression from older, bigger dogs. It's natural.'

'Your dog is *not* big, he is medium-sized.'

The man continues shouting and spitting, holding his dog up to his eye like a rare diamond. The dog plays up to it, looking panicked upwards to heaven, whimpering, panting and spinning in the man's hands, swivelling around nervously as though he feels Nero might be lurking at his heels with his knife and fork ready and a napkin tucked into his collar. The man clearly won't be happy – if ever – until Nero is wrestled to the kerb, muzzled by force, shot in the hind legs and then stoned to death in the Campo dei Santi Apostoli in front of a crowd of jeering Venetians.

Then he pulls out his trump card.

'I am a public official, don't talk to *me* in that way. I think you need to show me your papers, then we'll see who solves the problem.'

'You're a public official?' says Stef. 'Good. We can go to the police station and sort this out. I agree with you that it's the best thing to do.'

'No – we don't need to go to the police station,' says the man, caught out. 'It's enough that I see your papers. You can't talk to me like this!'

He reaches with some difficulty into his back pocket, gets his ID, which has police credentials on it, and pushes it in her face.

'No, no, I insist,' says Stef. 'If I've done something wrong then I want to take full responsibility for it. So let's take our dogs to the police station and see how it goes.'

The bluffing man backs away frightened and enraged, fondling the squeaking dog, which gives us an agonised look. He snarls that Stefania isn't worth talking to and lumbers away, muttering and still checking the dog.

'Seriously, Bidisha, people in this city are becoming more and more crazy the more time that passes,' Stef mutters, shaking her head.

We keep walking, looking around.

'Unbelievable,' says Stef after a while. Having kept her temper so beautifully it's now leaking out slowly in drops. 'He is the type of person who if you are not careful with him, he will try to make your life like hell. I mean come on, we are not living in some Mafia village in Sicily.'

'Yeah, what *was* that? "I am a public official." He probably cleans the canals around the police station at four every morning. I feel sorry for his wife, she has to take his shit all day. If he's not afraid to blow up like that in public you can imagine what he's like at home.'

Stef's boyfriend Bruno arrives to meet us and we set off for the boat stop together. Bruno's tall and attractive, with a shrewd, youthful face and an expression of permanent pondering, a tension across the shoulders. He's a documentary producer, always travelling, very urbane but with a sincerity and a gawky niceness that give him a teenagerish quality. I met him a few years ago when he flew over from Colombia to surprise Stefania on Valentine's Day. It's the real deal between them: they've been together for ten years, since their teens, and as Stefania says shyly, 'We are linked.'

'I think I should change my occupation and become a guru,' she says jubilantly as we walk, 'because last week I persuade this other friend of me, mine, to wear a bikini for the first time. Because she really has a beautiful body, why she not show it? And instead she wear this fifties-style black thing – boh! I mean come on... it was like made of wool. And now I persuade you to come to the beach. And if you have a crisis or a nervous breakdown you can come back. Bruno has brought you a special gift of factor fifty total sunblock lotion.'

'I bought it in the tropics,' says Bruno, handing it to me.

'Because I know you are a fanatic about the sun,' says Stef. True enough.

I pour some out: white emulsion paint, totally opaque. I've already applied it several times even before we leave for the Lido and all the other tourists have the pleasure of seeing Stefania and Bruno, a well-suited couple, and their friend the mime/clown/melting mannequin.

There's a large cinnamon-scented *pasticceria* nearby, its windows crammed with boxes of amaretto biscuits, wrapped loaves and sugared almonds, decorated with scrolls of ribbon and cellophane. Deeply suspect: too grotesque to be authentic. Stefania, seeing what I'm looking at, says:

'You will soon be able to tell which are the real *pasticcerie* and which are the touristic ones.'

'The not-authentic ones are the ones that have everything displayed in the windows,' says Bruno. 'Tourists like to see how much stuff the shop has. They do not trust the shopkeeper. Venice is always like this, of course, but it has changed even during my life. Now there is not one month of the year that we have no tourists. Everything is for them. Look at this.'

There are about forty teenaged tourists sitting in the middle of the Strada Nova for no reason, staring around vacantly and eating the dust kicked up by other people's shoes. I think about the number of times I've watched Nero defecate silkily onto those very paving stones and give a private shudder. We pass two Englishmen of about our age, both slim but already out of shape, dead white, topless, strutting and holding beer bottles.

'Put on your shirt,' Bruno mutters to himself.

'Is it illegal to be shirtless here?' I ask, half-joking.

'Yes, of course. The fine is like one hundred euros. This is a city. Nobody wants to see your chest.'

We go over one of the large bridges on the way to the station, one edge of it levelled down so that people can wheel their luggage along. Bruno says to Stefania in English, 'Oh, tell Bidisha the story of the *moneta* man.'

'Ah!' says Stefania. She and Bruno begin to smile. 'Every single day on this bridge there was the same man who ask for money, the same thing every day. He was bent over like this.' She hunches low and crooks her legs. '"Moneta,"' she rasps, '"moneta, per favore, moneta, moneta." That was all he said. He was, like, the famous moneta man. He had one leg.'

'No, two legs, but one was good and one was bad,' Bruno corrects her.

'Yes, one was good and one that was bad. Anyway, one day the moneta man was not there for some reason, and on the wall next to the bridge were, like, two big pieces of yellow paper. The first one had a drawing, the moneta man bent over, saying, "Moneta, per favore, moneta, moneta..."'

'Aha...' I say leadingly.

'And the second piece of paper,' she and Bruno start laughing, 'he was standing up, look young, doing a big dance, big smile on his face, with both legs working, next to his suitcase, about to go on summer holiday!'

We all stop spontaneously and laugh, me imagining the great cartoon grin and whirling legs of the second drawing.

'Someone had watched the man for weeks, drawn him and put the posters up on the wall in the night,' Bruno manages to say.

'And the moneta man?' I ask.

'The moneta man was never seen again!'

We catch a big white boat to the Lido. There's full yellow sunlight over the sea and nearly all the seats are full. The sea today is deep blue and full of brightness, with very precise silver and gold lines glinting on the surface as though a crystal net's been thrown over the water. The Lido appears in the distance, kitsch as all beach places are, peach melba colours and short buildings, cars parked everywhere. Odd to see them, but they make me realise how little I miss London – how, in fact, I haven't thought about it once.

'The beach we've chosen is good because it is organised and it is a good combination of popular people and working-class people and upper-class people,' Bruno and Stefania tell me.

I still can't tell the difference between the classes and in swimming costumes everyone looks the same anyway. There's a long, sandy walk to the beach. Everything's very pristine looking, even the paving stones. I suppose the sand scours them clean. Alongside the walkway is the stretch of sandy beach, open-air showers, bathroom shacks, striped cabins, groups of perfect unselfconscious teenagers and a volleyball court where some kids are trying to get a man to dislodge their ball from a tree. The man kicks a second ball hard up into the branches. The tree shakes and both balls tumble down. Cries of admiration and gratitude for the hero kicker of the day.

Every few yards behind the cabins the kids have set out a sort of garage sale of unwanted things arranged on beach towels: old books, toys and ornaments. We look at them as we go by, all the little children playing shopkeeper. The last towel's interesting. It's loaded with handmade glass bead necklaces in various colours: Masai primaries, Tibetan brown, red and orange wooden beads, chunky bracelets that look like they've been made from sweets, even jade glass and coral. The shopkeepers here are two fat, suntanned bull-boys of about ten, sitting on folding chairs to signal their status. An elegant lady picks up a coral and white mandala and asks about it.

'That necklace is Chinese, it costs thirty euros,' says one of the boys in a booming voice, not looking at her.

Everyone within earshot laughs and he looks cross. We walk on grinning to ourselves.

'Once at the beach I saw a child's stall,' Bruno says to me, 'and there were lots of things, and also two packages, "Surprise Package for Girls" and "Surprise Package for Boys", and I am sure that in those packages were the very *worst* things that she had!'

It's windy and very hot but not painfully so, and I can see the water like blue mist rolling close by. Stefania and Bruno comment on how crowded the beach is but it seems almost empty to me; I'd imagined throngs of greasy near-naked people baking it out, clumped together like bacteria on a microscope slide. Here we have lines of clean blue and white wooden cabanas, each with a table, chair and deck, hooks for hanging belongings and a curtain to change behind.

'They're very expensive,' says Bruno to me, 'so we all join together and rent one, about twenty families, and we share it. It's good because it's a social occasion too. We have all known each other for years. We saw the children growing up.'

Speaking of which, we arrive at the last cabana in the row, perpendicular to the water, and find a pink-swimsuited little girl making a mini city in the sand. She ignores us but doesn't mind us watching her work. First she digs a lake and fills it with water, then she produces a bag of excellent miniature plastic cats and dogs of various breeds. These are so perfectly rendered that we all spontaneously fall to our knees, reach for them and start asking about them: How many are there? Are they all different? Do the cats and dogs live together or separately? She's very cool under the attention and shows us the compound she's designed and built. There are separate areas for the cats and dogs to sleep, wash, swim and eat.

A woman of around seventy comes around the corner, very upright, pale, elegant and beautiful in a black one-piece swimming costume, her smooth white hair kept back with a Hermès scarf, a long face with a wide coral-lipped smile and watchful, bright eyes. We're all introduced – she's the girl's grandmother and her name's Anna. She talks about how soft and warm the water is, how lovely the colours are that day. She offers me some cherries (wonderful word: *ciliegie*) as I'm standing on the deck pushing my toes into the sand at the edge. I shake my head no before the others can translate for me and she says kindly, 'Ah! You understand Italian.' We smile at each other. Nice kindred soul.

Bruno and then Stefania go behind the curtain and change into shorts and white triangle bikini. I've come in a linen shirt and shorts and don't intend to remove them; the shirt hides a dark, bad, deeply regretted prison-style tattoo that covers the whole of my left shoulder and arm down to my wrist.

The girl with the cats and dogs is still playing by herself, very absorbed.

'How old are you?' asks Bruno.

'Only five,' she replies firmly.

'But five is big! Stefania was five when she first came here.'

'I'm the smallest one on the beach.'

We take our towels, say goodbye to Anna and the clever little girl and go towards the water.

'So, Bidisha, what do you think? A crisis?' says Stef.

'Not at all. When you said "beach" I was imagining a kind of Dante hell.'

We settle ourselves about thirty feet from the sea and there are eighteen feet of clean sand between us and anyone else. Stefania and Bruno lie flat on their backs and chatter while I apply sun cream to my entire body frenziedly.

'You are going for maximum protection,' says Bruno approvingly. 'That is very wise. Me, I put on myself – banana oil!'

A peaceful silence descends as we begin to soak up the sun. After half an hour or so Stef and Bruno go to swim. They stand at the edge, looking out and talking, a silver cloud of heat hovering over the sea. They wade in, knee-high, then waist-high. A smooth rolling wave comes to meet them and as one they dive bottom-up head-down like dolphins into the heart of the water. They surface, bobbing far out in the sea, and I see Bruno in one movement leap forward in the water and cling to Stef, kissing her cheek. They swim further out. The sun's straight above me and breaks over my head like an egg yolk.

From behind my shades I watch a group of women in front of me, all about sixty years old. They're sitting, nutty brown, bikinied, oiled, legs akimbo, on a row of brightly-coloured sun loungers under a closed, askew sun umbrella. One of them is sewing very firmly with a thick red thread, pushing the needle in so hard that she must be hemming tarpaulin or mending a canvas sail. Another woman mocks herself:

'Look at me: I have *this* [she slaps her stomach], I have *this* [she pinches her thigh]. Who cares? Here I am, take it or leave it!'

And with that she lies back, grinning, and gives herself up to the sun gods.

After a couple of hours the three of us decide to leave and go back to the cabana to change. A new woman's there, fabulous forties in a leopard print bikini and tortoiseshell Sophia Loren sunglasses (which reminds me, Loren was on TV the other day, prompting howls from Stefania: 'She is eighty-five years old! She last made a good film in the fifties! And she is really a man.'). The woman's there with her teenaged daughter and the daughter's friends, bikinis for the girls, tiny trunks for the boys. Every girl looks like Artemis and every boy looks like Pan. We all say hello and they look me over curiously. I'd thought I'd be able to blend in in Italy but I realise that I don't have the Italians' ease, certainty or charisma.

On our way back to the boat stop we pass Hotel Des Bains and the private beach where Luchino Visconti shot *Death in Venice*. It's become tired and grimy in the last few decades, all its pastel colours shot through with grey. The Lido's very quiet. On the boat I lean over and watch the white foam cling to the water, separate and disappear, rise and cling. As we approach Venice proper we begin to make out the series of bridges, St Mark's Piazzetta and the pointed clock tower. It doesn't loom over us but, as Turner knew, seems to come softly into being, materialising from nothing, a city made of icing dust and rice-paper. Stefania, Bruno and I get off the boat, take a side street and tread deep inside to secret, stony brown-and-grey Venice, into a tiny cubicle of a *pasticceria* with dark pink marble counters and rows of mad-scientist jars containing wrapped sweets. The air's hot and smells of basil and sugar.

'Usually they make a beautiful hot *pizzetta* but only on Sundays, they say,' says Stef disappointedly after consulting with the owners. 'I wanted to show you.'

Instead she has a cheese twist and I choose a pastry tart with green olives, which I eat leaning against the counter with the sun glowing in my bones.

'This is the traditional thing to do after going to the beach,' Bruno tells me and I nod lazily, too enamoured by the tart to say anything.

I insist on paying as a thank you for the beautiful day. They protest but I have a strong feeling that this is the correct thing to do; their vague remonstrations are merely part of the accepted etiquette. I must develop an instinct for when is the right time to pay and when to be paid for, when to insist and when to hang back, when to protest and when to murmur my thanks.

That night after Stef's gone upstairs I stay on her parents' balcony until one. The sky goes charcoal black and gold at the edges, the Canal Grande turns bottle green and a blurred solid rain begins to fall very quietly, so elegantly that I don't notice it at first. A strange grey mist comes down. The view is now all dark metallic greens, greys, silvers and blacks. The vaporetti and water taxis still go past but look as though they're struggling and the entire river seems to twist in one piece like liquorice, the power coming from deep inside. Then the water of the river begins to crinkle down from the direction of the station and fold itself into thin, strong, opaque green pleats. The rain comes down finer and denser and the water goes dull on the surface, its hard reflections turning into amber smears. In the rain the buildings become dull, soaking it up, and the windows go an absolute forbidding black. The rain stops eventually and the water turns black again, the sky purplish. The gold and white lights melt into the water. Time for bed.

Chapter Four

My moving out and Stefania's parents' return from their respective conferences coincide perfectly. Stef and Bruno are in Padova so on my last evening alone I jog up to the empty Fondamenta Nuove, opposite the cemetery. The view's pallid and the water looks as though it's been carved out of salt. Just before the hospital I take a right and find myself in countless courtyards, secret gardens, dead ends and capricious serpentine coils, up and down white stone bridges, red brick bridges, spindly black iron bridges, brown wooden bridges, past clinking tethered boats, canals foul-smelling, salty-smelling, reedy-smelling or eerily still. I'm trying to come out on the south edge near the Giardini, the public gardens with their crunching gravel walkways and the white live-looking statues, right by the Biennale pavilions. I pass a guy sitting outside with a young, small, chocolate brown lurcher puppy, soft bones, gleaming short fur, intelligent, questioning face (the dog), too-big paws and an adorable lolloping way of running, plus a way of sitting down, plonking itself onto the floor and staring up at passers-by, ergo very cute. It's not really the done thing to spontaneously pet someone else's dog in Venice so I keep my hands off but the puppy ups and follows me and nips the back of my ankle playfully before being called back.

As I leap down a bridge, having been momentarily spooked by the sight of my own shadow spreading along the steps in front of me, I see two little French girls, nine or ten years old, in matching white cotton dresses, hair washed and combed and pristine, playing a game of Simon Says.

'Now do it,' one commands the other in French.

The other bunny-hops three neat steps to the right.

'*Un, deux, trois,*' she says as she does so.

I jog past. They look up and grin.

'*Buongiorno,*' they call to me merrily in perfect accents. I'm a little way on before I hear them. After a spasm of shyness I turn back and call out '*Buongiorno!*'

The girls beam.

'*Grazie!*' they trill, and I scamper away ecstatically. Such elegant, touching, tactful behaviour!

Occasionally I pass people making their way out for the evening but mainly I encounter oldish well-dressed men who stop in their tracks and stare openly, grunting comments like 'Ugh, that's good, bounce down those steps,' in time with my footfalls. Venetians are so leisurely that they find the sight of anyone doing exercise unutterably hilarious, futile, absurd, pointing me out to their friends, turning to peer into my eyes to detect signs of madness as I hobble past, my head glowing like a hazard light.

I walk towards the public gardens trying to catch my breath, the water of the Canale di San Marco on my right. The sun's beginning to set and everything's gold – the cobbles, the water, the sky, the hotel windows. I hear the bell-tower ringing, see the church of San Giorgio Maggiore floating on its island in the distance, somehow a proud and unpleasant sight, set in plenty of protective green. The sea's a length of gauze with a haze of heat and milky colour oozing off it.

By the time I get to the Giardini it's getting dark and the statues look a bit too ready to turn their heads and watch me pass. The trees are full of the throbbing noise of crickets like cheering fans at a rock concert. The art pavilions are always sinister when not in use, waiting amidst the leaves and dark gravel. Great Britain's pavilion is one big imperial temple in Victorian colours, royal green and muddy red. By the kids' play area I see three wooden gypsy caravans, each one delicately embellished, with three steps and a ridged rose-painted porch. There are kids and men ranged around them, lean and brown, and the beginnings of a fire. The men are brushing their teeth under the drinking-water fountains. That's when I realise they're real, not some dedicated theatre troupe putting on a show *about* gypsies. They look at me warily as I run past, as if I'm going to tell on them. I don't stare.

Turning back towards St Mark's again I pass the souvenir-sellers who've packed up for the day and are now urging their stalls in front of them on rickety wheels. There are some pleasure boats moored along the edge of the water, big white things called *Athena* and *Diana*. Some men lean out to watch me – staff, not passengers, dressed in smart white uniforms with caps. One of them pounds on the railing and shouts jeeringly to me, 'Run! Run!' His friend laughs wildly next to him. I start passing the grandest of the hotels on my right, their waterfront restaurants full of tubby flushed people.

I turn in to the piazza just as the sky goes navy blue and all the lights come up. St Mark's Square is all confidence, dark gold, bronze, a giant gilded cloister lined with expensive shops, bustling gold cafes, pigeons, hawkers, Venetians and visitors. Stef has told me there's no point doing a racial comparison of London and Venice because there's no systematic immigration in Venice but I do make a few notes: African street-hawkers selling fake Louis Vuitton and Prada bags outside the (nice touch) actual Louis Vuitton and Prada shops; Sri Lankan waiters and trinket-sellers – I see them gathering at the end of the day; Bangladeshi guys on the beach going from group to group holding out belts, 'Rolexi' watches and hangers full of nylon sarongs; Japanese waitresses, nannies and cleaners. Stefania says that the immigrants here are part of the grey market, not quite legal, not quite not; they live 'a shit life' as domestics or peddlers.

I cut into the middle of the square and kick slowly through the pigeons. Then an interesting thing happens. From nowhere a group of geeky young people (seventeen years old? Sixteen?) with rucksacks, specs, bags and notebooks form a circle with their teacher in the middle. They begin to sing a devotional song in Latin, all tenor, alto and soprano, no bass. The song gathers in the evening, smoothly bending. I can't help but stop as everyone in the square is, like me, drawn towards the sound. It's impossible to tell who's making it as we all seem to join the circle. Children run forward, tugged by the harmonies. As it goes on, one of the singers, a beautiful girl with corn-yellow waist-length hair and long Mormon skirt turns her head, looks behind her and smiles at me while singing. I nod minutely. The song ends and with a laugh and a shrug the teenaged singers disband and walk off. Within ten seconds they're lost in the crowd.

Night falls. I get lost and find myself stuck in cold, dark, residential Dorsoduro in the south. I see the white church of Angelo Raffaele with its statue of San Tobiolino, the boy and the fish and the little dog, which I recognise from Salley Vickers' book *Miss Garnet's Angel*. The church has interesting proportions, very flat and big, square like a packing box, sitting at an angle to the other buildings, looking as though a harried housekeeper shoved it there in the hope that nobody'd notice.

I seem to be the only person in the city. I run through long dark alleys, past churches brown, black and white, up and down deserted canals. I keep going north and see nobody except, on one bridge, a slim man carrying a double bass taller and three times as wide as he is, in a coffin-like case with two wheels on the bottom. I'm about to ask if he needs help getting it down the other side when I see that there's a little strap on the upper side of the case so that he can hoist it through his shoulder, heave it onto his back and carry it over like Jesus bearing the cross.

Close by Stefania's house a young Sri Lankan guy spots me and walks out of the blue straight at me, very hard and strong and deliberate. Every time I change my direction he laughs and changes his. Eventually he gives up the game and simply walks fast and strong into me, clips me with his whole body and hisses 'Ciao' in my ear as I stumble, then veers away and disappears. I walk on, my muscles very hard so that it's like walking on stilts.

I turn in when I see the men's clothing shop by Stefania's house. Get home, peel off my clothes and hit the shower hard. Later I tell Stef about the singing group and my magic Venice music moment and she rolls her eyes, unsurprised. Christian fundamentalist schools from middle America have a habit of bringing their choirs over here for music competitions and staging impromptu imperial takeovers in the square, she tells me.

She wonders just how quickly the police and the haters would come running if a group of Muslim singers got together and spontaneously began whirling in the name of Allah.

The next day I pack my things and go for a short walk to the Campo Santi Giovanni e Paolo, whose church seems to have been constructed solely out of big round brown towers joined together like a bulbous chocolate sponge roll. The shops are all closed (usually ditto for Monday mornings and all lunch-hours) but I look in at some glass and mask memento shops. Stefania says that the famous annual *carnevale* is only for tourists and that the mask shops sell thin, cheap, ashy reproductions straight off a Beijing conveyor belt. There's perhaps one genuine mask workshop remaining in Venice, if that. I see some vile antiques: tin silver, plastic glass goblets, haunted old dress jewellery.

When Lucrezia arrives from her conference in London we lay the table on the balcony, light our citronella candles and enjoy a beautiful dinner made by Stefania: rice noodles with pesto, a kind of herbed flatbread, some flavoursome courgettes and red pepper and then, bliss, some wonderful ice cream from Il Gelatone on the Strada Nova. The flavours are yoghurt, grapefruit, yoghurt-and-sesame, strawberry (a great dusky pink colour), icy lemon and – my God – two blocks of iced whipped cream between wafers.

Lucrezia says I should go to Ca' Pesaro, the stippled white multi-columned museum that we can see from the balcony. It contains many past Biennale exhibits and, on the top floor, a key collection of Japanese art.

'Venice has a long history of loving art,' Lucrezia says. 'There were the schools affiliated to the churches, of course. They are called the *scuole*.'

School as in guild or workshop, not school for little kids.

'I know, there's the *scuola* of San Rocco right by my apartment,' I say.

'But the municipality also commissioned and bought work from Venetian painters as a way of sustaining them. They may not do that now, but whenever there is an exhibition, everyone in Venice goes to see it. There is a cultural and a social commitment.'

'I remember, once I met this horrible English man and he asked me if I had heard of this particular painter, a Venetian man, and I did not,' says Stefania. She frowns. 'Horrible man. This typical English man that thinks to know everything about another country.'

But the conversation turns another way and I don't get any more details about the myriad facets and expressions of his horribleness.

Instead we discuss my move. I'm supposed to meet Tiziana, the estate agent, who'll show me into the apartment and get me settled. Lucrezia gives me some essential information about her: she has a very old mother whom she looks after; she's Slovenian, although brought up in Italy; she has a thirty-year-old daughter, Elena, who in the recent past had a relationship with a gondolier and had a child with him. Elena the daughter is now in a relationship with a lawyer and this is deemed by everyone to be a more promising set-up, although I don't see how, particularly. I've met more evil lawyers than I have evil gondoliers.

Then I witness a perfect example of northern-Italian nicety, which goes like this: Stef and Lucrezia press me to finish all the pasta. I demur. They press me about six more times, saying that both of them are full to the brim and it'll only go to waste and that it's hardly a luxury meal which has to be split fairly three ways with every round. Eventually, because I'm very hungry, I relent and take the last big spoonful gratefully. After a decided pause Lucrezia looks at me pointedly, blinks once, picks up the bowl that the pasta was in, stares glumly inside it and starts scraping it with one tine of her fork and nibbling the minuscule leftover pieces of basil while I sit with the huge dollop I've taken on my plate. Irritated and embarrassed I realise I've done the wrong thing and insist that she takes half of what I've got. She refuses flat out twice as though she wouldn't dream of it, waving me off with a pitiful gesture, but accepts fully the third time I ask. Unable to help letting out a 'Why didn't you say so at the beginning? I would never have taken all of this if I knew you were still hungry. Give me your plate,' I heave up a ton of the pasta from my plate and hurl it onto hers, then stare at her in rebuke. Stefania understands all this in a flash, grins at me and says, 'On behalf of all the Italian people in the world I want to say: be less rigid!'

Moving day starts off grey and cold, with a clump of tarnished cloud floating above San Eustachio. That place is more of a miniatures cabinet than a church; there are statues in niches, statues on columns, statues in special alcoves and even stuck up on the roof like wedding cake decorations. Lucrezia emerges wearing her sleep-clothes but looking as though she's just stepped out of an appointment at Coco Chanel's atelier: a knee-length tartan flannel nightshirt and tan Birkenstock sandals. Her perfect white legs look as though they've been carved out of beech. I must be exuding some kind of psychological disorder because the moment I enter the kitchen she bolts out of it saying that I'm to help myself to whatever breakfast I want.

'I'm just going to get a cup of tea,' I say skittishly.

'As you like,' she replies, backing away.

Stefania's going to Padova especially early today in order to be back in time to help me. I forget about breakfast and go into the study to make the bed and change. I hear Nero barking on the stairs outside as Stefania leaves her apartment. Sometimes he barks for no reason: 'Oh *why*?' The existential canine query. Even dogs have their moments of angst and doubt.

Lucrezia's taken the opportunity of me being out of the kitchen to go back in there again and is just finishing her oats when I return to wash out my teacup. Whatever Stef says about her parents ('I think they love each other, but everything they do, there is a big argument about it') I can hear the feeling in their voices when they talk about each other. Lucrezia tells me twice in the space of ten minutes that Gregorio is due to be coming back from his conference in Brazil today. Then the phone rings and she leaps to her feet: 'Ah! That is Gregorio – I hope.' Gregorio also said to me on my first visit here, when we were in St Mark's Square, 'Florian's is a good place to go. Sometimes I go in the evening, with Lucrezia.' The sweet note of that shy 'with Lucrezia' said it all.

Lucrezia and I go out to meet Gregorio, dump some rubbish and walk the dog. The Strada Nova is full of fruit and veg stalls and tourists not keeping to the right. Nero is very lively and Lucrezia laughs:

'With all the female dogs it's lust, with all the male dogs it's a fight.'

I only have to ask twice and mount a reasoned argument before she'll let me take the heavier rubbish bags off her. We ask if we can dump them on some passing bin men but they're minimally apologetic:

'We don't have the boat today, only the carts, so we don't want to take anything we can't carry ourselves. Otherwise it gets too heavy.'

Eventually they relent and agree to take one bag of paper goods from us. As we walk away afterwards a bitter man complains because he almost tripped over Nero in the crowd:

'How can I be expected to walk in these conditions?' he spits into Lucrezia's face.

Lucrezia gives him a very cool shrug. She is not, but seems, physically frail. It's in her arid, chalky voice and her way of walking in small, fast tottering steps, as though she's very cold. Nero has been getting more and more excited the closer we get to the Ca d'Oro vaporetto stop, where we spy Gregorio waiting cheerfully, a clockwork owl in navy blazer and cotton twill trousers, the remains of his well-clipped hair in two white tufts above his ears. He carries a large navy wheelie case (to match his jacket) and an ochre canvas suit bag (to match his trousers). Nero gives no consideration to this *habille* and jumps up, around and across him, rolls on the ground, stretches, bows, leaps and so on. I hang back. Lucrezia rushes forward, they kiss and embrace and immediately start walking quickly home together. Eventually Gregorio remembers himself, stops, turns back and kisses me on the cheek politely.

'I have been in a conference in Brazil.'

'Ah,' I say, wanting to get away and leave them to it, but they're so keen to get back that I can't actually find a moment to stop and stage a leave-taking. I wind up trailing after them.

'Yes, the third-largest town in Brazil,' says Gregorio over his shoulder. 'Completely ugly. Whenever we tried to suggest that we see the town, the organisers said, "Why? There is no need. And you must be tired from the conference. Go to the hotel and sleep. We will send a car for you." They would not let us go anywhere. Everything was done for us and they would not let us pay for anything. And I caught a cold. Because everything was air-conditioned. From the car to the hotel, a twelve-hour coach ride, all of us together.'

'Air conditioning is the best way to catch an illness,' I say listlessly. All the while Gregorio has been talking, Lucrezia has not turned around once.

'Yes, terrible,' says Gregorio sadly.

Just as they're about to run up the last bridge with the dog I dig my heels into the ground and tell them I'm going for a walk.

'OK!' shouts Gregorio ecstatically before once again remembering his manners and adding, 'Ah, Bidisha, we are going to eat – Lucrezia?'

'At one o'clock,' says Lucrezia so unwillingly that she can barely open her mouth to speak, 'if you would like to come.'

'No, no,' I chirp, smiling at them both stupidly and patting my stomach. 'I'll get something outside if I'm hungry.'

Having paid our mutual dues we go off in opposite directions. I walk all the way across to the new developments, which face a stretch of murky sea and the industrial works. The buildings here are packed tight together, too symmetrical, inward and regular. But there are neat shutters and balconies, courtyards, benches outside, no litter, no gangs (or rather the gangs here are made up of plush old people out for larks), space for children to play and planted greenery. This is where, as Stef tells me, the poor and/or working-class people of Venice live. I see a young woman struggling up a bridge with a buggy, a kid and a tricycle: skin tight black jeans, hot pink stilettos, cropped white bomber jacket, tight ponytail. Beautiful of course. Funny, in London they'd think she was a rock star but here everything's about restraint, about not hurting the eye and showing that you can resist vulgar trends.

I go over the bridge at Ferrovia and cross into 'my' neighbourhood. Frari church looks like an enormous Bourbon biscuit, warm brown and exceedingly flat. Everyone crosses the Campo dei Frari: tourists, businessmen, families, children, students, and the tall coloured houses look down protectively. There are almost no tourist shops or restaurants, only an unwelcomingly dark paper shop, some cafes and an art print dealer selling Venetian etchings. I duck into my *campiello* and check that I know the three routes out again: one alley goes toward Rialto via Campo San Polo, the other leads out towards Campo Santa Margherita and then either to Zattere or to Accademia and along to San Marco; the third route takes me to Piazzale Roma where I get the bus to the airport or go over the bridge at Ferrovia and hit a right direct to Stef's house.

Back at the palazzo, Lucrezia and Gregorio are sitting opposite each other at the kitchen table sharing a bowl of cherries in companionable silence. I come in and put my head around to say hello but feel like an intruder. Lucrezia, I notice, never smiles on reflex; Gregorio always does.

'OK, I've packed and I'm ready to move,' I say in a loud jolly voice. Stef's organised for Tiziana to meet me at three-thirty outside Frari church.

'Excuse me,' says Lucrezia, 'I am a bit tired – it is all right to go alone?'

'Of course! I've already divided up my bags. It'll be easy. Stef and I can take the heavy one tonight and I'll take the lighter ones now.'

Gregorio jumps up, wiping his mouth on his napkin.

'What? You are leaving now? We will come with you.'

Lucrezia freezes where she's sitting and shoots him a look which he doesn't see.

'No need, no need,' I warble.

'But yes,' he says. 'We can take a coffee in Campo San Polo.'

Once more Lucrezia looks at him. Gregorio freezes and crumples a little, half-standing and half-sitting.

'We'll have a coffee tonight when Stef's got back and we're all together,' I say tactfully.

'We don't want to interfere,' says Lucrezia.

I can never work out if she means what she says or if she's so adept at duplicity, in English, that she means the opposite: 'We don't want to interfere' means 'We don't want to be interfered with'. I laugh gaily and go out with my laptop bag, my rucksack, a paper bag full of books and towels and my laundry bag. Then I have the most painful forty-minute trudge of my life, get to Frari pouring with sweat and ruin a lot of tourists' photo opportunities by leaning against the front of the church with all my things collapsing around me.

Tiziana comes up and touches my shoulder. I look like a melted greasy candle, she looks as though she's been meandering by a stream picking Alpine flowers. She always wears prismic sea-colours, I notice. To my relief she seizes the heaviest bag and carries me along with her to the apartment. She tells me I have to speak Italian.

'Then we need a translator,' I moan, but in Italian.

'But why?'

'Because I don't understand anything.'

I've practised all these phrases in advance.

'Oh come on. You speak it very well. And Lucrezia? Where's she?'

'She's something today.' I mime tiredness.

'And Stefania?'

'In Padova.' I mime typing.

'Oh well. Let's go.'

We go over the bridge and into my square. I look up and realise that they've repainted the sign: Campiello Ca' Zen. The Little Square of the House of Zen. I laugh out loud and want to explain, but can't, that 'Be Zen!' has been Stefania's and my catchphrase over the last few years.

Tiziana gives me the keys.

'My keys,' I announce. *Chiave.*

'Yes. There are two, so...'

'I'll give one to Stefania for safety.'

We go into the side alley and open the first door, number 2571. The flat's clean and in good order. The owner must be a seafaring man: all over the walls are paintings and photographs of boats, plus a naval map of the lagoon done in fine ink with handwritten coordinates and weather notes. No view downstairs, of course, but my left bedroom window looks all the way down the little street at the antiques shop, bookshop, ceramics place and art supplies shop.

Tiziana's rushing about opening all the drawers and telling me where everything is.

'This is my first apartment,' I say, but use the wrong word: *primero.*

'*Primo. Primero* is Spanish.'

'Got it... In London I live with my mother.'

'But in Italy this is normal. The family home.'

We go out to photocopy my passport so that the police know I live here. She recommends a few cafes and bars and tells me some final things – the owner prefers cash, to be paid on the tenth of every month; he's sorry he didn't have time to restore one of the walls, I'm not to mind the plaster-dust that's falling off it – and says as we're parting, 'I think that when you let yourself, you speak excellent Italian. What other languages do you speak?'

I tell her.

'You're on the right path.' She kisses my cheek. 'I hope to see you and Stefania soon, OK? We'll have a coffee or a drink together, or I'll invite you somewhere.'

Then I'm alone in my *primo* apartment. Stefania calls: in what must surely be a fit of relief at having me out of their house her parents have invited me back into it that very night for a dinner to celebrate my official (police-approved) arrival as a temporary citizen.

There's been a change of plan and dinner's at La Cantina, not Stef's parents' place. Stef and I get there early and take a seat outside. We notice that Tiziana's sitting a couple of tables down with two female friends and her dog, Coco. Ciaos and kisses all around. The head waitress tells us what's on offer that evening.

'In *osterie* here you have to trust the chef,' says Stef to me, translating. 'Now, there is the salmon, then there is the one that is with Santa Claus.'

'Reindeer,' I say, my mouth watering.

'Yes. And then there is pigeon. And then there is the one that is Bambi.'

'As young as Bambi?' I press like a long-time bordello client. 'Because you know you can get one that's like Bambi's mother.'

'No, no. Bambi. Baby Bambi.'

Stef then tries to order and is told directly, 'Actually your parents already called Marcello [the chef] and said what you were having.'

Stef and I laugh and are just mock-complaining about the tacit chef-parent treaty when the perpetrators themselves arrive. The sun's gone down and everything is lit and warm and dark. Chef Marcello comes up to pay his respects. He's small and round with a bald round head, round snowman face, a smiley expression and a low-key, professional but friendly manner.

'Marcello, we are in your hands,' says Gregorio.

He tries to decide what wine we should all drink and then leaves that to Marcello too. The wine arrives – a good strong red – and we joke about it as Marcello opens it and touts it around.

'And what price range is this? Are you robbing me? How much did you buy it for and how much are you charging us? I'm not sure I've got faith in your judgement,' says Gregorio. 'You've only been serving us for fifteen or twenty years, you don't know our tastes yet. Tell me about this wine, let's see what you know.'

'It was made for three euros, I bought it for ten euros,' says Marcello, his eyes twinkling, 'and of course it tripled in value on its way to your table!'

The meal: fresh smoked salmon with red onions, tomatoes and herbs to start. Then a platter of pigeon, reindeer, courgettes, carrot, mustard. Then various cheeses, including a very runny one, with bright-tasting bitter marmalade. Grappa to end for Gregorio, vapour in a glass.

La Cantina is opposite a Greek-style church.

'Just look at this church,' says Gregorio broadly at some point, having decided openly that I understand all Italian and stopped making any linguistic concessions to me. 'Just look at the columns. People don't realise that they are a single piece of stone, perfectly straight. One man made them with his hands, with no machine to help him. Amazing. Lucrezia, you're not looking.'

'I am looking, Gregorio,' says Lucrezia waspishly. 'I am fond of this church,' she says to me in English, 'because it was my church when I was growing up.'

Gregorio gets out his pen and starts drawing on his place mat. When he runs out of space he starts drawing on mine.

'Look. Christian churches have a layout like this – like the cross of Jesus. Greek churches have a layout that is even-sized along the arms – like the red cross. And also think about the Apollonian principle. Rationality.'

Gregorio tells me about the beautiful hotel architecture he saw in Brazil.

'So good to see something with an *idea* behind it,' he says. 'I have always wanted to live in a hotel. This time in Brazil I asked the manager how much would it cost, and every time I asked, the price came down and down.'

'Laundry...' I say dreamily.

'And every day you come downstairs, you are like a famous person. "Ah! Good morning sir!"'

'Are there any messages for me?' I say arrogantly, miming collaring a hotel employee, 'and is there any post? Could you check, and could you book a car for me for later?'

We're laughing and joking and he claps me on the back. In Gregorio's presence Lucrezia becomes very still; in her presence he becomes very animated.

We people-watch for a while.

'We are living as though we are in the seventeenth century,' says Lucrezia. 'Because we walk everywhere, because of the town planning and the restrictions on new development, because we are not a colonial country, because of the conservation of the city. There are some old families here, that can be traced back to the Roman Empire. And because Venetians love the idea of Venice and perpetuate it.'

'It's beautiful,' I agree – my standard line – 'but that's its danger. One could quite easily spend the whole day shopping at the market, going in and out of the churches, waiting and drinking or just looking...'

Stefania says, 'I have a friend. She say that Venice is like a golden cage, that she doesn't want to leave, but that when she is here, even checking the Internet feels like the big job of the day. And she said a beautiful thing: "Well, I feel about Venice the same way I feel about my mum. I may criticise her but really nothing can touch her. Nothing comes close."'

As we're finishing up a very tall, big-bellied African man with a slow-swinging walk, all the weight in the heels and calves, passes by in a floor-length ochre, brown and orange printed kaftan.

'Mustafa!' Gregorio calls him excitedly. 'Mustafa! Mustafa! Mustafa is our friend,' he says to me.

The man has an even, plain face that reminds me of an English pastor, small eyes, snub nose, small mouth, dark skin and a slightly too-small melon head. He's carrying two very full black but not heavy-looking bin bags. He wanders over with a smile, very polite.

'Do you have a friendship bracelet for our guest? She is from England, staying for four months,' says Gregorio to him.

'Yes, definitely,' says Mustafa in plain pleasant-sounding Italian.

I'm watching all this in puzzlement because I don't think that Mustafa is actually Stef's parents' friend, he's a sort of novelty over which they exercise their grace and patronage. I can't figure out quite what he does. Neighbour? Professor? Hawker? Friend of a friend? Artist? He reaches into his bag and pulls out two brightly-coloured friendship bracelets.

'The colours of the freedom flag,' he says, holding them out to me. 'Take them, take them, they're a present. For all of you.' He gives more to Stef, Lucrezia and Gregorio.

They chat and I watch. Mustafa has a shifty uninflected way of talking. He's invited to sit down and does so rather watchfully, not putting all his weight down or letting himself relax. He doesn't like to talk too much and I get the feeling that he wants to scarper before anyone finds out too much about him. We chat about friendship bracelets and what the colours mean. Lucrezia ties Gregorio's and Stefania's. I tie my own loosely as I don't want to have to wear it 'til it falls off (when I get home I tie it around the front door grille for mystic protection).

'Mustafa, what else do you have to show us? Any new CDs?' ask the parents.

Aha. Mustafa the CD man. Out of the bag come a handful of pirated CDs with laser-printed copy covers. Stef's parents let her choose, just one at first, then in a mood of increasing conviviality and hysteria, two, then three, then four CDs, all current. Mustafa keeps a straight face, says nothing and sits at the table looking carefully left and right.

'You are one of the first people to come to Venice from Africa, weren't you?' says Lucrezia.

Mustafa clearly doesn't want to answer, and why should he? Immigration chat is for immigration officials. Lucrezia merely stares at him and repeats the question. Mustafa says he was in Brescia before he came to Venice a long time ago. He's originally from Senegal – that's where his family are. He says something else which I don't catch.

'He has thirteen children from three different women,' Gregorio whispers to me, 'he *says*.'

I'm shocked by the functionality of the exchange. Everyone's all smiles and family-friend joviality, but when we've had our fun, inspected him like an object, extracted our information and palmed him off with some money for the CDs (he says he'll take anything and can't be pushed to give a price – of course this pushes the price up) Mustafa's immediately dismissed with a happy 'Ciao!', Stefania, Gregorio and Lucrezia turn away from him and he obediently gets off his chair and walks away.

'He is a wonderful man,' says Lucrezia without a second glance.

'A wonderful man,' says Stefania quickly, 'so friendly and nice. And quite a beautiful man,' she adds with a patronising smile.

'Ah yes, of course, of course,' says Lucrezia as if it's in no doubt, 'very impressive. Very handsome.' She squares her shoulders to indicate a good bearing. 'Mustafa is a lucky symbol,' she tells me. 'He just appears from nowhere. The first friendship bracelet he gave me, he gave it to me on the day I learned my niece in South America was pregnant. It finally broke when Sandro, the baby, had his one-year anniversary. The second bracelet Mustafa gave me, it broke on the day I entered an academic competition – which I won.'

'I remember, Mum, I helped you,' says Stefania. 'I made two photocopies of your proposal.'

We finally finish the meal, very satisfied. As we're getting up, Tiziana comes over to say hi-bye.

'Tiziana,' says Stefania, 'Bidisha couldn't believe you're a grandmother.'

'No!' says Tiziana in her flat sardonic voice.

'No, really,' I insist, smiling at her.

'Actually, when I took the little one to the doctor, he wouldn't believe I wasn't his mother. He thought I was hiding something! I kept saying, no, I am not the mother, I am the grandmother, I beg you.'

We're introduced to her friends, two equally *soignée* and well-dressed women in silks and furs and jewels.

'Four books published so young,' one exclaims in Italian, smiling at me elegantly after explanations have been made amongst the party.

'No, no, only two...' I say with a nervous laugh.

'Oh, *only* two,' she teases.

'Are they published in Italian, so we can read them?' asks the other lady.

'No, only in –' I randomly mention some languages I know the Italian words for.

I smile modestly, they smile kindly, they go away.

'But I do not like this kind of person,' says Stef immediately: '"We are Venetian, but we are still so international." They do not do anything, but they think, "We're the cream of Venice," meaning the cream of Italy, meaning the cream of the world.'

After the meal we go back to the palazzo to pick up Nero for a walk. Big mistake – Gregorio and Lucrezia have laid out their presents for Stef from Brazil and London all along the table. There's a beautifully packaged box of candied fruits, lots of surfer-looking flip-flops in yellow and orange with criss-cross rubber straps and square soles, bowls made from the dried skins of fruits and countless other things in shiny blue-starred wrapping paper. All three of them run forward and begin exclaiming over the things, laughing and joking excitedly, holding things up, getting Stef to try on the flip-flops, talking about other nice things they've seen on their travels, asking her what else she might like. Suddenly painfully homesick, I retreat further and further away until I'm standing in the doorway facing the stairs. I know that Mum does exactly the same for me when she has been away (with more presents! A longer table! A greater variety of flip-flops!), but not when we have guests. Eventually, after a long time, Gregorio recollects his manners:

'Eh! Bidisha!' He comes creeping forward. 'Take these!'

In his hands are the cheapest, ugliest pair of prosthetic grey rubber flip-flops I've ever seen, clearly huge so I have an excuse to refuse them, which I do, elegantly, and neither Stefania nor Gregorio nor Lucrezia insist on it.

Chapter Five

I make the bed in my new apartment and sleep well until I'm woken by loud talking from the guy who runs the newspaper hut in my *campiello*. The hut looks like a peaked theatrical hat with its black brim and streamers of magazines hanging in lines; the guy, I eventually learn from the dozens of greetings he receives, is called Massimo. One businessman jokingly strolls up and says to him, 'Ah! Well! This morning let's have a discussion about the deposition of the president – what say you?' He is humoured, the transaction's made and he's sent off with a slap on the back. Repeat tomorrow and every day for the rest of his life. Massimo's average height, thick and heavy with a fat mud-brown ponytail at his nape, a heavy red brown clayey face, about forty or so, probably really beautiful for about six months when he was a teenager, small dark brown eyes like commas, small mouth in a line. A booming voice which he likes using. His uniform, even in this heat, is a farmer's shirt, jeans, heavy boots and a safari waistcoat. As he's wandering around the *campiello* in front of his hut he looks up and catches my eye by accident. I give a small, horizontal smile, tokenly friendly, cautiously civilised. After a pause he hands me back an even smaller, flatter, more token smile, with an extra shading of mockery.

I spend the day shuffling furniture about, taking down the boat paintings which clutter the walls and make the place seem smaller (I remove all except for the nautical map downstairs) and listening out insect-like for the life of Venice – doors, footsteps, people laughing, singing and talking in the *campiello*. There must be a music teacher nearby because I hear piano, violin, oboe. Then a baby crying in a strange deep hoarse voice, regular short cries like a car alarm, and a young couple who talk to each other constantly with calm, friendly voices. The lads who run the antiques shop spend the day hanging around the *campiello* gossiping loudly, sitting outside on chairs they've brought out or lounging on the steps. There are two or three main ones, all in their twenties, tall, very thin and lanky in the Venetian style, hot-shit nonchalant oafs with fashion haircuts. One of them has a big, dumb, woofing black wolfhound.

There's a distinct pulse to the day: early in the morning there are hundreds of map-clutching tourist families, businessmen going to Ferrovia or Piazzale Roma, kids on the way to school, housekeepers going to the market. Late morning, university students and young tourist couples. A lull when the sun's at its highest, except for some roasted dazed tourists. And in the evening, returning students, young Venetians on their way out, everyone going for a *sprizz*. The tourists are all soaking their feet in their hotel bathrooms. A lot of passers-by look up and spot me as I'm doing my arranging because in Venice everyone's always scoping the buildings. There's a quick mutually curious flash and then they're gone. The antiques shop guys stare up brazenly, standing in the middle of the square and craning their heads back with an unwavering, unsympathetic look. Whenever a beautiful girl crosses the *campiello* (about two hundred times a day) they and their friends stop talking, stop moving, look her up and down with their mouths grinningly open and turn their heads to follow her as she passes. I see girl after girl notice this, grit her teeth, duck her head and frown on her way out of the *campiello*. Massimo, the antiques shop lads, the pale stocky guy who owns the art shop and the guys who run the bookshop together form quite an impressive fraternity.

I hear the clatter of the postman's, bin men's and delivery men's trolleys and carts throughout the day and the dry shush of the sweepers' brooms as they clean the square at dawn. I also hear exuberant birdsong from the caged birds upstairs, close and loud enough to drown everything out: chirrups, clicks, chirps, then long formless trills on one note, an electric streak. Even with the sun up my room is cool and not too sunny, but bright. The other buildings in the square shield me a bit. The bells of Frari church ring every hour and half-hour (the half-hour is denoted by the number of rings of the hour followed by a single ring of a different, higher pitch: 'one, two, three – *thirty*') although there's another that seems to come from a different direction and rings in deep earthlike peals for different services. At around six o'clock, Mass time, all the churches in Venice and Giudecca ring their bells and the sound is glorious.

The next day I dress carefully (imperative in Venice) and go to visit the bookshop, Einaudi's. I open the door and the shop bell tinkles. The three people standing around a desk by the door look up in surprise and stare at me coldly. I stare back, go to the shelves and started looking around at what's on display, with my back to them. Silence. At one point I turn back, unnerved, and they're all still staring at me. I realise that all the books on the shelves look the same. I'm in a publishers' office, not a bookshop. I count... horribly... for every twenty men they publish, they publish only one woman. There are some of A. S. Byatt's books. A woman comes up and asks if there's anything I want and thank God I say quickly that I was wondering if *The Matisse Stories* have been translated. She's complicit, pretends to look it up in the catalogue, I pretend to be anxious for it and after a while I'm able to leave, my entire body prickling with embarrassment.

I turn back and cross the square, monitored by the fraternity, and wander around in the pounding heat looking for food. Eventually I get down to Zattere, the southern edge, blasted by sunlight with flashing heat coming straight off the sea. I go to the Billa supermarket there and pay a nosebleed-inducing fifty euros for what I'd thought was going to be my weekly shop: a tub of floating mozzarella turds, carrots, yoghurt, salad leaves, vegetables, skimmed milk and cured venison. This place is too expensive, no wonder Venetians are all thin.

On the way back I notice that in Venice nobody wears 'ethnic' dress. There are no overt references to other cultures, no prints, no gypsy styling, no hippy or traveller dress, no African, Indian or Japanese influence, no found-on-my-travels jewellery. It's all strictly Italian style. All day long I see people staring hostilely, first at my Indian printed top, then up at my face.

Eventually I make it home, more by chance than design, pouring with sweat. As I'm trudging down my twentieth brown stone alleyway trying to keep the top of the Frari campanile in view, a young pretty guy of about my age comes running after me. I think he's French. He asks me in soft English where the supermarket is. Ah, another hungry hopeful, tall, slender, olive-skinned, long wavy chocolate brown hair in a careless ponytail, floppy blue shirt. Some girls would fancy him – not me though. Why? Because when I finish giving him directions I spontaneously flop back against the wall in exhaustion and he says, 'Do you want any help, or...?', stressing the 'or' and clearly wanting me to refuse, to the extent that the moment he utters the question, he looks frightened. I good-naturedly wave him off, thinking, Why did you ask, if you so obviously didn't want to help? Why don't you just stay quiet? Or say 'I want you to think of me as a nice boy but I don't want to perform any action to justify it.'

On the way back I solve the mystery of the Buddha-like Mustafa that Lucrezia's so in love with. He doesn't just magically appear, he lives near me and I hear his voice morning and night as he passes. I've seen him twice around Rialto, on my side, gliding cool in his kaftan.

I get home and inspect the venison, which looks and smells weird, livery and dark. Then I look up *cuore* in the dictionary. It doesn't mean 'cured', it means 'heart'. Oh my God, I've got Bambi's heart marinating in my fridge. I cook the heart: slimy, skinny, tough, salty, stinking and inedible.

I go out again just as the Mass at Frari church is about to begin. A great Bauhaus-sounding organ harmony reverberates through the walls, music full of dread. No wonder everyone's so scared of God, if this is his theme tune. The inside of the church is dark and red-lit, the side door's open and there's a guy stationed there turning tourists away and pointing to a sign that says 'Mass. No tourist visits.' Well-dressed old Italians are filing in two by two like ark animals. I hide behind them and go in too. The church is vast and dark. The red glass lamps have been lowered from the ceiling on chains and are full of lit candles. This would be a great place for a cocktail party. The intricately carved treacle brown choir stalls are empty but the pews at the front, before the Bellini altarpiece, are slowly filling up. I see two very young (eighteen?) Benedictine monks in black robes with white belts. They're arranging stuff on the stage, lighting candles, laying out a big Bible and putting the gold brocade marker in the right place, testing the microphone by the lectern. Compared with the size of the building they look like kids setting up a school play. Given that Frari church was originally Franciscan, not Benedictine, and the monastery behind it was turned into the state archives years ago, the monks must come from the monastery on San Giorgio Maggiore or be visiting from another city. Or are they theology students being tested for something? On goes the organ, awe-filled and histrionic, not stirring the soul so much as battering it down. I let my gaze range around the front of the church. One of the young brothers glances up and notices me. He has a clear, beautiful, sincere face. Curly soft dark hair, tanned skin. I'm sweating as usual, fanning myself carelessly with the Mass guide. I accidentally catch his eye and a slow, natural, gently interested look passes between us for two long seconds. I drop my eyes and direct an amused smile into my lap. The young monk's yearning, boredom and lack of vocation are so clearly written across his face (and may I say, obviously: what a waste!) that I feel rather tempted to stride up and murmur, 'Darling. Let me take you away from all this.'

I proceed to run/walk/trudge over the Rialto Bridge (thronging) and down through St Mark's Square (ditto plus pigeons), then the coast, the Riva dei Sette Martiri and onwards into the Biennale gardens and Sant'Elena, a basketball-courts-

and-tall-trees area that feels, frankly, like the Bronx. This is the only place in Venice where you see second-generation African-Italian and Asian-Italian kids playing.

I notice that Venice is getting ready for the Festa del Redentore that night, the historic post-plague jubilations, celebrated these days with fireworks and a bridge cast between Zattere and the Redentore church in Giudecca. All along the St Mark's coast there are hundreds of boats crowded to the rim, full of people oiled and dancing, many-coloured flags strung in lines, long tables set out outside the houses all the way to the public gardens, entire families getting ready for a meal, barbecues sizzling, wine in fat bottles and children playing out. Half the public gardens are cordoned off because the Architecture Biennale pavilions are being set up so I wander close to the sea, tracing the white stone balcony walls. A hot mist comes in off the sea, a warm ice-blue wash smelling of simmering water, sun and light. There are groups of slender young policemen gossiping prettily together; maybe they fight crime in between going to model castings and film auditions.

That evening I purchase a comically large pizza from the place adjacent to Frari church, next to the *gelateria*. Plain cheese and tomato, thin as tissue, it fits through the front door with just a millimetre to spare. There's always a crowd of people outside the pizza place, buying a quick slice to see them through the next couple of hours – kids, visitors, locals. They sit against the church railings and scarf it down. While I'm waiting for my pizza to be baked a craggy Venetian guy – nervy and wiry, older, linen clad – comes up and buys single slices for himself and his wife. All single slices are sold for €1.50. He complains bitterly that all the slices aren't the same size and that he's been ill-favoured compared to his wife, who wears a diplomatic smile and pretends that she hasn't heard him. He makes the girl give him a bigger slice, which she does in a bemused and silent way, with a slow, pitying look.

I then go next door to Gelateria Millevoglie to keep my sugar psychosis fully functional. The girl behind the counter gets frustrated (and shows it) with a couple of very young, trendy Chinese tourists who want one scoop each but don't know any Italian. She rolls her eyes, turns her head away, tuts, makes a disgusted face when they point, taps her toe, sighs with irritation, repeats herself loudly in Italian and gives me baleful apologetic looks as though I'm complicit in her game. When they eventually get served she turns to me with a big relieved sigh and an expression of sympathy, as if to say, 'I know – these foreigners are such pains.' I order two scoops of yoghurt flavour, one of tiramisu and one of nutty stuff. Afterwards I say to her questioningly, 'My Italian isn't bad, is it?'

As always the shop-people's brisk friendly manner freezes when I ask something genuinely small-talky.

'Your Italian? No, it's not bad,' she says nicely, 'I can understand you.'

And she waves me off cheerily.

The next day is a work day for me, enlivened by a bit of amusingly shaming news from my mum, who is in all circumstances (usually) the most efficient, capable, clever and versatile person around. Not today though! Today, worried after not having heard from me in forty-eight hours and knowing I was in a despondent mood about my bad book, Mum phoned Stef's mobile and asked if I was OK. Great: I am thirteen years old again.

'Mum! She's going to think we're all mad. The last thing I wanted to do was be a liability and now Stefania has to be *your* mum as well as mine.'

'I know, Min [my pet name], I'm sorry,' says Mum regretfully.

An hour or so later the doorbell rings, very shrill, making me jump, and I hear someone shout 'Bidisha?' loudly. I dart to the door and pull back the curtain. Oh dear – it's Stef and her mother, the former looking at me with a bright, concerned look, the latter very steely indeed. They also boggle at the state I'm in: dusty feet, grey shorts, grey vest (both quite stringy), tattoos, a light dusting of armpit hair. The flat is so dusty, a Venetian problem. It only takes one humid day for it to be full of fine, clingy, pale grey silt.

I stand there in astounded clown humiliation.

'Good God! Stef.'

'Are you OK?' Said as a token and a rebuke.

'Yes, yes, I'm fine. I'm so sorry my mum called. So embarrassing,' I say shamefully, because of course the fault is not that of Mum but me.

'But no,' says Stefania, 'my mother has done this hundreds of times.'

'Yes,' affirms Lucrezia remorselessly. She hasn't moved a muscle nor shifted a hair since I pulled back the curtain.

'But I called you yesterday, like, one hundred times,' Stef goes on.

'I thought you were away yesterday?'

'I got back at eleven and there were the fireworks, for the Festa del Redentore... I called you, like, one hundred times and I thought, oh no, the phone is switch off... your mum call me...so now we come to see if you are dead.'

'No, I'm fine, I'm sorry.' I'm so mortified now that I am unable to meet her eye, plus I'm giving a really creepy, shifty laugh.

'Why didn't you call me?' says Stef. She is really annoyed.

Then Lucrezia (rightly) tells me off: 'Of course it is all right. But if she calls us and she is worried, of course we are obliged to do something.'

'I understand, and I apologise. It won't happen again.' This, I realise, is what I ought to have said at the very beginning.

Stef then tells her mother off in Italian and says to me, 'Look, Bidisha, we were only worried about you. Call me, OK? Use your phone.'

I invite them in but they can't oblige because they've been walking Nero, who's tired (I see him lurking around the corner). Stefania continues to be lovingly severe with me and tells me off for not calling to let her know I'd spoken with Mum. When they're gone I go upstairs, cry with embarrassment and then reach for the phone.

'Hi Mum, I just thought you'd like to know, Stef and her mum just came and knocked on my door and told me off in the street. Can you imagine how humiliating that was?'

'Oh dear, Min, I'm sorry. But why did they come?'

'Because they were worried. Well, Stef was worried and Lucrezia was annoyed. They're like my Venetian family now, if I don't behave they'll send me away.'

The next day, very contrite, I fix to meet Stefania at the station bridge, on her side. I see her from the top of the bridge, a vision of Pucci, black gypsy linen, green flip-flops and a thin, droopy, exhausted-looking Nero. We go to the Vodaphone shop together, close to tinselly, crowded Campo San Marcuola. It's a terrifying and even quite a morally defiling experience: a spanking clean, fully-branded red and silver shop staffed exclusively by fast-talking ten-foot-tall Vodaphone babes, all tanned, all bodacious, all made up, all hurried and fearsomely efficient in their uniform of black skin-tight trousers and tight red polo T-shirt with – oh my God – a great big bunch of keys hanging down between their breasts. There's no way my three lines of Italian would stand up to them; they'd decimate me in a second. Stefania does it all for me, gets me an Italian SIM card and number, gives them my address and tells me how much it all costs. All around us there are gleaming little Italian-designed mobiles, phone/camera/e-mail gadgets with spaceship-control buttons and slick black bodies.

'You realise we're witnessing the death of human civilisation?' I say to Stef in a low voice.

She nods slowly in depressed affirmation. We're surrounded by salivating young people playing with the phones and handing over their money.

'God Stef, those Vodaphone women were scary. I never would've been able to manage without you. Thank you so much, I owe you – as always,' I say when we're out of there.

'You know what I said to the girl when we were leaving? "I can tell that you're having a very stressed day, so thank you and bye-bye,"' says Stef wickedly.

I laugh: her kiss-off to the shop assistant is a classic Venetian-style put-down: an elegantly cutting way of telling her to be less brusque and harried next time. Before I walk her home we sample the sugary finger foods and creamy coffee of the Pasticceria Dal Mas on the Lista di Spagna by the train station. The key there is to whisk in, sup quickly and whisk out, smacking your lips as you go. A note: the lady in charge is very nice but the serving staff never smile. Another note: when having your coffee it's rude to look at anything. Do not watch the other customers or the staff.

Don't admire the decor. Don't read a newspaper. Don't look at yourself in the mirror. Don't slouch. Appear to be perfectly at ease at all times. Look at your friends (you're supposed to be with friends) or look at the ceiling.

Outside we bump into Gregorio, looking very smart and trim (as trim as a square-shaped person can look) in bright white chinos and floppy linen jacket, a folded white cotton handkerchief in his hand.

'Gregory!' Stef calls to him sweetly and teasingly in English. 'Gregory! Where are you going?'

'For a walk and to buy some bread,' he replies. He greets me and smiles. 'You are wearing beautiful colours today.'

I'm in a cream smock shirt and dark pink linen trousers.

'I look like an ice cream,' I say in Italian.

He laughs.

'Take the dog,' says Stefania to her dad, handing Nero over.

'I have to walk Nero again this evening. It – he – will be too energetic otherwise. Nero is a he, yes, not an it?' he says to me.

'Yes. A he. Unless you hate dogs.'

He mops his forehead.

'It used to be that you could phone the shop and they would deliver to you all the heavy things. The bread, the pasta, the oil, the flour. Delivery would be free if you lived three bridges away or less. So you could telephone and say, "Eh, yes, hello, I would like... three kilos of pasta. Three kilos of rice. Please hurry. I am hosting a dinner party tonight." They do not do that any more, since the Billa supermarket opened.'

We part and Stef and I make an arrangement to meet Ginevra for dinner at Zucca. On my way there later that evening I slip my feet out of my flip-flops and lay them on the broad stones on the street for a second: the stones feel warm and curved, like human backs. Quickly duck into the Chiesa San Pantaleone in Campo San Pantalon, which smells fantastic, old incense deep in the woodwork. An astonishing, visceral-looking crucifix too: Jesus, rendered in chocolate brown marble, writhing graphically, his loincloth almost flying off in the marble breeze, his hair windswept, his face coy and pretty, his body in excellent jogging condition. Then, in the Cappella del Chiodo, I see an amazing Coronation by Vivarini and d'Alemagna from 1444, chock full of glowing gold haloes.

I come out and spot Ginevra from a distance. Tonight she's looking sleek and mannish like an Yves Saint Laurent model, with lean, bare forearms, black linen shirt and trousers, Birkenstocks, long, clever catlike eyes ringed with heat-smudged eyeliner.

'You look very beautiful, Ginevra,' I say.

'As always,' says Stefania, joining us.

'No, no,' moans Ginevra, 'when you have seen me for the tenth time in the same clothes you will not think so.'

'Oh come on...' we groan. Ginevra is turning out to be quite the Eeyore. I'm worried by her strange, clammy touch, as though all her humours are out of balance. Whenever she touches me it's as though someone's poured cold water down my back.

We walk to Zucca, fighting through the humidity. There are lots of people out. We're in my area, walking along the bars, restaurants and narrow streets of San Polo. Zucca is as close as a sauna and quite full. There's some kind of drama with the staff: the waitress is red and flushed over pale colouring. She runs into the kitchen and bursts into tears, pursued by two other staff members, re-emerges sunny but crimson-cheeked. Mysterious.

Stefania and Ginevra ask me how I've settled in and agree on the niceness of my apartment.

'At least you can see the sky from your windows,' says Ginevra. 'I have to —' She mimes sticking her head out of the window, squinting up and craning her neck to see the sky.

'It's not bad,' I admit. 'The only thing is that it's very dusty. It's everywhere. I can even feel it in my mouth. And I've been swatting a few mosquitoes, but nothing serious.'

'Now we have the tiger mosquito but a few years ago — do you remember, Ginevra?' says Stefania.

'I do not know what you are about to say,' says Ginevra despondently.

'We had the male mosquitoes,' Stefania wiggles her fingers to indicate wings, 'and they were very stupid. They were so stupid that they would just sit on the wall,' she makes a face to indicate a rapturous idiocy, like a kid entranced in front of a TV set, 'and then die.'

'Like a terrible existential allegory,' I say.

'Yes! And I remember, when I was a kid, the whole wall was black with them.'

'I do not remember that,' says Ginevra sadly.

The two of them talk about a piece of local scandal concerning one of the big white boats that took us to the Lido the day we visited the beach. Apparently the other day a small fishing boat collided with it. The fishing boat contained a man, a child and a woman. The woman just happened to fall out, hit her head, drown and die. But they never recovered the body, despite sealing and dragging the lagoon. The man has now been imprisoned because the very next day he was seen out at the Redentore fireworks parties with a young woman, drinking, singing and celebrating. Plus a few years ago he robbed a lot of banks at gunpoint.

'He killed her and made it seem like an accident,' says Stef.

'How did he get the body to disappear?' challenges Ginevra.

'The current. Or he put stones on it.'

'When he was in the fishing boat?'

'Yes.'

'In front of the child?'

'Yes!'

'Are you sure?' Ginevra flaps her hands and puts on a baby voice. '"Mamma! Papa?"'

'And what is so funny,' Stef says to me in English, 'is that the local papers – I mean, they are crap, but they write everything like a novel: "You would think that on the night of the Redentore this man was at home, alone, in the dark, grieving about the terrible accident which he had witness, alone, the loss of his wife, at sea. But no! He was out!"'

We eat. I have a delicate vegetable lasagne to start, followed by *vitello tonnato*, tender veal with tuna mayonnaise, a speciality of the season. Followed by a rich chocolate mousse. After dinner we walk out into the still-humid night. It's about ten o'clock.

'Now, Bidisha will take us to Campo Santa Margherita,' says Stef – and I do! Without any glitches.

Campo St M is thriving as usual. We sit down at Caffè Rosso, right in the centre. Stef tells us she and Bruno are going on holiday to a nudist camping site in Croatia. Ginevra and I are appalled. Stef is defensive and gets a little annoyed by our immaturity:

'But the sea there is very beautiful. And it is a kind of law, that when the scenery is the most beautiful, the camping is naked.'

Ginevra and I giggle stupidly.

'But why are you laughing? I do not understand your point,' says Stef, getting cross.

'Why do you have to be naked? What's the benefit of it? Nudity is not more honest than being clothed. It doesn't have more integrity. It's not true that you're more free when you don't have any clothes on. Quite the opposite,' I protest, trying to make a reasoned argument.

'Because you can be like an animal,' says Stefania.

'That is not my goal,' I say primly. 'If I was surrounded by naked people I wouldn't be able to stop myself from looking, even if I didn't want to.'

'But you are an athlete. You love bodies.'

'Not like that!'

'It's quite cold at night,' Stef remarks, which of course makes Ginevra and I laugh even more childishly than ever.

'A hat and a scarf and gloves, and nothing in between,' says Ginevra as I howl. 'And at the supermarket — just a handbag.'

Stef gets ever crosser.

'Both of you, be less rigid. We will have a good time. My parents used nude camping places a lot when I was growing up. They are very civilised. If we are lucky we will be between two polite German families, not any Italian families talking all the time and cooking pasta... not that Italian families do this. If we need to buy food we will drive to the town.'

'Naked?' I prompt, and we start laughing again.

On the way home they ask me domestic questions...

'But you have not visited the Rialto market?' says Stefania.

'I don't like markets for political reasons.'

'Why?'

'I told you, they make me feel like a housewife,' I snap.

'And how do supermarkets make you feel?' she deadpans.

Just as we're about to part that evening we see a girlish nun of about seventy clipping past smartly, the white starched folds of her knee-length frock dancing in the gloom. She's accompanied by a school student, a slim docile boy of about twelve.

'Look, a white one,' Stef hisses, pointing openly at the nun's frock. 'Get back inside the nunnery.'

Apart from the white-dressed Cistercian nuns there are some grey-dressed ones too but they have a bad rep in Italy, everyone can remember being caned/thwarted by one at school.

I clock up about ten days without seeing anyone, until one night I'm working at the kitchen island when I hear 'Bidisha?' whispered piercingly through my letter box, nearly scaring me to death. It's Mara, the vivacious buck-toothed friend of Stefania, waiting outside the door with eight other people and wanting to know if I'd like to go for a drink. I'm very charmed and touched and say yes, come outside and stupidly shake everyone's hand: Mara's boyfriend Dario who likes to read to her in German, Bianca whose elderly neighbours do it like buffaloes, a couple of Spanish girls whom Mara used to study with, two Spanish guys, assorted others. The hand-shaking (and the time it takes) successfully embarrasses the entire party. We go to Caffè Rosso, and over drinks one of the girls tells a funny story which Mara translates for me. The girl's boyfriend's aunt and uncle, who're in their seventies, took the young couple out to dinner upon hearing of their betrothal. The aunt and uncle are very liberal.

'They are seventy years old, but they ask them a lot of personal questions,' says Mara. 'They say, on the night of their own wedding, they do love seven times.'

'Seven *times*? Oh God! *Complimenti!*' I splutter. I don't know why this shocks me: what did I expect a young couple from a more buttoned-up generation to do on their wedding night? Play cards?

I am grateful for the cordiality which has been shown to me by Stefania's friends. They've offered their friendship with an unintense readiness and consideration that seem almost miraculous after the (as I now recognise it) insularity of Londoners. But who can say? There's such a contrast between the learned, solicitous and truly elegant-minded women and men I'm meeting through the Barone–Ritter dynasty and the constant goading comments, looks, theatrical panting and blown kisses, even the little pushes and shoves I get when out alone.

Sometimes I feel like I'm on an endless food-hospitality relay which I could never hope to repay, given the paucity of my own skills in that area. I'm invited for dinner at Lucrezia and Gregorio's place a few days after Stef returns from her camping holiday. Before going there I take a walk in Zattere just before sunset. Warm porcelain blue sirocco light. The sea's very blue and glows opaquely. The water's high and splashes across the stones, reflecting countless lights, some twinkly and distant, others warm and close. I buy a big pack of Millevoglie ice cream as a token of apology for the Mum-calling-Stef diplomatic incident.

I arrive to find that the lights in the main chamber of the palazzo have been dimmed and Gregorio and Stef are setting the table with rough earthenware dishes, a nice contrast to the fine silver forks and the long candles burning in the candelabra. Lucrezia's in the kitchen.

'I'm sorry for disappearing,' I say bashfully to her. 'I brought this for dessert.'

The grovel goes down well:

'It is fine. Of course,' says Lucrezia kindly. 'But do not disappear again.'

She takes the ice cream smoothly and I realise that she'd expected me to bring something all along. Relief — another social hiccup averted. I am consigned to a chair and not allowed to help, so watch Stef, Lucrezia and Gregorio preparing the meal around me while Stef shouts 'What a ball breaker!' whenever her mum asks her dad to do something. I go to meet the other guests: an Italian guy called Guillermo who was an ex-student of Lucrezia's, chunky, round, pale, bald, young but ill-kempt, badly dressed, works in the City in London; accompanied by Claudia, Spanish, his partner, tall and very thin, well spoken, quiet but not shy. They've both been living in London and have very weak, open handshakes.

I'm next to Claudia on the balcony. We lean out and admire the view, which seems to rock gently. No land in sight, only black water, black sky and lights.

'Are you living here?' Claudia asks me in English.

'For three or four months. To relax. And you?'

'No, I am from Madrid, but I have spent the last four years in London, but now... I don't know. I have met Guillermo and he would like to stay. But London is not my city.'

'No? And what about Venice?'

'Ah, Venice.' We smile at each other. 'I could be very happy here.'

Guillermo comes onto the balcony, sits down and starts talking. He speaks excellent English with a clipped accent:

'In my opinion you can learn more from walking around Venice for two days than spending four years in London. I'll tell you how – you just get lost. Every new city I'm in, I don't take a map, I just go for a walk and get lost and keep my eyes open. I am passionate about history and it's amazing what you can see. In my opinion you can learn much more that way.'

Claudia listens to this (and much more) respectfully and, I am astonished, makes no gesture of impatience. I listen respectfully for the first sentence, politely for the next, peevishly for the third and tend to my own thoughts thereafter. When the silence gets too long I say something mild and meaningless.

'But in my opinion,' Guillermo answers quickly, 'it is the wrong mentality to say this about Venice. I have seen, since I've been in London, a lot of people say they're going to come to London to learn the language, get a job, and in three, four years they haven't done anything. They just go out to have fun, put it on the American Express, Visa card, and if you say, where did you get that? They say, oh, my dad gave it to me. On the contrast you can come to Venice and grow – you can expand your spirit in two days more than you would expand your spirit in four years in London.'

'And do you think I've expanded my spirit by having met *you*?' I want to say, but only reply, 'That's a good way of looking at it. I have to bear that in mind.'

'It's obvious to me. Not that I don't love London. I do.'

'I don't,' laughs Claudia next to me. 'That is why we're in Venice. We have a few things to discuss.'

'I want to have kids,' Guillermo states as though placing an order at a drive-thru.

'I am not so sure,' Claudia tells me. 'Marriage, yes. Kids, I don't know.'

But wait – Guillermo has yet more opinions to give:

'The problem for Claudia,' he says, 'is that she has just finished her degree and she has to look for a job. When she has a job she will feel fine about London.'

Claudia looks at me, rolls her eyes and shakes her head: no way. After being called to the table we turn off the main lights altogether and light the citronella candles on the balcony. Gregorio laughs:

'The tourists passing on the vaporetti will be looking at us and saying, "Really, poor things, in these ancient Venetian palaces they don't even have electricity."'

To get the food facts out of the way, the dinner goes as follows: prosecco, very crisp and dry; risotto with shrimp and wheat with tender beans; prosciutto and melon; roast beef loaf and rosemary, grilled tomatoes, char-cooked parsnip, cauliflower; three cheeses, one soft blue, two harder, and some special bread; ice cream for all. I eat until I can eat no more and am greatly pleased. The only thing I do mind is the excessive solicitude, being asked ten times if you want coffee, tea, a second helping, etc. Imagine if you said yes every time.

Gregorio kicks off the evening with some academic chat:

'In my department there is working with me a very interesting, intelligent woman. There is also, above me, a very intelligent, interesting woman. But the professor of the department is a man, very old, about one hundred. He sits all day by the door, asleep. When a student comes out after a lesson: "Ah! Professor! Good day!" "Ah! Student! Good day, good day!" He leaps up, bows, sits down and descends once more into a slumber, bent over the hook of his cane. And that is the professor's job.'

I'm sitting on the church pew between Guillermo and Claudia. Opposite us are Gregorio, Stef (directly opposite me) and Lucrezia on the Louis XIV chairs, pale pink and gold brocade, curly backs.

'Lucrezia, I have a *Death in Venice* question to ask you. What is this sirocco that everyone talks about?' I ask.

'This is a south-easterly wind. Some people say that it is south-westerly but I think it is south-easterly. But perhaps it is a case of where you are. It flows in from Libya. Sirocco is an Arabic word.

It blows through the whole of Italy and at first it is very dry, a desert wind. It blows through all the towns. Then, eventually, it becomes very wet and very heavy.'

'This is sirocco weather, now,' says Gregorio.

'It pushes the seas against the coast,' says Lucrezia.

'I noticed. This afternoon in Zattere it was very high,' I say thoughtfully.

'I do not like the image of Venice that *Death in Venice* presents,' says Stef, frowning, 'as if it is all about decay.'

'I'm obsessed with it,' I say. 'Not the book, the film.'

'Dirk Bogarde was gay,' says Lucrezia with malicious delight, adding in Italian, 'and he was a major faggot in that film.' Poor old Dirk.

We're all speaking in English as our common language: Lucrezia and Stefania speak Italian and English. Gregorio also speaks Spanish. Claudia speaks Spanish and English, Guillermo English and Italian.

'I am sorry,' says Lucrezia suddenly, looking at me, 'I have cut the cheese in a very ugly way.'

I look down and realise that what she means is that *I* have cut the cheese badly, and that she's had to follow the crooked line I left. I blush, apologise openly and don't add, 'Just as well it's only a piece of cheese.' Stef looks daggers at her mother while Gregorio teaches me how to cut the cheese lengthways, holding the whole thing in the palm of the hand and slicing off the flat facing side, not cutting off the nose and working back — otherwise the last person just gets the rind. It strikes me that holding all of the cheese in all of your hand is less stylish and certainly less hygienic than simply lopping off its nose, but say nothing and receive the lesson dutifully.

We talk about jobs in different countries and Stef grumbles, 'I do not like this Anglo-Saxon way of life. In London there is always this feeling of competition.'

'I like London because I like working in the City,' says Guillermo of course. 'I always wanted to work in the City. When I was a child you could ask me what I wanted to do, I said Secretary of the Treasury! I would take all my coins and pile them up – I didn't want paper money, only coins so I could make piles.'

The entire table has become silent and sleepy with boredom since Guillermo opened his mouth.

'When I first came to London I thought I would get a job in a bank,' he goes on. 'Instead I worked in a restaurant in Heathrow Airport! I told so many lies at the interview. "How many months have you been in England?" "Six!" It was three. "What were you doing before?" "Assistant manager in a restaurant in Milan." I was a waiter in a village near my house. I got the job and every single person I worked with was Indian. On the bus to work in the morning there were twenty guys and I was the only white one. Everyone else was Indian including the driver. But I have to say I made eight friends there. In the City I have made only two.'

Nobody says anything. Presently Guillermo does us the favour of contributing something further:

'Now in Italy there is this new job: independent financial advisor. Anyone can become an independent financial advisor. It is ridiculous. That is my opinion, anyway. I knew someone – a woman, actually. She was a painter and then I heard she is now an IFA. I am sure she is a very good artist but what does a person like that know about finance? And that is not to say anything against artists, my brother is an artist. A proper one. But I would not give him my money. That is my attitude, anyway.'

By now Gregorio is slumped in his chair staring slack-mouthed at the floor and nudging a prone, heat-destroyed Nero with his foot. Lucrezia's watching Guillermo with a cold smile. She attempts something unimaginably banal, about which Guillermo could not possibly have anything to say:

'There is great excitement in Cannaregio because they are finally renovating the Billa supermarket. At the moment it has an atmosphere, a little bit post-war, a little bit Yugoslavia.'

'This idea of having huge supermarkets is a relatively new thing. It is not like London,' says Stefania.

Oh no. With this mention of his current city of residence Guillermo's ears prick up:

'In London it is a very big issue. You need a car to go to the supermarket in the suburbs and in the inner city there are some places where there is nowhere to get even some small thing,' says Guillermo.

I say, 'The biggest supermarkets are in the suburbs.'

Lucrezia: 'Or there is Harrods Food Hall...'

Stef: 'There is a good supermarket in Hendon.'

Me: 'Hendon is major suburbia.'

Lucrezia [making a gesture of shooing away a cat]: 'Oh, who lives in Hendon apart from the Jews?'

'You shouldn't say that,' I say immediately.

She's defiant though: 'Every time I go to Hendon I see it is full of...'

She makes the gesture of pulling a wig straight and I give a shocked abrupt laugh.

When dinner's over Stefania and her parents play with the dog. Stef stands over him, pulls his ears and arranges her tropical print skirt around him like a cape.

'We are a bit fanatical about this dog,' says Lucrezia apologetically, but not apologetically enough to stop.

'I notice when I am walking Nero around Venice, I frighten a lot of Japanese girls, tourists. Perhaps the Japanese think dogs are impure,' says Stef.

'Indians see dogs as impure because there are lots of strays around. It's only with the recent Western bourgeoisification that they've started keeping them as pets,' I say.

'They hate dogs but they *love* cows,' says Guillermo derisively. I wonder what his eight Indian friends would make of that.

'Japanese girls find it unusual to see a girl with a big dog. They find it powerful,' says Lucrezia. 'They are brought up to be afraid of everything.'

'I have also noticed a lot of Japanese girls put their hand over their mouth when they laugh,' says Stef. 'To preserve their modest image.'

'In Italy a lot of old women do that too,' says Lucrezia. 'And they also pretend to be frightened of dogs when really, they do not give a fuck.'

'It is really just "Oh, macho, please save me,"' says Stef.

The evening's over quickly after that.

'Ciao Biddy,' says Gregorio abruptly, standing up and opening the door. I'm realising what the Italian 'Ciao' really is – a dismissal. You're not supposed to linger after you've been given it.

Stefania says she'll walk me halfway back. There are lots of people still around the main streets. Rialto's dark and all the stalls are shuttered. I feel guilty about Stef going to the effort to walk me and keep saying, 'Do you want to say goodbye now?' to give her the opportunity to turn back. Which she misunderstands and says, 'Why, do you want to be alone?' Excessive politeness has been the downfall of many a cross-cultural friendship.

'So, Bidisha,' she grins. 'You were very bored tonight.'

'No! No! I mean, I was personally bored. But I thought Guillermo was, ah, an interesting phenomenon. Imagine if they have kids though. Who wants to be lectured by Mr Opinion every morning at breakfast?'

'It is an anthropological investigation,' Stef concludes. 'It is good to meet people from a different world. You can see that they lead a completely different life to us. And he is my mother's ex-student, and you are always different with your ex-professors.'

'Yes, you always want to show them what you've become. And your naked camping? How was it?'

'It was beautiful,' she sighs. 'The sea was beautiful. And in the restaurants and supermarket everyone was dressed. There weren't many Italians. Mainly Germans and people from the Netherlands. But I got burned on my back.'

'Oh, I'm sorry!' I'd been walking along with my hand on her shoulder.

'No, no, not there. Lower down.'

'You mean your bum!'

'Yes,' she blushes. 'It hurts to sit down. And also my chest. I am wearing a human sunburn bikini.'

She ends up walking me all the way home. Later that night Lucrezia and Gregorio get the car out of the car park at Tronchetto and go to the countryside for the weekend. Which reminds me: Ginevra was stopped by a crazed and claustrophobic French girl in Accademia Gallery the other day. The girl asked her feverishly where 'the exit' was. She didn't mean the exit of the gallery, she meant the exit of Venice itself, 'You know, where all the cars are.'

'Makes you realise how foreigners see Venice,' commented Ginevra later, 'like a little bottle with only one way out.'

Chapter Six

Stefania's been telling me about the sunglasses guy for some time now as he's the only person she trusts herself to buy sunglasses from, and enough of a local character to be of interest to me. He has a small, chic shop near Campo San Bartolomeo on Stef's side of Rialto Bridge. We visit on a bright, busy, sunny day.

Inside the shop, the sunglasses guy's dealing with a customer. He's tall and slimmish with cropped hair and very clear pale skin, in fashionably preppy clothes. He has the standard northern Italian graceful chirpiness, a way of greasing the wheels of social intercourse. As he winds up his previous appointment (with a middle-aged man in an excellent lightweight suit: 'Oh bravo you, sire!' I mentally hail him), he murmurs to everyone, 'Now, sir, I'll put your new glasses in this case to protect them from bumps and knocks, and I'll slip in a piece of paper with your prescription on it, and if you just give me a moment as I tot up the final sum...'

Meanwhile he slickly flashes a hello at Stefania. I sit down in front of a pile of *Vogue Uomos* and look around. The place is bare, stylish, with a few trendy major brand glasses displayed on sculptural tree-like, bendy metal structures. In Venice shopkeepers guard their wares and shoppers must petition humbly to see them, submitting themselves to the shopkeeper's superior aesthetic knowledge. In short they are allowed to see only what the proprietor wishes them to see. It is OK to spend a lot of money, but not on two versions of the same item (like two jumpers of similar design but different colours), which is vulgar, or on two logically unrelated items (like a cotton vest and some woolly socks), which shows an unseasonal lack of forethought.

Finally the older chap leaves and sunglasses guy turns his full attention on Stef. He has a nice manner, bright-eyed and present. Stef says hello to him and introduces me — 'I'm just out with my English friend today' — and the guy and I greet each other. I always feel I'm doing this wrong, showing too much stiffness or too little poise, smiling too narrowly or too fully, unable to decide between a chirpy *ciao* or *buongiorno* or *piacere*. What sounds frosty? What sounds childish? They smile back but there's always a slight question or falling-off in their eyes, the politeness of a covered-up faux pas. It's as though I've dropped something and they've tactfully toed it under the carpet.

'Sorry I haven't been in for a while,' says Stefania. 'I need some sunglasses.'

'Ah, yes, the sun is so piercing at this time of year,' says the guy sympathetically, as though this thought had only just occurred to him.

'But I do have a budget,' says Stef cautiously.

'But of course you do,' says the sunglasses guy. 'You're young, and one doesn't need to spend a lot of money to look stylish. Tell me your budget and I'll find you some beautiful glasses to wear.'

While talking he looks smilingly and gently at both Stef and me and everything proceeds in the atmosphere of flowing goodwill which Stef always creates around her. I smile back when smiled at, understanding about three quarters of what he's saying but really just wanting to watch the two virtuosi at work. The guy begins to produce glasses from the slender tray-cabinets around him, which slide open noiselessly, and pays tribute to them:

'Fendi. Black, square, minimalist. They block the sun completely but if you just... there we go... the question is, how do they blend with your skin tone? Do they sit at the bridge of your nose or are they falling forwards? Let me see – now, if you observe yourself in the mirror...'

'I *quite* like these...'

'So! We'll put them on the "quite like" pile. Now, something completely different. Wire rims, a lightly tinted lens, golden tones to pick out the pink here,' he playfully pinches her cheeks, 'and bring out your lovely hair colour. Now – Prada – a classic style, light, elegant, very discreet.'

'But the lenses... I'm just wondering about the lenses. Won't they let in the sun through the sides?'

'Perhaps, and that's generally true. But the genius of these frames is that they sit very close to your face, really inside the socket, and they never seem "too much" – too aggressive.'

'I'm always so uncertain of these things. And glasses are a difficult item to choose. I wonder, if it's all right, I might come again with my friend Mara. She's a designer. She has an excellent eye.'

'But of course, I would love to meet her. Now, we'll put these on the "maybe" pile, and don't worry, I have many more to show you, and all in your price range.'

After a few minutes of similar chat, looking at us both, the sunglasses guy turns his head and says to Stef very sweetly, like a nurse, 'Does your friend not understand Italian?' I wake up and say, 'Hey!' He looks down at me as though I'm a cute but senile Labrador. 'It's just that I could tell... something wasn't quite connecting,' he says kindly. I am aghast with embarrassment and can think of nothing to say to redeem myself. Stefania, always at ease, says firmly and affectionately, 'No, she understands.'

'I understand everything, but I don't speak it well,' I say, before falling back on my usual lame explanation of my reticence: 'And I'm tired.'

I have by now established myself universally as the most tired girl in Venice. My tiredness is legendary, I have been tired in bars, shops and restaurants all over the city. Stefania has frequently told me off for being quiet during coffees, lunches and dinners (to which I consistently reply with reference to my monumental, chronic and famous tiredness) when all I'm really doing is enjoying the meal and listening to the other guests. Stef interprets this as (a) not understanding Italian, (b) being worried about something and/or (c) having been offended by something someone said.

More glasses are tried. I favour a pair in a warm camouflage green and reject the opaque black pair because they're too harsh for her colouring. We leave, having bought nothing. Venetian shopkeepers become your friends for life if you exhibit a stylish and prudent decorum in resisting the lure of base greed (yours and theirs). The sunglasses guy happily packs away all the sunglasses and makes a note of what Stef liked. We take our leave.

Stef as usual misreads me.

'Sorry, sorry, Bidisha. It took too long.'

'It didn't. I was enjoying myself! Sometimes I don't think you understand me at all.'

Stef smiles sunnily and I laugh.

29 July rolls around: my twenty-sixth birthday. That evening I'm waiting outside Frari church as per instructions. Very gratifying to see five people (Stef, Ginevra, Bruno, Bianca and Mara) coming over the bridge – my new crew. We start off having drinks at Imagina in Campo St M. We'd agreed on no gifts but Ginevra surprises me with a book of Huck Scarry's Venice watercolours. She's wrapped it beautifully in brown paper and even made a paper rosette for one corner. We have a private thank-you/no-no-it-was-nothing exchange. The others are joking about when they all went camping in Valencia together about nine years ago.

'The ground was so hard we couldn't put the tent pegs in,' says Bruno. 'We tried all night and then when we were thinking, Oh God, what are we gonna do, a man drives up, a Spanish man, and says, "Excuse me, would you like to borrow an electric drill for making holes in walls?" "Ah! Yes, thank you very much!" "Where would you like a hole? Here? No Problem. Vvvoooo! And here also? One second. Vvvoooo!" Problem completely solved. And also in Valencia there was a Dutch family, really nice, who gave me an outdoors grill because they were leaving. Nine years later I am still using the same grill. Oh, and there was also a woman there, Italian, with two little kids called Asia and Africa.'

'Too much,' says Stef grimly. 'Can you imagine calling to your kids across the camp site? "Asia! Africaaah..."'

We go to a secret fish restaurant: typical Venetian unassuming style, handwritten menus, wood everywhere, mouth-watering odours, a tough waitress who gives short shrift to — well, to everyone. She rolls her eyes at us because we said we were going to be five people and we're six instead. We sit down (Stef, Mara and Bianca squashed onto one bench, me at the head of the very small table, Bruno and Ginevra on the other side) and great hilarity ensues as we all try and decide what to have.

'Since we all have an economic problem I think we should all pay for what we order instead of dividing it six ways,' Stefania proposes.

'What?!' shouts Bruno. 'Are we German? Do you want to get out your little calculator and work out who had a bread roll and who had a water?' Bruno leans over to me:

'I had dinner with some German finance people one night and they were fighting about the bill for half an hour. They're all like that.'

We order: clams with spaghetti for Bruno, squid in black ink with polenta for me, Stef and Ginevra have a huge platter of langoustines and spaghetti for Mara and Bianca to share. White wine. We set about eating and talking with no mind for noise or mess. The squid is brilliant and I love the glistening blackness of it.

'Smile,' Bianca commands me. I give a big Mickey Mouse cheese-grin and make it as grotesque as I can. 'Black smile!' she laughs as I show off my ghoulish black teeth.

The food is pure, hearty and plentiful. I take some of Bruno's clams (after having been offered) and exhort him to have some of mine.

'No, no,' he says, 'I will take some from the monster over there!' (Meaning Stefania.)

Watching them I can almost believe that some loves were written in the stars. When we were walking up to the restaurant I caught sight of a couple I've seen about six times now. They were standing unhappily by a phone box, their faces creased with despair. I pointed them out to Bruno.

'See them? They're always arguing. I don't think I've seen them once when they haven't been arguing about something.'

'But it's a way of living,' he said generously. 'Stefania and me, we sometimes spend months fighting and fighting!' With a look of flushed playful joy on his face.

We're talking so much in the restaurant – about silly things, like how the design of the chic wine carafe is such that it spills every time you pour it – that someone at an adjoining table shushes us loudly. They do it quick and sharp so that it pierces everything but we can't tell where it's come from. We stare at each other, wounded, comically ashamed, and I learn a new phrase – *scopa in culo*: a broomstick up the bottom.

'Global phenomenon,' I say. 'We have the same phrase in English: "That guy has a major stick up his arse."'

'In Italy there is a famous song by this pop singer, a really strong-woman song, and it goes, "What d'you want? D'you want me to stick a broom up my ass so I can clean your house?"' says Stefania.

We all laugh at her efficiency with the langoustines (there were so many in Mara's dish that she passed them over). She can get the maximum meat out, leaving only the legs and a few slivers of translucent pink shell.

'Stefania always inspires me when she is eating shellfish like this,' says Bruno. 'Three twists and it is all out. She is like someone with a Rubik's cube. I always try to follow her strategy when I am putting up a tent.'

'It is a natural talent,' says Stef. 'Once when I was little, I was in a restaurant with my parents and we ordered a crab, and the waiter bring it and he say with this look on his face, "Oh but I do not think *the child* will be able to manage." I was like, "Please. Hand it over. I will show *you*."'

We pay and leave and walk back towards Postali on Rio Marin. Outside Tonolo *pasticceria* we bump into Stef's delectable young cousin Renato. Fitted black T-shirt, slim nothing hips in baggy jeans, a small bag across his chest. We chat with him and watch Mara as she comes close to him, very friendly, and asks to see his bag, saying 'May I?' and cringing submissively as he takes it off and hands it to her. She crowds over it and praises its design, shape, purpose and practicality. Note: the bag, though cool, is a completely plain black nylon square with a black leather flap. Prada, possibly. But still, easy to understand with one short glance, and not worth all Mara's salivating. However, it gives me an opportunity to do some salivating of my own.

'Your cousin is so beautiful,' I groan to Stef when we pass on.

'Yes,' says Mara, 'with Renato and his brother I am always, like, OK, grow up, and then we'll see.'

'They don't need to grow up, they're fine as they are,' I say.

'No! Seventeen is too young.'

'Too young for what? Seventeen is perfect.'

'It is just as well that he is leaving soon,' growls Stefania.

We're all in high spirits as we walk back to Frari and pass the archway that leads to my *campiello*. To reach Postali we have to go by the Millevoglie ice cream place and can't resist a few scoops. At Postali we sit by the canal drinking prosecco. The usual old friends pass by and greet Stefania. Everything is dark and warm, liquid and convivial. Ginevra and I talk about *Death in Venice*.

'I watch that film obsessively,' I say. 'I love what the camera does. Every time he sees that boy Tadzio...'

'And everything stops,' Ginevra says, nodding.

'Everything stops and goes bright and glittery as though he's looking at the sun.'

The others are talking about the tradition of putting up a public poster around Venice when someone graduates. The posters are usually well-decorated and contain a witty description of the person's past bedroom exploits.

Mara is dreading her architecture graduation poster.

'But I have had thirty boyfriends,' she says, looking exhausted.

'You have to try before you buy,' I remark, and she agrees with a leaden sigh and nod.

'I think, to find a boyfriend, you should start with a tour of the bookshops,' says Ginevra, 'and then the Film Biennale – the special feature on the work of the French existential directors. And one or two design exhibitions...'

The evening goes on 'til one. We take a walk afterwards, close to Piazzale Roma and then along the Canal Grande opposite the train station, where the big, plain hotels are. Mara is so desperate for a man's attention that she ushers us into the freezing cold lobby of the Carlton Hotel because she knows the guy who's working there. I even watched her dancing around Bruno at some point in the evening.

After standing around in the lobby for twenty minutes while she basks in man-rays we decide to leave her behind and go our separate ways. Ginevra, Bianca and I say goodnight to Stef and Bruno, who go back to Stef's place. We three drift back in the direction we came from. On the Rio Marin Ginevra points out a beautiful palazzo that's currently undergoing restoration.

'That is the house that Henry James's *The Aspern Papers* is set in. It's haunted.'

Immediately I get the chill. We peer inside at the museum-lit ground floor.

'And you see the garden,' says Ginevra. There's a tall and very thickly planted fertile garden above stern walls and grilles. 'Once it was a private garden that used to stretch all the way to Piazzale Roma.'

'Ginevra, did you read Henry James in the translation or the original?'

'In English. But even though I can get a general idea of the story I can't get the finer meanings. For example, why did he use this particular adjective instead of another?'

'Oh, why are you so modest?' I cry. 'Why don't you come to London? You could be an editor, you could be a writer, you could be a scholar.'

Ginevra recoils dramatically, goes pale and stammers,

'No, but you do not understand, everyone in Italy is taught English at school, this is not something special.'

'It *is* something special.'

'How do you know?'

'Because I've got eyes in my head and I can see you,' I say crossly.

In the Campo dei Frari Bianca bumps into a male friend. He's forty or a little older, bull-like, small and square but in tough good shape with wiry grey thinning hair and an intelligent, animalistically attractive face. They enter a wild private discussion, she pleased with him, he with her, both seeming to ask 'Why?' of each other while standing right in each other's space. But this is standard behaviour, he could just as easily be the family plumber explaining something about the dodgy pipes. Bianca introduces us as Ginevra and Bidisha, 'my English friend'. The guy thinks that pale Ginevra's the English friend and says 'Nice to meet you,' in English. Ginevra is so surprised that she answers, also in English, 'Nice to meet *you*?' Then Bianca says, 'No, *she's* not English.' To top off the confusion I say '*I'm* the English one' – in Italian. We explain that it's my birthday.

'How old?' he asks.

'Twenty-six.'

'*Vecchia*,' he jokes. Old.

This is what every single person has said to me today on hearing my age. *Vecchia*, old. Old, old, old. They all seem to mind the oldness, except me. I look at the guy and feel tempted to say to him, 'Honey, if I'm old then you're bloody ancient and knocking on the gates of hell.' Smile sweetly instead.

I kiss Bianca goodnight. She'll be busy writing her architecture dissertation over the next few weeks but urges me to meet her for a drink one night:

'I'll stand in the *campiello* and call up at your window. Don't lean out and pour water on my head!'

Over the next few days the humidity increases and the sea swells high, almost level with the ground at the St Mark's edge. It's dangerous to run there, the marble's too slippery, so I take to darting around the residential areas in San Polo and Castello, discovering random niches containing a plaster Virgin Mary and some fresh buds in a vase, well-tended courtyards, stray cats, a family motto or Roman Empire rubric carved into the stone.

I visit Frari church, smell the marble, look at the tombs, the slabs, the chapels, the altarpieces, the great lacquered wedge of the choir stalls and the candles. There are no hot young monks on show, sadly. My secret wish, when I take up one long, fresh candle and light it from another, is always the same: 'Give me the strength to see the way'. Tacky, I know, but it sounds better than 'I don't believe in you, make me famous'. Close my eyes for a moment to concentrate, then I fit the candle between the jaws of the black iron clip where it stays, leaning slightly and burning down among its forty or fifty fellows.

When in Frari church I often linger around the relics, noting people's genuflections. The Virgin Mary Worship Look is an expression I've observed on the faces of the beefy granddads who come to the Mass. These old men gaze up at the Mary statue, their eyes suffused with submissive love and beseechment as though they were beholding a scene of the greatest maternal tenderness. They go down stiffly on one knee, they cross themselves, their eyes fill with tears, they bow their heads and make a wish. Exactly the same guys who bug me on my runs and congregate with their buddies to idle, stare and bullshit in the darker wine bars. Exactly the same guys, in short, who have never behaved with real respect towards a real woman in the entire course of their life.

By now I've settled into my triple life, and each one has a different Venice to go with it. There's the existence I lead with Ginevra and Stef and her family, when we're part of a young, artistic, thriving and civilised city. There's my solitary work life, listening in on the small community around the *campiello* and all the people who pass by in the course of the day. I often go to Frari church just to think, or to Campo St M for a break and a coffee (I've elected the blue-and-cream Caffè Causin as my solitary favourite, despite a certain irregularity in the pricing, and Gobbetti's *pasticceria* for its pear tart and friendly auburn-haired owner), and the Venice I see there is one of families, daily errands, visitors, relaxed students and children. The chairs at

Caffè Causin are so comfortable, really cupping your bottom, that it's not possible to spend less than an hour over your coffee.

Finally, there's the Venice I see when I'm running through the city every other day. Each trip resembles a Leviathan-type trawl through all the strata of society, from the built-up trashery of the Mercerie luxury shops to the loose, open canals in northern Cannaregio. The harassment I 'attract' (am subjected to? Am obliged to receive?) is so keen, so vicious and so plentiful that it is almost (but, in fact, not) comical, and certainly wouldn't be believed if I told anyone. Indeed even if I recounted the episodes in detail, in person, under oath, in a dock, I may not be believed.

Running in Zattere one afternoon one of the Sri Lankan mystery men, possibly scenting a sub-continental connection, comes close as I crawl past, older, fat, smiling horribly, and mutters '*Sì,* ciao' caressingly into my ear. I stop dead and spin around.

'What?' I say in English. 'Come here and say it again, since you're so *friendly*.'

He looks surprised, backs away, his eyes swivel left and right, he pretends he doesn't know what I mean and mutters, '*No...*'

More amusingly, in the same place later the same day, as the sun sets, I am trudging away and get overtaken by a showily snorting, coughing, puffing jogger of thirty or so, who is completely naked except for a pair of very small black shorts and jogging shoes (no socks). Model on a break? Arch-narcissist? Manorexic? He has a fatless V-torso, no-carbs body with every muscle strenuously defined, matte opaque turkey tan, clipped executive haircut. Having lodged himself in front of me he then goes through his circus routine: eight steps with a great exhalation every other step, and then... a star jump and a full twirl with his arms out and his back flexing. He gets to the end of the coast, crosses the wooden platform over the sea, bends over and begins, for my eyes only, doing a series of revealing stretches, press-ups, leg-lifts and so on. I usually do my final stretches on the platform too, but only when alone. This time I stop dead, give a groan of irritation, turn on my heel and go back the way I came. When I glance back the guy has stopped doing his press-ups (a fancy variation: throw yourself up and give a little clap before you hit the ground again) and is lying forlornly on the floor watching me go.

Because Venice is so small, joggers often choose the same routes (note: one is not supposed to greet or acknowledge other joggers even if you see them every day or indeed every lap). Later I see joggy-boy prancing and stretching in the very middle of Campo St M, sprinting hither and thither among the cafes, the restaurants, the tourists, the students and the children (*all* of whom ignore him – three cheers for Venetian diffidence on this one occasion), grunting heroically and wiping the sweat manfully from his forehead like someone in an aftershave advert. Is someone in search of validation? I think they are...

By the first week of August I'm noticing that a lot of the shops and *pasticcerie* around San Polo are shut for something called *ferie*. At first I think this means refurbishment but no, it means holidays – they've all gone to the mountains in the north or the dry sun in the south. It's so hot that my ears are aching from the air pressure.

Stefania goes away filming and Ginevra and I have fallen into the habit of having the odd coffee here and there. One day we visit Il Prato, the paper shop, together. The woman recognises me: 'Were you in here a few months ago? I remember you because of your beautiful rings.' I'm pleased, and Ginevra whispers to me later, 'I wanted to say, "Yes, she was in here before, and she will be in here again, many times!"' Ginevra tells me that Lucrezia Ritter's design eye is so sharp that she can go into a stationery shop and tell which ones use machine-printed paper and which ones use hand-printed paper. At Il Prato I buy a paper-covered ledger in a rusty vine design. It costs nearly fifty euros and the only way to justify it to myself is by saying I won't do any food-shopping that week. Following this new tight budget I go to the 'everything' shop in Campo St M and buy the cheapest shampoo I can find – €1.60. Exactly the same shampoo is €1.90 in Billa. The market's so small here that competition never really drives prices down and shops can charge what they like.

Ginevra escorts me around town while I make notes.

'Let's go to Florian's one day,' I say, thinking about the day I'm supposed to finish my book and how I'll celebrate.

'To Florence?'

'No, Florian's, the cafe.'

'Ah! Florian's. Because it would actually be cheaper to go to Florence.'

We visit Gobbetti's, 'my' *pasticceria* in a little corner of Campo Santa Margherita, just before the bridge to Campo San Barnaba. There are big round cakes in the window, each one like an exquisite hat, piled high with rice-paper birds, berries, leaves, flowers and candied fruit. I order a chocolate mousse and the friendly auburn-haired lady laughs and makes a 'delicious – good choice' face and asks, '*Una brutta giornata?*' Bad day? Literally: an ugly day. She adds in Italian, 'When you've had a bad day, have the chocolate mousse! It's the only medicine you need, and it's *very* effective.'

There seem to be no Venetians around, only travellers munching on sandwiches and studying maps. Ginevra's family are in the process of redecorating their bathroom. The original's all black marble and pink tile, seventies nightclub style, 'like something Gianni Versace designed on a bad day, perhaps when he had a headache'. We talk about the various public restoration projects in the city – each project has a printed sign hung outside it, giving the name of the company, the names of all the major participants and managers and a prospective completion date (usually long gone). Ginevra says they're all half in the pay of the Mafia.

'I thought the Mafia thing was a myth?' I say.

'No. It is not as though it's one organisation that you apply to, but if you want anything done, the official bodies and the police do not do anything. You have to speak to someone alternative: the Mafiosi. But it is not true that they are busy shooting each other in restaurants all the time.'

'In India, in certain areas, if you're known to be rich and you move house and don't want to be robbed or hit up for money, you have to speak to "someone" and pay them off. It's like protection money.'

'Ah! It's the same thing, and it exists in every area of life. Nothing will ever change it. You can talk about progress and civilisation but I think this is *us*, this is the Italian characteristic.'

A few moments of drinking and enjoying the shade. A policeman strolls past, barely eighteen. They keep in touch by mobile phone but as there appears to be little violent activity in Venice they don't have that much to do. I do see them talking into their mobiles, but the two times I listen in it's never to do with matters of polity: one guy's fixing dinner arrangements with his wife and daughters; another chap whispers lovingly into the phone a dramatic 'Darling. Tell me *everything*.' Others stare around hard-eyed.

Ginevra says that she's noticed how easy it is to get to my window by climbing on top of the newspaper stand, which is easy to get to by climbing on top of the bin. I've thought about this too. People say there's no serious crime in Venice but who knows? Judging by the street-harassment the crime which dare not speak its name is probably just around the corner.

'I love living alone,' I say. 'As long as I have work to do. It's when you don't have an occupation that you go crazy...'

'Thirteen cats...'

'Going to the supermarket every day...'

'To buy just one thing: one tomato and one little cucumber and one egg to boil.'

I don't say it but even that sounds like a good life.

Another of 'our' places is Gelateria Nico on Zattere with its wide sea terrace and crowded tables. We choose seats the furthest out, right over the water, get hypnotised by the waves and spend the afternoon clinging to the railings, trying not to throw ourselves in. The decaf is rough and hot, arrives on a square silver tray with water. The waiter, Moroccan-looking, sweating hard and harassed under the sun.

'We are going to the mountains for two weeks, they are only one or two hours from here in the north. The south could be better, like Tuscany, but my father was like no, the mountains, the mountains,' says Ginevra.

'You too? I'm going to be the only person left here... Isn't the south really hot at this time of year?'

'Yes, but it is a good, dry heat. Venice is a wet heat. You go to the south to dry your bones – is that a phrase in English? You store the heat inside you before the winter?'

'Yes: get some sun in your bones.'

I look over at Giudecca, the long flat mirror-line of it, the same for hundreds of years, the three white thickset churches spread out evenly on the coast.

'Very difficult to get a grip on yourself here,' I murmur.

'Don't try! This is what Venice is for.'

We eventually drag ourselves out of our seats and walk for all of two minutes to visit the church of Santa Maria della Visitazione (commonly known as Artigianale). There's an amazing ceiling like a dark chocolate novelty chessboard, each square painted with a portrait of one of the saints, the glowing pale walls breaking apart slightly, the floor laid with long stones, yellowed cream and the lightest pink, also crumbling – the whole church is sun-baked and sun-bleached (I remember something Stef said: 'Sometimes I think that in Venice there's no distinction between inside and outside'). Horrible wooden confessional like a public toilet.

That night there's a crashing storm: thunder, rain, crackling darkness. I listen to the grinding thunder outside, industrial barrels being rolled over our heads. The lightning plunges all the way to the ground, licking the sides of the buildings. It's like the flash of a camera, flat and white and motion-freezing, as though God's taking photographs of Venice. Makes me feel close to the other people who live in the *campiello*, sure that we are all looking up and thinking the same thing.

Chapter Seven

A couple of months into my stay I break up the humid August stasis with an art-and-coffee odyssey, urged on by the beseeching plaster eyes of the Virgin in Frari church. Her face is so well-rendered, her gaze always slipping away, inward-looking, even as she reaches out. What I really like are images of the Annunciation — the ones by Fra Angelico are among my favourites — the stillness and the waiting and the watchfulness. I always imagine Mary sitting in her room, turning the page of her book, feeling a change in the air and then glancing up casually to see Gabriel alighting at the high window with a slight smile on his face. Some of the Venetian Gabriels, I do notice, are remarkably agile and sexy, and it does make me wonder about the painters... for example, in the Chiesa di San Vidal, a *very* interesting sculpture/marble relief of the Annunciation by Tarsia: Gabriel naked, young, toned, looking half-coy, half-proud and fully expectant, swathed (just about) in a little cloth and holding flowers as if presenting himself to Mary as a consolation prize for the diplomatic hassle of having God's baby.

From there I visit the gloomy Chiesa di Santo Stefano. There are large, bitty, bricky, diamond-shaped marble stones on the floor, coral and cream, a square worked ceiling, insubstantial sentimental paintings. I find the prize in the dark leftmost chapel, the Cappella di San Michele, in the form of an anonymous white marble sculpture of St Michael, skirted, winged, gorgeous, spear-carrying, pre-Christian in appearance, barely visible in the shadows, in a sort of niche framed in gold fronds and leaves painted onto black – what utter beauty. I stare into the shadows... I turn away and find myself face to face with a red marble Jesus, very sinewy and mangled, swinging from the cross, clearly in a great deal of pain – and a bank of lit candles in front of him, all the little devotees.

Afterwards I venture into Toppo, the bistro-style bar at the bottom of the Ponte dei Frari. The guy who owns the place barks at me but I detect something friendly in him. He's fifty-something and handsome, with strange colouring: cold, absolutely grey skin, iron grey hair cut long and floppy to the ears, iron blue dark eyes, bloodless grey-purple lips, all angular. A good-looking corpse. I stay upstairs and watch the bar downstairs (the upstairs is designed like a gallery, with a big hole in the centre to look down). I sit in my own lino booth. The dead owner comes up and turns on my personal art deco-style lamp for me.

Later I visit the Guggenheim museum, drifting through examples of the very worst of several major artists' work (a really *bad* Picasso, a really *bad* Ernst) until I come across an amazing Jackson Pollock, black and neon, vibrating ominously against a wall, called – oh, I don't know – *I'm Depressed and I've*

Been Drinking All Day. Plus a vivid Francis Bacon painting of a monkey. Virtually no women artists, even in recent acquisitions. Maybe four out of three hundred? It isn't worth making a precise tally. Very peculiar – the curators just don't see us. The Guggenheim house is itself very beautiful and soaked in sadness. Iron grilles like symmetrical vines, a view onto the blurred, bright Canal Grande, a room dedicated to the colourful artworks of Guggenheim's self-taught daughter Pegeen, who committed suicide. The best things in the gallery are the black and white reportage photos of Peggy alone and with various artists, her gaze so strong and powerful and yet full of humour and vivacity. Peggy Guggenheim didn't think she was beautiful but she was, and charismatic too.

I visit the church of San Trovaso to see some Tintorettos but can never be touched by him, his characters always fleshy and pale and lumpily swaddled in clothes, blank-eyed and in ridiculous perpetual motion, reaching, pointing, staring, leaning, exclaiming, yet devoid of life, soul, intention and always in this peculiar light, not sun and not candle, something like a dingy table lamp under a polyester scarf. As Ginevra and I were saying earlier, these churches would be fantastic if they had a cafe in the back and the priests doubled up as waiters.

I duck into the Chiesa di San Pantaleone on the way home and clock a very funny ceiling by Fumiani: lots of angels' legs and knickers going up to heaven, promising all the faithful that when they die they'll achieve – what? Seraphic panty-sniffing nirvana? There's also a notable sculpture of St Anna depicting an older, rigorous-looking woman smiling like a tax inspector.

A few nights later Ginevra invites me to dinner at the Al Nono Risorto pizzeria, a bustling brown-wood place with a huge, shingled, ivy hung garden. We have a drink beforehand at Toppo. Ginevra orders a *sprizz* and says,

'How can you drink water all the time?'

'How can you drink that orange stuff?' I defiantly respond.

'I heard a funny story about London in the news today. Apparently so many people are taking Prozac that it has entered the waste system from their urine, and now it has entered the drinking water. So the drinking water's full of Prozac and everyone's very happy... but it may not be true. In August they invent the news because nothing is happening and they have to fill up the gap. Also, this is the time that the government introduces all the worst laws because everyone's away on holiday so they can't protest.'

We go to the restaurant, get exactly the table we want – in the corner of the garden, under a canopy of trailing stems and leaves – and order. While we're waiting, Ginevra happens to mention that she's teaching herself Ancient Greek from a book. She already knows Latin. Unable to stand this provocation I burst out, 'Oh come on! We have to do something about your career. I've decided that we're going to translate your book into either English or French and publish it. The English have a fascination for Italy. It'll do very well.'

'Just like that?' she jokingly replies, clicking her fingers like a genie.

I haven't yet mastered the art of Italian delay, prevarication and general Zen flow, probably because I think it's an illusion. The thin little perfect-blue-suited businessmen I see racing to Piazzale Roma every morning don't seem very Zen to me.

I eat a wonderful gooey pizza, thin as paper, topped with prosciutto, gorgonzola and mushrooms, all washed down with prosecco, then astound Ginevra by wolfing down an enormous tartufo nero and three quarters of a long tiramisu.

'You know what "tiramisu" means, literally?' she asks me. 'Take me up. Carry me up.'

'That's beautiful,' I say genuinely, charmed that such transcendent raptures can be attached to a pudding.

We talk about writing.

'As a Venetian,' says Ginevra, 'I see too many books about foreigners coming to Venice and "discovering a magical place". If I were to find my ideal book —'

'What would it be?' I urge.

'A book about an ordinary Venetian family, not the very poor underclass and not the famous nobility who have a name going back to the Roman Empire. With a few characters, not ancient history, going back perhaps fifty years. Just their ordinary lives.'

'That's one for you to write,' I say. 'You're the true Venetian, not me. I could only see things as an outsider... the magic and the beauty and the decay and all the clichés, the legends.' Thinking about a recently published book of Venetian myths and ghost stories I've seen on sale around town I say excitedly, 'I want to stay in a haunted house one night. With friends. With the lights on.'

'No, looking at Venice you would think that every corner must be full of ghosts, but there aren't.'

'Do you believe in that stuff? Premonitions...'

'Yes. Absolutely,' says Ginevra. 'There are a lot of stories in my family. And Stefania too. Nero's dog-sitter's house is this ancient villa and there is one hallway hung with all the paintings of the ancestors, and one day a person who they do not like came to visit and all the paintings come, go...'

'All the paintings crashed to the floor?'

'Yes.'

'Oh God. Oh God!' I shiver and look around me for any loose-hanging portraits. 'I believe in magical incidents,' I say.

'Nothing magical ever happens to me.'

'It will.'

'Yes. Perhaps when I am sixty years old.'

'Oh Ginevra,' I say, annoyed.

Ginevra cuts a slice of pizza, curves it in her large hand, bows her head and eats elegantly. I cut mine into rectangles.

'You can tell everything about a person from the way they eat a pizza,' says Ginevra. 'My mother begins at one side and slowly cuts the whole thing into tiny little squares. And some people get the whole pizza, fold it into four and put the whole thing in their mouth.'

'I wouldn't trust a person like that.'

'Me neither. Too demanding. They want to *dominate* the pizza.'

Afterwards, Ginevra walks me home through Santa Croce, dark, black shadows, brown and grey stone, empty. A fat, bald Sri Lankan man in front of us keeps turning around, eyeballing us and muttering, 'Yes, that's it, come here darlings' and holding out his arms to us. I scowl.

'You are too expressive,' says Ginevra to me.

'Right! It's my fault.'

We take a shortcut but soon reconnect with the Sri Lankan man, who laughs aloud, his belly bursting through his shirt, and holds his arms wide open.

I see Ginevra off, wishing her a good holiday, and spend the rest of August listening to life in the Campiello Ca' Zen. At any one time I can hear one or all of the following: an opera singer rehearsing arpeggios. She has a good voice but can't hit any notes with it, all the tunes sound like they're melting. The caged birds above me. The people who come to Massimo the newspaper guy for their daily chat, and some of the local children, who seem to love him: 'Ciao Massimo!' they cry, giggling as they run through the square. I can't criticise dour old Massimo too much as I suspect he's inadvertently taught me Italian. He talks all day, we're only separated by one wall, suddenly I find I can understand what he's saying. Next up is a stupid yapping little dog called Luna and its stupid yapping little owner, whose response to the dog's yapping is a long ineffectual 'Shhhh....' repeated about ten times, along with 'Luna, Luna, behave, be quiet, come, quietly, quietly,' in a whining, hoarse, defeated voice. The dog is so stupid it can't tell what 'Shh, be quiet' etc. means. The owner is so stupid she can't tell how stupid the dog is. I hear them come out and return about three times a day, always the same script. I also keep an ear out for the old woman with a hacking cough who's friends with other old women in the square, talking about domestic matters every day. As Ginevra says, '"How's your son? How's your daughter?" Always the same...' The women conclude their chats with '*A domani!*' ("til tomorrow then!') Depressing... An emotion also felt by the ponderous person whom I can hear listening to mournful violin sonatas in the afternoons.

In the evenings I've taken to killing mosquitoes with a triumphant 'Yeah pal, there ya go!' One night I close my window to reveal a pale beige, paper-dry locust the size of a kitchen knife sitting silently halfway up the inside surface of the glass. I let out a cry, hunt about and eventually, for some reason, squash it with the most expensive, rare and beautiful thing in the room, my big Il Prato journal (as Ginevra asked me later, why not a shoe?). Neon yellow goo comes out, the locust is stuck to the window with it, eventually rustles down to the windowsill and I flick it out with another guttural cry. What did I think it was going to do to me? Although Ginevra says that I did the right thing and if I'd simply shooed it it would have hopped circles around me – terrifying thought. The journal is sadly ruined.

As it happens, I do see Ginevra once more before her holiday. We have a late drink at Bagolo. The sky's dark and clotted and I say something about the frequent thunderstorms we've been having.

'I have become afraid of the storms,' she tells me.

I look at her closely. It's rare for her to make any reference to her feelings.

'Why, do you think they're going to whip your house away like in *The Wizard of Oz*?' I ask.

'Yes... no, it's that I can see the power of nature. I've noticed that I have many fears which I did not have before.'

I wait for her to tell me something more but she doesn't.

'That's a sign of depression,' I prompt.

She makes a short 'hmm' sound which means, hey, well, who knows, maybe you're wrong, maybe you're right, and the subject's closed. She tells me she's spent the day visiting her grandparents.

'They have a beautiful house on the Fondamenta Nuove, opposite the cemetery.'

'That's my favourite view in Venice.'

'It's a nice story, because they were not born here. They are not Venetian. My grandfather is a carpenter, and when he arrived here he was really poor. He had to work so hard, and he did. Finally, he and my grandmother could afford the house where they live now.'

'Well that's your novel right there. That's the story.'

'It is a good story,' she admits. 'I grew up with the smell of the wood and wax and polish.'

'Beautiful! That's a story for George Eliot. The poor family that arrives with their clever granddaughter... Or Umberto Eco?'

I only say it because there's a big display of his books at the shop behind St Mark's. Ginevra waves her hand dismissively:

'Eco is the great unread author. If you want to feel that you are an intelligent person, buy a book by him – but don't keep it. Give it to someone as a Christmas present. That way you extend the compliment: "I think I am an intelligent person, and because I think you are an intelligent person too, I give you this book." Nobody has ever read one of his books, apart from *The Name of the Rose*.'

'But did you see the film?'

'Oh my God...'

'Right, and all the monks were like, "I can't believe Sean Connery's come to investigate the murders at our monastery. I thought he was an actor..."'

Eventually we do part, she does go away on holiday and I'm left to my own devices. One day I'm waiting at Il Gelatone for a scoop of ice cream and who's in front of me in the queue? A tiny slender Japanese nun, speaking full fast Italian, in spotless white little-girl tea-party frock and wimple, buying two enormous packs of ice cream and wafers to go with it. The nuns're having a party, the nuns're having a party! She must be a regular too – some of the other staff members come out the back to have a humble friendly chat. Come to think of it, every time I see a nun around Venice she's always holding a big cake or a loaf of olive bread.

Sometime in August I finish a section of work and decide to present myself with some tickets to a dance performance in Campo

Pisani, off Campo Santo Stefano. The dance is choreographed by Mauro Constantini.

'Are you eligible for any reductions?' asks the girl at the booth.

'No...' I'm looking at the list of possible concessions. 'I don't have a Rolling Venice card... and I'm not a PhD student.'

'But you're under twenty-six?'

'No, it was my twenty-sixth birthday, not yesterday, a few weeks ago yesterday,' I explain brokenly.

'Ah, well then! I'll give you a birthday present,' she rejoins, and lets me have it at the lower price.

I heehaw with delight, run off to Campo St M, choose a cafe at random and treat myself to a lasagne dinner. Of which: the cheap price (seven euros – cheap for Venice) should have warned me. Along comes the waiter and sets down a paper place-mat and a plastic pack containing a flimsy plastic knife and fork and wet tissue. Along comes the lasagne, bright orange and raging hot, fresh from the microwave and angrily blitzed around the edges. Accompanying it are two stale white rolls. Aeroplane food. Oh well.

I watch dusk fall. Just before nine o'clock I make my way to Campo Pisani, lean against the wall and watch everyone lining up, the usual impeccable older Venetians, groomed audacious women with heat-smoothed bobs, rather silent men. Almost no tourists (I count myself as a half-tourist). Suddenly I spot Tiziana, the estate agent – unmistakable slender, shrugging body, long arms and floppy mermaid clothes. She catches sight of me, looks amazed, opens her arms, smiles and raises her eyes to the heavens. I beam shyly. She comes straight over.

'Are you alone?' she demands in Italian.

'Yes,' I bleat.

She links her arm through mine: 'Come with me.'

And she introduces me to all her friends: a woman whom I met before at the Metropole cocktail party, a couple of men in their fifties, all the soft-faced civilised linen type. Also her mum, who's sitting down and has a pair of crutches. She is solid and very healthy-looking, with a strong, square, tanned face and short grey hair, in a silk overshirt and trousers.

'She has something wrong with her back,' Tiziana explains. 'She's seventy-six.'

'Oh my God! Youthful looks run in your family,' I say in English. Her mum looks about fifty.

After this we chat in Italian because Tiziana refuses to let me speak English. As people begin to file in I manage to garble out, 'I've got to go, I'm in the middle of my row,' cautious about outstaying my welcome and unable to read Italian politeness very well. Tiziana makes me promise to find them at a nearby *gelateria* after the performance for an ice cream.

I've got an excellent seat in the second row with a small kid sitting in front of me. Her huge dad sits next to her with another kid on his lap. The woman next to me gives a lazy Italian laugh of frustration – she can't see anything. 'This always happens to me,' she murmurs, smiling resignedly. She is early sixties, ballerina slim, Mattel pretty, frosted blonde bob, neat white linen skirt suit. Her husband is slumped in his chair next to her, occasionally leans in and whispers babyishly in her ear.

The performance is great. The most impressive dancer is a rope thin, dead white, bony, sharp-faced, sinewy woman, her every limb like a long needle, who moves like a spider. Absolute control. The performance is ruined slightly by the choreographer running out every ten minutes to explain what's just gone on and take questions. He's short and bald with a muscular, heavy build. He has a plain, round, smiley face, rimless glasses, skintight T-shirt, jeans and designer trainers. He talks with his hands, crumbling the air between his fingers and spilling it out up near his mouth as though tasting every morsel of what he's saying. At the final Q&A session he says, 'I'm so happy. Venice is always something special; usually the moment it's over the audience gets up and flees for the exit but you sit serenely, and I'm so grateful because you give me the opportunity to talk about what I love and what I'm passionate about.'

There's a pause, during which the entire audience thinks quite blatantly, 'We sit here because we are Venetians and you are not; therefore *you* should leave first.'

Eventually we get out and I stand around until everyone's gone, not sure whether Tiziana's invitation was sincere or just the Italian way of saying 'See you around.' Go to the ice cream place where they're all sitting, look down at them tentatively – Tiziana immediately jumps up and makes space for me.

'What did you think?'

'*Danza bellissima, conversazione brutta*,' I quip, grammatically incorrect. Great dancing, bad talking. Tiziana finds this so witty – I had been preparing it for forty minutes – that she repeats it around the table and everyone laughs.

'This girl is a phenomenon. She's only been here a month and she speaks Italian.'

'I can't speak Italian,' I say modestly, in Italian, loving Tiziana with heart and soul at that moment. 'But I can understand a lot.'

Talk turns to other cultural events in Venice. Plans are made.

'I think, an opera by Wagner,' suggests someone.

'I think an opera by Wagner would be extremely long, hard, boring and tiresome,' says Tiziana, resting her elbow on the side of my chair.

As per usual various friends walk by and everyone at our table calls out, 'Ciao! Ciao! Ciao Roberto/Paola/Maurizio/Otto.'

Tiziana's female friend, sitting close by her, is a lightly wrinkled, dark-tanned woman with pretty, doll-like features, bow lips, bow eyebrows, almond eyes and a beautiful slim figure with sharp wide shoulders. Soft, simply-cut tawny hair that falls to her shoulders. She's shy and doesn't have charisma like Tiziana.

'Is your ice cream good?' Tiziana asks her.

'No, it's all cream. It's supposed to be a cup of ice cream and then some whipped cream on top,' she says, poking at it with her spoon.

'I had a very good ice cream in Denver, Colorado,' says Tiziana's mum suddenly.

'No! America? Are you sure?' says everyone in disbelief.

'It was made by an Italian couple.'

'Ah! *That's* why...'

Some friends of Tiziana's walk past with a sweet brown basset hound, shining and friendly and syrupy all over, who walks between our feet and looks up at us in chummy regard. When he's gone, Tiziana says, 'That dog is amazing. He knows two hundred words. If you say to him, "Where's yesterday's newspaper?" he goes to the bin and gets it out. And he can sing. He lives in a house by a *fondamenta* where the tourist gondolas pass by, and every time one of the gondoliers is singing under the window, he runs to it: "Aroo, awoo!" If you turn on the radio, suddenly he adds "Aroo, awoo!" – not bad either. And one afternoon when the gondolier wasn't singing, he rowed under the window anyway and said, "But signora, where is the basset? I have a concert tonight. I need the basset!"' She adds, 'My own dog Coco knows about five words: bed, food, Coco, door and mountain. So she knows roughly where to go. And she is a bit deaf, so...'

Someone pays (not me) and we disband for the night, all very low-key and friendly. This sort of spontaneous collaboration, which seems so normal for them, is so revolutionary for me that I have to stop myself jumping up and licking all their faces in glee. Instead I go to Caffè Rosso in Campo St M and celebrate with a glass of water, noticed curiously by the surrounding groups of sociable young people. I can't wait 'til I'm a serene fifty-something and can do this kind of thing with impunity.

Chapter Eight

After two days of dictionary research I call Tiziana because I have to pay my rent. I've got the script written out in front of me. She's nice on the phone, speaking in slow, clear Italian: 'Let's meet at Campo Santo Stefano — you remember, the place where we had the ice creams on the night of the dance performance?' I'm amazed that I can understand her. Then she says, 'What time is it? I can't see the clock...' and I understand that too! Why? Because I had to change the battery in my watch so I looked up all the appropriate words, burst into the watch shop and delivered them, only to gag mutely when the lady followed it up with, 'Would you like to wear it home or shall I put it in a bag?'

I turn up on time but there's no sign of Tiziana, so I loiter and watch a row of older Italian ladies in pretty printed dresses sitting on a bench talking and bursting into laughter every few seconds. Behind them is a group of friends at the designated ice cream place. One of the men sitting at the table has a rough-hewn handsome face, sunburnt skin, sailor-cropped hair and the strangest ice-blue eyes, like lasers, noticeable from a hundred yards away. I wonder where the cliché of the dark-haired, dark-eyed, chunky, curvy Italians came from. The ones I've seen so far are uniformly willowy, delicate and slender and with features that seem to unite in the best combinations all the best elements of every race under the sun. In front of me is a little boy of four or so, with a pale blonde bowl haircut and caramel tan. He's running about amongst the pigeons, chasing them and trying to clap both hands around them, singing to himself, completely oblivious and happy. I watch him and find myself grinning along.

Eventually Tiziana appears, Coco the German shepherd following with a put-upon tired look on her face. Tiziana beckons me over with a curve of her long arm – I pop up – then to my surprise she catches the blonde kid, hoists him up and kisses him squashily on the cheek while he gazes down into her eyes holding a chunk of her hair in each damp hand.

'Bidisha, meet Luca,' she says.

'Ciao, Luca.'

'Luca, be polite and shake hands.'

We do, then he neatly removes his hand.

'This is the son of my daughter,' Tiziana explains, all in Italian.

Ah. Luca is the son of Tiziana's daughter Elena. The kid's father's the famous rotten gondolier... who's sitting at a table at the next cafe along. He has straw-like sexy blonde hair, a ruggedly attractive face (if you like that kind of thing), a tight black T-shirt, a solid torso and a sour expression. He's with a group of people, all of whom look a little careworn, pale, dishevelled, druggy, hungover and generally (let's not be prim about it) not in the same league as Tiziana. The gondolier deliberately doesn't look at Tiziana and I can see his dislike of her as a solid shadow in the air. Tiziana takes Luca by the hand and then rushes off towards Rialto, beckoning me to follow.

'I'm sorry I'm late,' says Tiziana, 'I had to take my mum somewhere and she took so long to get down the stairs with her crutches. Now we have to go because I said I'd buy her some carrots [or a chariot].'

I realise that my Italian is not quite up to scratch. Anyway, we're off to get something or other so I'll stick with Tiziana until she boots me off the ride. And I do have 800 euros to give her. I follow her and Luca and Coco follows me, the oldest, shaggiest, most unfit dog on the planet. Kids on the way want to stroke her and ask her name.

'Her name's Coco,' I explain, 'but she's a bit deaf so if you want to be nice to her you have to smile a lot.'

I follow them down alley after alley, keeping an eye out for carrots/chariots, until eventually we come to a large apartment door in a dead end. It's opened by the guy I recognise from the other night, who passed with his chocolate basset hound, which runs out – Coco is suddenly magically enlivened – perhaps she's just lonely – and is now gambolling around the entrance hall. Tiziana hands the basset hound guy a black rucksack she's been carrying. I am stumped. Luca is very cool and stands there looking around. We walk back, Tiziana with the satisfied air of having performed a duty, and pause to look in at a shop with the shutters drawn. Is this the carrot shop I wonder?

'It's closed,' says little Luca.

'Yup. Closed,' says Tiziana.

No carrots today, I conclude. We walk around a bit more but I don't know why. Then Tiziana stops and takes off her flip-flop, leaning against a wall.

'Why did you do that?' asks Luca curiously.

'I have a problem with my sandal,' replies Tiziana.

'Why?'

'I don't know. It's rubbing.'

'My shoe does that too.'

'Does it? Show me.'

Luca bends down and undoes the Velcro strap on one of his sandals. One of his long, very sweet tanned toes has a little red mark on it.

'See, it's a burn on my toe. From my shoe.'

'That's true,' says Tiziana.

Luca enquires after his great-grandmother. More Italian I don't understand.

'Why isn't she here today?' he asks.

Tiziana replies either 'She's got a hump like a camel' or 'She had an accident – she was on holiday and got stepped on by a camel.' Something to do with a camel at any rate.

I'm a couple of steps behind, guiding Coco and listening intently.

'I don't know what a camel is,' Luca announces after a few moments.

'Do you know a horse?' Tiziana enquires.

'Yes.'

'A camel's like a horse, only much bigger and yellow, and it has a bump on its back.'

'Why?'

'I don't know, that's its characteristic. It keeps its water in there because it lives in very dry, hot countries.'

'Why?'

'I don't know. That's where it survives best I suppose.'

'And the face of a camel is like what?'

'Shorter than a horse's, and more square.'

'And the teeth?'

'Big teeth.'

'And does it have a tail?'

'Oh yes. All camels have tails.'

'And what's that like?'

'The tail of a camel...'

Tiziana mutters to me, 'What's a camel's tail like?' I freak and make a long thin worm shape with my hands. She continues, 'The tail of a camel is long and thin but it's like a rope, not hairy like a horse's.'

'Now I know what a camel is,' says Luca, satisfied, then grabs his crotch. 'I need to do a wee.'

'Oh. OK... where?'

'In the canal,' he says decidedly, and I think about all the hapless tourists who think it's charmingly bohemian to sit on the shit-streaked steps and dabble their toes in the water amongst the litter, the algae, the slime and the swimming, black, piss-drinking water rats.

The three of us (four including the dog) make sure to take up a proud position high on a popular bridge, ascertaining above all that it's a place where gondoliers, tourists and Venetians are wont to gather at all times of the day. I direct my attention towards the window of a shabby pseudo-antiques junk shop. Behind me I hear a surprisingly strong stream as Luca urinates through the iron rails of the bridge down into the canal.

'What's she looking at?' he asks, meaning me.

'The shop with old things in it,' says Tiziana.

'Yes, I'm sorry I'm not watching,' I say sharply in English.

Tiziana gives me a quick, humorous, understanding look. I would like to see Luca at the age of twenty, wonderfully free and proud of himself, feeling that the city is his and marking it by whipping out his dick on every corner.

Once sated we walk back towards the *gelateria* in Campo Santo Stefano. Prompted heavily by Tiziana, Luca says to me, 'When I am four years old I'm going to go to the big school.'

'Fantastic!' I reply. 'When? In September?'

'No, in February next year,' Tiziana explains.

'But I can't believe he's so young, he has so much charisma.'

'He has an independence and a self-possession which are incredible. His mother was exactly the same at his age,' said Tiziana serenely.

When we arrive back at the *gelateria* we find a group of Romany buskers with accordions and acoustic guitars and violins, entertaining people. They collect coins in a little plastic ice cream cup. Luca immediately rushes forward, gets in between them and begins a fantastic stop-start robotic dance incorporating sudden stamps and freezes. He runs to his dad, who's still at the neighbouring cafe. The dad collects him and again doesn't look at Tiziana, although one of his friends, a wan, bashed-looking younger girl, does say hello very nicely. Luca runs up to us to say goodbye as we sit down at 'our' *gelateria*. He plonks himself down for a second (more flinty non-looking from the father) and then sets off again. Eventually the dad, still most definitely not looking, hoists Luca up onto his shoulder and the whole party moves off (happy waves from Luca).

'That's the father,' says Tiziana. 'He loves Luca a lot, and he takes very good care of him.'

'But he doesn't act in a good way towards *you*.'

'Because I am the mother of the...'

'You're the mother of his ex-partner, who –' I mime making a big damning cross in the air – 'but so what? If you're only nice to *some* people then you're basically nasty.'

'And how are *you*?' says Tiziana laconically.

'I'm good. Sorry for being so badly dressed, I was doing sport.'

'But tell me, how did you learn Italian? I don't understand it, if all you're doing is staying indoors working.'

'Me neither. I think it's because the newspaper-seller in my *campiello* doesn't stop talking, and when I'm asleep in the mornings my mind records what he's saying.'

'Unbelievable!' Tiziana likes this story. 'I have an American friend who's been here a year and a half and she speaks worse than you. She only speaks Italian when she has to.'

We order drinks and she asks about the book. I tell her a little bit about it.

'Do you know the crime writer Donna Leon?' she asks.

'Yes, of course,' I say.

'She's one of my best friends. She writes about Venice. She's American but she's lived here for years.'

'But she's famous!'

'Yes, she's very successful. But she works incredibly hard. I knew her before she was famous and I've seen how much she's had to work.'

'I see her books everywhere,' I say admiringly, remembering something from my dinner with Ginevra, who also mentioned her: 'The thriller is the best type of novel, because it is a box into which you can put anything you like. It can be a history lesson or a love story. You just have to make sure the lid fits neatly at the end.'

I eventually hand over the rent money and call for the bill. Tiziana insists on paying and says to me, 'Next time.' We bid each other goodbye and I stroll off, very happy. Only in Venice could a rent appointment with one's estate agent turn into a cross-city carrot trek, topped off with a nice aperitif and a chat about books.

The first signs that autumn's coming are the daytime storms and an increase in general humidity, with the exception of a five-minute coolness at the beginning of the evening. One Saturday it rains heavily from morning 'til night, sunshine cracking open and thunder pouring out. One night, carrying a slice of pizza home, a chunk drops off onto my trousers and everyone looks askance at the smear it leaves. In London I could walk around covered in blood with a knife sticking out of my neck and nobody would blink an eye.

I have a few minor linguistic triumphs, like buying an opera ticket and communicating with a shop assistant regarding the purchase of a vest. I get the feeling that I'm a bit of a laughing stock in the cake places I go to. Only businessmen go anywhere alone, yet there I am, always in clown pink trousers and a white shirt, my errand clothes. In Tonolo I order a coffee and the waitress says something about me to her colleague, who's working the till. I only catch 'See that girl there, she always...' I turn my head, the colleague's eyes shoot to mine and she blushes. On the way home I bump into Mara's boyfriend Dario outside Frari church. I like this Venetian practice of chirping 'Ciao!' and then gliding by. It gives a sense of the ease and continuity of life: no need for a heavy chat every time we see each other, we'll all be here tomorrow.

One afternoon I'm walking alone among the crowds on the Riva degli Schiavoni, close to San Marco. The water's by my side, bright and vast. I pick out a boy's voice, young and harsh, repeating the same few words over and over again. We're on one of the tourist-clogged shallow bridges. The words are 'Get lost, go away, why don't you go away, go somewhere else, get out of here.' It's a local boy of about ten, stocky and alone, with pale features, in T-shirt and long shorts. He's bending over a Romanian beggar woman who's huddled on the ground. She's about seventy, dusty, hump-backed, crumpled right over with her face inches from the ground and both her arms spread out, one hand holding a small ice cream pot for loose change. In this heat she's in all her clothes, all black, and a headscarf. The boy is stooped over her, his face a few inches from hers, hard with hatred. His feet are close to her face. The woman is mumbling, keening, crying, grovelling, begging, denying in a continuous mumbling loop but the boy doesn't stop – indeed, he edges closer. His mouth is slack with hatred. 'Go away. Can't you hear me? Get lost. Go somewhere else. Get out.'

I am nauseated, not only by him, his satisfaction, curled fist and obvious desire to strike her, but also his fearlessness and my fear. How does he behave with the women in his own family? If at ten he has no qualms about stepping up to a stranger, a woman with literally nothing, who may have struggled and fought all her long life, on a bridge full of witnesses from all over the world, in the middle of the day, what will he have progressed to by the age of twenty? Worse, I don't do anything. I'm frozen with disgust and fear and darkness. An older man sidles up and puts fifty cents into the woman's bowl, with a baleful glance at the boy – but this glance isn't enough, in fact it's almost apologetic. The boy ignores it.

In the last week of August there's a sudden flare of dry, strong heat captured in a dreamlike peach light. The smell of dry tinder. Calm grey light in the evenings. I work my way through an excellent, lucid translation of Iris Murdoch's *The Bell* (in Italian: *La Campana*) that's just come out. Easy to follow, too, because I know the original almost word for word. I wake up to (but not because of) people chatting in the square, and the stupid dog Luna and her stupid owner:

'Yap! Yap! Yapyap!'

'*Shhhhh, Luna, piano, piano, shhh, andiamo, Luna...*' comes the old, parched, begging voice.

'Yapyapyap! Yap! Yap!'

'*Shhh, Luna, piano, andiamo, piano....*'

Stefania comes back from filming for a few days but we're both so focused on our work that it's like two fighter jets shooting past each other in opposite directions. On receiving her call I head off to Gobbetti's to replenish myself and the red-haired lady grins and says 'Cappuccino, *deca!*' when I walk in. 'Cos I'm a local now, and that's my usual. I have a pear *crostata* too – delicious, and you can taste the almond paste in the crust. If only they had tables and chairs instead of a little shelf to lean your elbow on, but this is Venice. They like a quick turnover.

After that it's off to meet Stef for the evening. There's a thirty-year-old slob guy high on a balcony outside one of the apartments by the side of Frari church. He's sitting legs apart on a plastic chair staring down through the railings. When any woman walks past he makes a loud, puckering, popping noise with his mouth. When they look up automatically he jeers at them. Ten minutes later I'm getting money out in Campo San Bartolomeo. Two young Sri Lankan guys strike up next to me and hiss teasingly: '*Ksss, kss-kss-ksss*'. I snatch the money out of the machine and they walk alongside me, turning to me with teasing smiles and hissing, until I turn off and take another route.

I spot Stef and Mara outside the train station and rush down the broad bridge to meet them. That evening – I've been looking forward to this for weeks – we all go to see *Harry Potter and the Prisoner of Azkaban* which is showing in the open air in Campo San Polo. They've set up a huge screen surrounded by tiered seats and a security barrier, with a row of ticket huts outside. I take the responsibility of queuing up to buy our tickets. There are several huts open and a full line of excited, expectant people in front of each one, families, kids, teens, a few tourists too. Then Stef and Mara smoke a last-minute cigarette each while I drop into a pretty shop by the side of the square, that sells drop earrings in semi-precious stones. I buy a pair of simple jade ones for my mum. The woman in the shop's friendly and soft-spoken and gets me into conversation, which I fluff terribly:

'Are you Italian, or... Oh! You speak it. Because sometimes one can't tell, Venice is always so full of foreigners... and you're a student, a language student?' she says.

'No, a writer.'

'Ah! And you've come in search of ...'

'A piece of piece.'

Yes. Oops. I mean 'a bit of peace' of course. She lets it slide. She finds out where I'm from, sighs and says, 'If you've lived in London you come to know the whole of the world. Not so in Venice.'

'But it's very lively here.' I indicate the square, where the auditorium lights are just coming up and people are milling around buying ice creams.

'Yes,' says the lady, 'it's quite normal for people to go for a walk at night. There's a good street-life here.'

I rejoin Mara and Stef. We sit right up at the top and realise we're next to a bunch of thirteen-year-olds who keep talking and laughing and going up and down to get junk food. The film starts. Mara shushes them and then says to me, 'I love to shush people in the cinema.'

They carry on. Stef goes over to them and hisses, 'I'm sorry to be bitter, but shut up!'

They apologise and carry on. We spend the whole night tutting to ourselves and recrossing our legs.

'It's because we're in the area for young people,' says Mara. 'Usually I sit more or less in the centre, only with adults.'

The film's excellent — darker and cleverer than the first two of the series. Shamingly, I fancy all the boy actors and therefore view the whole thing through a slight erotic mirage.

Stef and Mara are trying to decide where to go next as the credits roll.

'Postali,' I suggest as we climb down.

'Postali is always the best place,' says Mara appreciatively. 'Always appropriate.'

'And we have to go there, because every time I walk past, the owner says hello to me,' I add. 'The guy with the grey hair.'

'Roberto. Yes, he's very friendly. And a little bit —' Mara makes a snatching motion, a snake on the attack.

'He is a sexy man,' says Stef briskly.

'But he's old,' I say, although I've recently discredited myself by saying 'But did you notice all the sexual aspects?' when we were talking about the film.

'But he carries it well,' Mara decides.

After our drink Stef and I want some private time so we slip over to her half of the Venice biscuit and I walk her home through deserted Cannaregio.

At the end of August I notice that (a) it's almost getting to be jacket weather, and (b) there are noticeably fewer tourists around. The *campiello*'s empty for much of the day. The light's different again, red–gold, shaded, more remote. The sun's setting earlier and faster. The moon here is always orange or red, rarely white. The stars are so close and bright that they resemble a child's painting, and they really do twinkle when you look at them: hard, big, cheerful white asterisks above the roofs. The music-loving person in my square is very deeply affected by the prospect of autumn and is now listening to maudlin flute music, organ recitals and piano sonatas day and night... melancholy soul. There's also a new addition to my roster of people to listen out for: the person who stirs their afternoon tea for an entire minute, thirty seconds deep at the bottom of the cup and thirty seconds high and tinkling at the top of the cup. Imagine living with that every day for the rest of your life. Divorce!

Stef and I meet for dinner at Muro, a new spanking-trendy New York-style restaurant at Rialto, on my side, close to the *pescheria*. Designer bar, designer staircase, designer chairs, designer people. It's an odd juxtaposition which doesn't quite work, sitting by the glass walls and looking out on a big blank square of ancient stones, cobbles, pillars and Canaletto water. I order a chunk of beef and they give me an enormous black-handled homicide knife to cut it with. The knife is such a statement in itself and so impractical to use that Stef and I laugh at the pretension.

We catch up with each other's news. Stefania's exhausted because she's been stuffed in a truck with six of her colleagues following a theatre troupe up and down the country:

'I discover that when you are a producer you have to be a little bit of a psychologist too. If there is a problem with the director you cannot say, "Look, you are acting like a stupid arsehole."

You have to say, "Maybe the participants would feel more able to engage with you if you were not looking inside the camera all the time, because they respect your opinion and they would like to speak with you directly."'

'You diplomat!'

'But you, Bidisha? When you finish the book? What happens?'

'The marathon.'

This is what all my training has been leading up to. It's at the end of October.

'No. You are really doing it?' Stef asks.

'I want to. I like collecting the medals.'

'I think you are more Catholic than me.'

'Yes, my reward for the mental pain of scholarship is the physical pain of the marathon!'

Stef heaves a yawn:

'Maybe because I'm Mediterranean I need three weeks in the year where I go to the mountains and switch my mind off and be with nature. Well, maybe two weeks, or ten days. That lets me recover. Just one week of doing nothing, just being a body.'

'Why d'you keep reducing the time? You deserve three full weeks of break,' I say firmly.

I tell her a little bit about my new favourite break place, Frari church, and this sets us off on one of our favourite topics, the attractions of the contemplative life. Cue Stefania:

'I have been speaking a little bit with this friend of mine, who is producing a documentary about a convent in Rome. It's called *Devotion*.'

'Ooh! Tell me.'

'But what is strange is that many people who are there can't explain why they are there. And half of them are lesbians. She says you can just tell. At least four of them. Because the director is Mariella, this beautiful woman who we met in London. You remember.'

'Ah yes. She is unbelievably beautiful but,' we both instinctively put our hands up to the wall, 'she has a face as hard as a piece of stone.'

'And they all want her,' says Stef. 'They're gay but they can't admit it, so they become nuns – and it's very easy...'

'I think it's quite common. Monks too. I'm sure they have secret fantasies *all the time*,' I put in.

'Not *all* the time?' Stef queries.

'Why not? What else do they do? They do some sweeping. They polish the Jesus...'

'At the end of the day it is an easy life.'

'Yes, it's harder to live in the world.'

'I have to say, I have some problems fitting in with the world,' she admits.

'So do I. But I think the answer, instead of having to do the whole God thing, is just having, you know, a really nice apartment.'

'And a lot of money,' she adds.

'And some professional recognition, and good friends, and a bit of work to do, but not too much.'

'But it is hard to get into a convent in Italy,' says Stef thoughtfully. 'They want people who are graduates, who've studied philosophy and theology together. There's a big exam you have to pass. It takes two years to prepare for it.'

'Really? In England the convents are *begging* for new recruits. Nobody's interested. I read about it.'

'Mariella says there's one interesting girl there. She was young, she worked in documentaries – I mean, she was completely like us. And one day she came to the convent for a conference about the arts, and she was impressed with the atmosphere, and she went back to talk to them. Within one year she was studying for the exam...'

'And now she's a nun.'

'Now she is a nun.'

'What a waste. What a waste!' I say. 'Wouldn't it be better if she became an award-winning director and hunted down sex traffickers? Instead of wiping down the convent cafeteria every day.'

By now our fashionable food's arrived and we're eating it. It's average.

'There are one thousand churches in Venice,' says Stef. 'I have been into them all and I don't feel nothing... anything. Yes! This is the very simple rule of the double negative!'

'Me neither. Some of them have even less atmosphere than a museum or a gallery, and at the very least that's what they're supposed to be,' I say. 'The only places I feel anything are galleries and bookshops. And sometimes Frari church, especially when the monks're around. Oh, and when I'm sitting outside Caffè Causin having a macchiato...'

'At the Basilica of San Marco, I can feel something, among all that gold. Also, in mosques, and in Greek Orthodox churches... but I think it is just a question of decoration!'

Eventually, about four hours later, we pay and leave.

'That was a bit expensive,' Stef murmurs once we've said goodbye to our waitress. 'The amount we got, for what we paid.'

'And a cow's a big animal! Why did I get such a small piece?'

'And two little bits of tuna they gave me... Never again.'

'Never again, Stef. We've learnt our lesson. The fashionable world is not for us.'

The next day I experience the inexpressible delight of being welcomed officially into the Venetian community: I go to Gobbetti's, order a coffee, drink it, want to pay for it (one euro) but discover that I have only eighty cents or a ten euro note. The lady takes the eighty cents and says I can pay the twenty cent remainder the next time I come. I do manage to stifle the impulse to jump up and down and cry 'You trust me! You trust me!'

Later, walking in Zattere watching the sea and sky turn Quink blue I notice that Venetians' clothing has indeed changed, as if by governmental decree, all on the same day. We're now talking light autumn wear – russet, gold, fawn and buff linen suits, toffee-coloured hard leather shoes, a heavier bag perhaps, plain but weighty jewellery, shades. Jacket obligatory, sandals banned and if you're dying in the heat, pretend otherwise. That night I fall asleep listening to the clattering rain and a howling werewolf wind.

Chapter Nine

As soon as August ends the film crews arrive. At the moment there are two versions of *Casanova* being shot, one for English TV and one for Hollywood, plus *The Merchant of Venice*. One of the crews has blocked off a portion of St Mark's and constructed an elaborate wooden gallows/stage/courthouse set. At night the tourists gather to gawp, the technicians turn up the floodlights and Venice looks like it'll crumble in the beam. A note: star actors are always smaller than you imagine but the extras are *huge*.

As a result of all this activity a lot of the young filmy people in Venice (including Stef and many of her friends) are involved in the production and second-unit side of things. The big-budget foreign crews are despised by the Italian production companies for their ignorance. For example, the Americans have brought tea, mineral water and other foodstuffs over by sea thinking they won't be able to get it here. Stef and I joke that soon they'll start shipping over prosciutto and cheese from Little Italy in New York. Another example: a Hollywood senior executive came over to check on how the production was going. He took Stefania and her team to lunch to thank them for all their work. Tall guy in suit trousers and white trainers, desperately wanted to relax and fit in but couldn't – didn't have the mental vocabulary for it. He gave her a bottle of wine that was worth 200 euros and the guy at the wine place who sold it to him (who, of course, has known Stef's family for years) told her privately that if she took it back later that day, he'd give her the cash.

Back in Campiello Ca' Zen, it doesn't take me long to discover that Massimo the *giornalaio* is nowhere near the twinkle-eyed prole newspaper seller that the local schoolkids think he is. Every day he gets asked for directions about thirty times by tourists. Each time, even before the desperate heat-muffled smiles of the tourists have stretched to full imbecility, he shouts 'Rialto. Rialto Bridge' at them, regardless of whether they're asking where the WC, St Mark's, a map, a particular shop or a good restaurant is. If they carry on asking he just repeats 'Rialto' over and over again, more loudly and clearly each time, chin up, eyes hard. This is for the amusement/benefit of the antiques shop lads, who stop talking and watch slackly. A young woman who lives above me comes out and says hello whenever she passes Massimo. He looks at her and never replies. Afterwards he smiles to himself, turns away and begins tidying a pile of newspapers. This happens about three times a day. Massimo gives me a small-eyed stare whenever I come out.

One day I'm walking in Zattere when someone calls out to me from ground level. It's Tiziana, sitting at the lip of the sea on the marble steps. The sun's sparkling so brightly that she looks like a part of the water. She gets up and peers into my face. For some reason she speaks English and I speak Italian.

'What are you doing tonight?' she asks.

'Tonight? Nothing. Stefania's filming, so...'

'There is a dance performance in the Lido at midnight. Would you like to come?'

'Oh! I wish... I'd love to but... I think it's a bit too late for me.'

'Before that, we are having dinner at a place called Do Forni. Do you want to come? There will be seven of us.'

'I'd love to!'

Tiziana takes out one of her many notebooks and draws me a map, repeating the name of the restaurant clearly several times. An older male friend in a suit comes up to meet her and I am introduced. I've forgotten how to issue a formal greeting so we end up shaking hands in silence while he looks at me in puzzlement before escorting Tiziana gently away and (I presume) enquiring concernedly after her poor mute friend.

I go off in the opposite direction, pleased. That evening I shower and change (fresh white shirt, jeans, fitted jacket – I realise I haven't brought the right clothes with me, nothing really smart), thinking all the time that I've made a mistake and that Tiziana's invitation was mere politeness, not meant to have been taken up. I imagine turning up to a table full of strangers, all of us smiling weakly with embarrassment, glancing at each other, unable to understand why I'm there.

The Do Forni restaurant is on the Calle Specchieri. A young, fresh, wet-faced waiter in a white jacket is on guard at the door.

'The name of your reservation?' he asks.

I give it.

'And how many people?'

'Seven, I believe.'

As soon as I get in I realise that I'm severely underdressed. I should have worn silk and brocade, not tweed and cotton, and carried a beaded bag, not my little canvas square. The young waiter (I'm even worse dressed than the staff) leads me through a series of dark, crowded, lively dining rooms full of red and blue glass, burgundy velvet, dark wood, no natural light, touches of gilt, everything a little flushed, resembling the banqueting suite on an ancient frigate. There are American families and Italian dynasties alongside well-groomed power-people who're here for the film festival, sweating money and perpetual dissatisfaction. I'm led to a long table with two mystery women at the far right, next to the wall, the doll-faced lady from after the dance performance and a guy with a thick moustache. I stand at the end of the table and beam at them. No reaction.

'Are you the friends of Tiziana?' I say in a small voice in Italian.

A few more seconds of nothing, then the moustache guy grins up at me and says '*Sì!*' in a friendly way. I sit down gingerly next to him and there are introductions all around. The moustache guy's youngish and has wavy dark brown hair. He's wearing an expensive monogrammed shirt and bespoke shoes. Next to him is a slender intellectual-looking woman with a lean face and very short auburn hair, a slight tan, small eyes and mouth. Opposite her is a petite woman with a small, rough, animalistic-pretty face and a hungry leaning-in way of sitting, too much make-up and a hoarse voice. She stares at me openly but not hostilely. Her name's Caterina.

'Do you speak Italian?' she asks me in Italian.

'A bit.'

'Because we don't speak English.'

'We'll manage,' I say chirpily.

The way to get by is smile and wrack one's brains at every moment. I fall into conversation with the guy, Emanuele, who pours me some water, sits close by and talks to me non-stop, feeding me easy questions and generally being attentive. How long have I been here? What do I do? How did I learn Italian? Kind as this all is, I tell him it's hard to communicate searching for each word and he apologises jokingly for making me tired before the meal's even begun. He asks me what I'm doing at the moment.

'Working on a book,' I say brokenly. 'But it's hard, hard, hard...'

'Discipline!'

'Yes, but all I want to do is go out, it's so difficult.'

'Hey. You could be working in a factory.'

I laugh heartily at this, swallow my ego and have such an excellent time that I forget to ask him anything about himself.

Tiziana and her mum arrive. Everyone shoots to their feet out of respect for the oldest member of the party. I am a beat too late, still slumped blindly in the chair so that everyone looks down at me disparagingly. I flush dark red and half-stand foolishly, making myself even more conspicuous. Emanuele rushes around and pulls the table out for Tiziana's mother to get by before I've even realised that there isn't enough space for her. Luckily she likes me and remembers me from the dance performance; when she finally sits down we grin at each other over the glassware. Tiziana smiles a kind hello too.

The waiter comes over and then begins a long, long conversation about what the kitchen can make us, what we prefer and don't prefer, fish or meat (we choose fish), types of fish, number of fish, size of fish, number of courses, perhaps a little meat to start...

Caterina is a vegetarian, what does she like?... and I *must* try the soufflé here, it's famous. Seeing me hesitate politely the entire table leans in my direction and mounts a campaign.

Prosecco's served. The food begins to trickle in too: beautiful thick slices of prosciutto and black bread. I accidentally use the fish knife for the butter. People notice and silence descends once more. Emanuele tells me kindly not to worry.

'I'm using the wrong knife,' I say through gritted teeth, failing to make a cool joke of it.

'Don't worry about it,' says Emanuele sweetly to me in French (we'd been talking about his trip to Paris the previous year). 'Use whichever one you want.'

These rules! Who cares how I eat? As long as I'm not patrolling the restaurant shooting people dead at random I think I'm doing OK. Anyway, the food: fat king prawns, tight little shrimps, soft crab meat, scallops in sour vinegar and onions, a Venetian speciality, juicy squid in tomato sauce. Tiziana notices that I've got a spot of the sauce on my shirt and shows me how to dab it off with fizzy water. I do so for the next two hours. At some point I catch her watching me and mumble '*cazzo*' – 'prick', but used here to mean 'shit' – making her laugh.

I realise that I've spent the first bit of the meal only talking to Emanuele so I ignore him for a while, even though I notice that we sit similarly, leaning our breastbone against the edge of the table with both forearms along the surface. I have a little trouble following all the conversation, especially the off-the-cuff jokes. Still, my Italian's holding up amazingly well.

'I hate hearing my voice on the answerphone,' says Emanuele to me suddenly.

'Me too, I always think it sounds too nasal,' I reply.

'Me too! But doesn't it?'

'No! You have a nice voice,' I say gallantly. It's true enough.

After vegetarian over-bronzed Caterina has had her second long dialogue with the waiters about what she can eat for the upcoming courses, Emanuele grumbles to me, 'I don't like vegetarians. They can never give you a reason, if you ask them.'

I say slowly in English, 'And whenever you get into a debate with a vegetarian, they say, could you kill a cow with your bare hands? And I say no. But that makes me squeamish, not a hypocrite. I like clothes but I'm not willing to weave my own.'

Emanuele begins nodding and agreeing fervently:

'I don't like radical positions. We all have to exist in society and continue together...'

I say nothing. This is the key, I think, to the essence of Emanuele, the point of Emanuele, so I preserve it in my data bank. After a while I say, 'It's always the people who care about animals who don't give a damn about the human condition. If you want to talk about violence against women or the gap between rich and poor they get bored, but *my God*, if you want to talk about the poor little rabbits with their little broken floppy ears and their red eyes, oh, you should see the tears... and why *not* have a steak? It's only a cow.'

'This is the global system,' says Emanuele in English. 'The mans eats the animals.' Switching to Italian he says, 'Cows are hardly an endangered species.'

'Right! It's not like we're eating lions.'

'No.' We both begin smiling wickedly. 'Although I would like to taste one. You know, these animal people remind me of the people who go to the post office every month to pay five euros for some kids on the other side of the world. If you care about the poor then go there and see it with your own eyes and do

183

something to help. If you're a doctor and you say you care, go over and be a doctor there. Donate your – *capacità*?'

'Your capacity, yourself.'

'Exactly. Give something of yourself.'

'But that is a radical position,' I joke.

'Is it? Maybe I should modify it.'

'You're saying that if you're a doctor you should go and...'

'No, OK... just give something more from yourself, from your life.'

'Yes. Don't make yourself feel better by doing the minimum and never thinking about it again. But then doing the minimum is better than doing zero. How much do you do? I do zero.'

'I also do zero!'

Having bonded by these means we return to the general conversation, which is about that season's theatre programme. The biggest buzz in the city is about a series of Sarah Kane works that're being put on.

'I'd like to see the plays,' says Emanuele to me.

'I hate theatre. It mortifies me. I can never suspend my disbelief. Ninety-nine per cent of actors don't have charisma in real life,' I complain.

'I also like audio books...'

'No! Horrible.'

'What? A little bit of Dante...'

'Oh – yes, OK. Maybe a bit of Dante,' I relent, and the thought left hanging in the air is *you, me, and a little bit of Dante...*

The others are talking about Botox and joking about their ageing even though they all look marvellous to me, Tiziana most of all. Tiziana's mum, whose name I never catch (but it's rude to use it so directly anyway) says that she had black spots all over her complexion and bought every cream going. In the end it was natural oil that saved her:

'The doctor laughed at me and ridiculed me when I told him.'

'Doctors don't know anything,' I say.

'Not a thing.'

'Can I ask, signora, how long did you use it for?' asks Gina the doll-faced woman, who I've learnt is Emanuele's mother. 'I have two pretty little age spots, one here and one here.'

'Four years,' comes the unbending reply.

'Every day?'

'Every night. Except when I have a gentleman guest for the evening.' Tiziana's mother mimes messily putting oil all over her face and then calling out sweetly, 'My love, I'm ready!' We all guffaw.

Then Gina, who's a little nervous and pretentious, notices that Tiziana's mother's wearing a chic herringbone-shaped gold ring and asks to see it, then comments, 'But you have such beautifully soft skin, signora.'

Caterina feels the signora's hand too and agrees. La signora puts on a queenly face and holds out her arm disdainfully:

'Would anyone else at the table like the honour of touching my hand? I won't offer it again.'

I laugh and she half-winks at me. I realise I'm having a brilliant time. I take this realisation and tuck it happily into my breast pocket. The focus then turns to me, led by sexy veggie Caterina. Is it my first time away from home? Do I miss my parents? I must talk to my mum a lot on the phone. How old am I? And also, where's my name from?

'It's Indian,' I say.

'It's beautiful,' says Gina in her timorous way, 'the most beautiful name I've ever heard, it's like the name of a goddess.'

The talk progresses and I lose track.

'Can you understand what they're saying?' says Emanuele to me.

'I can't hear much.'

'Ah. Because of the background noise,' he says considerately.

Gina repeats herself more clearly:

'We were talking about the beginnings of novels. I like it when a book begins with an ordinary scene, and then all the little details flow up and connect to each other and you realise they're all significant.'

'Me too,' I say keenly. 'I like good stories.'

'A few hours with this lot and you'll have more stories than you know what to do with,' says Tiziana broadly.

The meal's been going on all this time. Tiny exquisite course after tiny exquisite course. The food isn't haute cuisine or nouvelle cuisine, it's just small. Yes, it tastes good – but Lucrezia could do much better, and in less time too. I'd told everyone that I was allergic to alcohol but now find myself on my second full glass of prosecco... or maybe the third. How did that happen?

A hot crumble of golden soufflé arrives, served with molten dark chocolate. We all worship. Talk turns to facial hair.

'Do you like men with moustaches?' Gina asks me.

'No!' I cry, grinning. 'Clean for me.'

Emanuele's playing with his thick moustache self-mockingly.

'When he came back from travelling in Guatemala he had a full beard and moustache,' says Gina.

'OK. This weekend the moustache goes,' says Emanuele in response to the onslaught.

We have coffees.

'Now, aren't you glad we had the fish?' someone asks me.

'Yes, it was perfect. Usually I'm a big meat fan but this meal was exquisite. I'm satisfied.'

'You like meat? Then you've found your soulmate, Emanuele's the same,' says Gina.

There's a flash of laughter. Emanuele and I are too embarrassed to look at each other.

I notice that throughout the meal Gina hasn't eaten anything. Her method is to take a bite, light up a cigarette and then pass her plate around exhorting everyone to try a bit. She only accepts the plate again when it's empty. I remember her not eating her ice cream after the dance performance and want to ask her about it but can never find the opportunity. Whenever Emanuele passes something to me I take a bit and he says, 'You take so little. Take more!' He asks, half to himself, 'Is there any prosecco left?' and I say no, I don't think so, then spot it in the ice bucket at the end of the table.

'Oh yes. I'll get it,' I say.

I half get up and reach for it –

'No, no, you don't need to do that,' he says, putting his hand on my arm to keep me in my seat – but not putting his hand on my nearest arm, no; putting his arm right around me and holding my left bicep.

I've always been able to tell what someone's like from their touch and his, though pleasant enough, is forceful. Firm, confident, very warm in temperature, but there's real aggression there, which I suppose only his closest people see. Another one for the data bank.

When I reached for the prosecco my shirtsleeve rode up a bit.

'I see you have a tattoo,' says Emanuele, looking at my forearm. 'I've never been tempted myself, but a friend of mine asked me to design one for her. And I did, and I sent it to her, but I enclosed a note of disapproval.'

I rejoin the general conversation to find that we're back to facial hair:

'Some of them have two thin little lines down the sides of their jaws and a tiny triangle under their lip,' says Tiziana's mum.

'Horrible. Like facial bonsai,' I shudder.

'It's an awful lot of work,' she agrees, 'for something so small that's also very ugly.'

The bill arrives and I experience cardiac shock. Fifty-two euros each for those morsels? I'd taken out fifty euros thinking it'd cover dinner and the next two weeks' worth of food-shopping. I have another twenty euro note but no loose change for the two. Silence and embarrassment as the table looks on. I feel Gina chill slightly towards me.

'You don't have *any* change?' she asks me, exasperated.

And yet Venetian etiquette is such that they're so embarrassed about talking money at all that they won't let me even things up by taking all the coins and putting my other note in. I blush so hard with confusion, embarrassment and frustration that it feels as though there's steam coming out of my ears. Emanuele grins and tells me it doesn't matter at all. The tight faces of everyone else (even the deliberate deaf blankness of Tiziana and her mum) tell me that it does.

When we leave it's past midnight, one group to go home and the other (Caterina, Tiziana, Tiziana's mum) to go to Rialto and then, very late, to the dance performance. We stand for a moment in the street outside the restaurant, Emanuele sticking close by me. We swap numbers. Ciaos and goodnights all round. He bows to me. We part. I've had a brilliant time.

'Are you going home?' Tiziana asks me.

'Yes, but I'll go with you to walk your mum home. I need some exercise.'

We walk slowly through the crowded streets, Tiziana's mum careful on her crutches. She's just here for a visit though, usually lives in Geneva. Caterina and I chat and I discover that she actually speaks excellent English. And is unbelievably rich. She tells me that when she's in London she stays at a friend's flat, which has an excellent bedroom window view of Harrods.

'The service at the restaurant took so long,' she says, yawning. 'The waiters had to be very nice to Gina because her parents own the building. They had to show, "Yes, we will get the kitchen to do anything for you, we will dedicate ourselves to you all night long. We will not rush you. Your patronage is our honour."'

'I still prefer it to London. If you stay longer than an hour and a half at your table you feel them wanting you to leave.'

'Yes, they want to kick you – off?'

'Out. Yes.'

We pass a group of young sailors dressed in white, gawky and painfully skinny, tanned, either fresh from the naval college at Sant'Elena or just docked, wearing too-big uniforms. How old are they? Sixteen, if that? They blush to the hilt when we pass them.

'I always wonder about these groups of sailors I see around,' I comment to Caterina.

'I bet they're looking for a brothel. There can't be much to do on a ship,' she replies in Italian. This is exactly what I'd been thinking too. 'But then, they always have each other,' she adds.

'Hey, when you're in the middle of the Adriatic, Africa's way over there, Europe's way over the other side, you've read every book you brought with you, eventually you're gonna find yourself knocking on the door of the next cabin,' I say. 'What I don't understand is how they keep their clothes so clean. There's not a single stain on their bottoms, they must never sit down anywhere. If they're not on the ship having sex with each other they probably spend the rest of their time doing laundry. Trying to keep their whites white.'

Tiziana's mum and I fall into step.

'Tomorrow will be the day of the apples,' she says. 'One in the morning, one at lunch and perhaps a third at dinner. In the last few years I've observed an escalation in my numbers. I was a size forty, then I watched it go up to forty-two, forty-four, forty-six. When it reaches forty-eight, *basta*, enough. I'll stop eating, get myself back down to forty and start again. Unfortunately I love to eat.'

'Me too!'

When we part she strokes my face, pinches my cheek, winks at me and calls me *bambina*. Mutual fandom. I beam back, kiss Tiziana and Caterina goodbye and stroll over the bridge, pass the darkened market stalls and closed shops on my side of Rialto, the silent route home. Remember to turn right when I see the bag-and-gloves shop...

I get home and crash about tipsily, strangely excited, angry with myself – that all it took was one ordinary meal for me to be pleased with the world; because I like Tiziana so much; because I was too afraid to really turn and look at Emanuele in a frank way, I didn't get a proper look at his face... and I'm angry with myself, after years of blissful celibacy, for still being susceptible. It makes me doubt my vocation, about which I am vague but serious. What has celibacy taught me if I am still attracted by the sight of a couple of beautiful young monks or a young male dinner companion? What if I am more easily temptable now, if my thoughts are darker, lewder and more predatory? Thoughts like these keep me occupied well into the night and continue, not unpleasantly, it must be said, even into my dreams.

Chapter Ten

The next day I feel too bright to lock myself away and concentrate, too ill to go for a run. Is this how drinkers feel all the time? Never fully present? Tiziana's invited me to a gallery opening and even though I know I have to work, I still go. Dressed: white silk shirt, aubergine silk harem trousers, flip-flops, canvas bag on a string.

It's a stifling hot evening. I've arranged to meet Tiziana at Campo Santi Filippo e Giacomo at seven-thirty. I'm five minutes late, hastening down a narrow side street towards San Marco. It's not dark. A fat, pale, sweating man with a takeaway kebab carton in his hand falls into step with me. His trousers are stained and his soaked polyester shirt is, er, also stained.

'Quickly, quickly, step-step, off we go to Piazza San Marco,' he goads, mocking my fast walk.

The alleyway is long and narrow with no turnings.

'I'm not looking for Piazza San Marco,' I say coldly. The alley's too thin for me to shake him off without simply running ahead.

'What're you looking for?'

'A street near there,' I say reluctantly.

'Mind if I come with you?' he grins.

'Thank you but no.'

He laughs to see me wrangling with my own politeness and tails away when we burst out, thank God, into the chaotic space of San Marco.

Get to Campo Santi Filippo e Giacomo. It's *sprizz*-hour and everyone's out drinking aperitifs, seemingly oblivious to the humidity. When I spot Tiziana I realise with a terrible slump that I've got my clothes completely wrong *again*. How can I tell? Let's see what she's wearing: fitted, straight, pale blue jeans, a faded silver and white top made of gossamer silk, a pale green linen fencing jacket, possibly couture, and black suede stilettos with arching gold metal heels. Gold-blonde hair, gold-blonde skin. In Venice all this does matter, unfortunately. One must spend an awful lot of time, money and effort to look understated... and yet at the same time as looking understated one must drop thrilling little surprises here and there, cufflinks matched to briefcase-buckle, bracelet matched to hair slide. Therefore a completely plain slip-it-on-and-go Armani suit (a note: nobody in Venice wears black, it's too hard on the eye) with no accessories is just as much of a style cop-out as a wrinkled tracksuit.

The gallery's in a tiny lane nearby, even hotter and more humid than the square. There's a crush of well-off people outside, all talking and drinking. Nobody seems interested in the art. The women are exquisitely dressed, with forensic attention to detail, the men in the usual draped linen ensembles. Tiziana instantly begins talking to a hundred people and I linger behind like a long-faced boring ghost.

I go inside the first room of the gallery, which contains a single huge wall-painting, black lines on white: vegetables turning into dicks, industrial tools turning into dicks, household objects and plants turning into dicks, musical instruments turning into dicks. This is when I miss the London bullshit filter. The work irritates me, not just because it's lazy, puerile and self-indulgent but also because it's phallocentric and arrogant: I am great because I have *this*. I am going to stick *this* in your face, and if you don't like it, you have a problem. Machismo has destroyed the world and all the women of Venice have flocked to worship it.

Except that they haven't, because the gallery's empty. Ah, Venetian complacency. Tiziana comes in, sticks a press release in my hand and then pulls me out again. I am introduced to a cold English woman who has no interest in me (or, I suspect, in any woman) and barely moves her mouth when she speaks. Tallish, with olive colouring, a light tan, curly russet hair, red lipstick, smart black dress. I fan myself with the press release and make an inane comment about the heat.

'You're lucky,' she replies, 'last summer it was so hot we used to get up and walk around at three in the morning. We couldn't sleep at all.'

We, we, we. Her partner's Italian, an older grey-curly-haired, intellectual-faced linen person.

'Never go to bed with an Italian!' the English woman bursts out with a brittle laugh, and I think, oh, yes, I know who you are: the woman who can't talk about anything apart from men. She's panicking slightly at having been left to converse with a female and waits for me to say something about *my* man but I excuse myself politely.

I see a miniature collie-type dog, black and white and little and soft, in the arms of a stunningly beautiful possibly mixed-race woman: African-American, Native American and Anglo combination? Huge amber-green eyes with thickly curling lashes, glowing toffee skin, toothily full Barbie smile, light-coloured Afro hair, all amber and gold, with a great strong figure, wearing a shimmering green and gold silk tunic. We're introduced – yup, she's American – and I realise that this is the woman Tiziana told me about, who's been here for one and a half years and doesn't speak Italian unless she has to. We shake hands but I'm whipped away again to say hello to Caterina. What a fashion diva, I must worship: yesterday, black and white with diamante-strap high heels; today, sequinned dark pink and silver chain mail against matte black. With her is a tall, solid, grey-haired, grey-faced, dry, grave, distinguished, completely silent man. Name, Salvatore. Profession, banker? Don? Executioner? I'm too frightened to shake his hand, plus I don't know whether to say hi, hello, good evening, goodnight or simply bow.

The American woman, Charmaine, returns and looks Tiziana up and down fawningly. I've been listening to her for the last few minutes as she answers someone's Italian questions in English. I wish I had the confidence to stride in anywhere, speak English and expect everyone else to fall in line.

'Tiziana!' she says. 'I love what you're wearing. I love that jacket on you. I love that colour and I love that shape.'

'But what you are wearing is also very beautiful,' Tiziana replies in very slow English, 'is it from India?'

'No, it's not from India,' Charmaine scoffs, 'or China. It's from Cambodia.' Tiziana looks puzzled so Charmaine speaks more loudly: 'Cambodia? You know? Cambodia, Laos, Malaysia?'

'Ah yes, of course,' says Tiziana mildly. 'Cambodia. I didn't catch the word.'

I escape upstairs: more dicks. Lots of press releases and biogs and postcards by the dick-artist lying around everywhere.

Tiziana, Caterina and I find a corner to sit in. On a shelf are some lumps of discarded bronze metal, kids' clay worms bent or flattened. I push them out of the way with my elbow.

'These are the sculptures of the artist,' says Tiziana.

'What!' I hurriedly shove them back into place. 'Are you joking?'

Caterina, who's been thinking the same thing as me, picks up one of the 'pieces' and inspects it.

'I thought it was part of an old coat hook,' I say.

'I thought it was a hanging of the door,' she says in English. 'A hang... a handle.'

Giggling, we pick up the 'sculptures' and fit them to the door and walls – even so, they're still ugly.

'But we must be careful,' says Caterina, making eyes around the room. 'The enemy [meaning the artist] may be listening.'

I get up and have a wander. In another room I find a lot of little square canvases covered in various slop-colours, with some dots and squiggles on them. On one wall five are laid out in a row at regular head-high intervals. On another wall they're clustered together. I spot Charmaine, monochrome yap-dog in her arms, staring brightly with her luminous amber Barbie-eyes at the paintings.

'So! What d'you make of these?' I ask her.

'Well, that's an interesting question,' she says in her flat cyborg voice. 'I'm not sure what to say. If I saw this kind of thing on the street I'm not sure what I'd think about it, but the way it's presented here, maybe it gains something in value just because it's in a gallery. I mean *that* wall has a pretty traditional presentation, and *this* wall makes it all a bit more random... I think what'd be really great is if you could say, hey, why not give a space and a presentation like this to some homeless kids? I think that's what would make this artist really special, if he was big enough to say, "OK, my own stuff's not too great, maybe I should open it up to people who aren't as lucky as I am."'

'Ouch! But how many terrible artists really know they're terrible?'

'But how much more special and unique would it make him if he admitted it?'

We stroll around the gallery a bit more.

'How long have you been in Venice?' she asks me.

'Not long. Eight weeks.'

'Well you're lucky because wherever you go in the world you'll fit in; if you go to Peru they'll think you're Peruvian, if you go to Thailand they'll think you're Thai... you have a beautiful face, beautiful eyes.'

'I'm very ill-travelled,' I say. 'I need to undertake some sort of world tour.'

'Where to?'

'New York, Berlin –'

'I'm from New York, I miss New York. But what about the Eastern territories? Singapore is great right now. Tokyo's cool, that's a good scene. Hong Kong's OK, a little bit commercial. Shanghai, have you been to Shanghai?'

'Er. No.'

Then, out of nowhere, she hits me with the Big Bitter Speech of Inspiration:

'Listen, when you're in a new place... when I'm in a place like this I'm not interested in ninety-nine per cent of the people here, most of them have nothing going for them. Completely average, never gonna enhance your life. You have to do your thing and keep your eyes open, and I can say this to you because you're a beautiful girl and you've got your whole life to make it in front of you… I can still remember my grandmother telling me, when she was growing up she had to straighten her hair, she had to hide her lips, she got *nothing* for it, she didn't experience *anything* in her lifetime to make up for it, the civil rights movement came after her. I grew up in upstate New York in a tiny little town full of assholes. And I never once thought I was beautiful, not once, until one day when I was about fifteen, I had this Chinese dress, all silk, and I wore it out, and I felt so – oh – I felt like a princess. And I was standing in the street and a woman came up to me, very beautiful, she was Argentinean, extremely rich. And she was trying to inspire me – she already had all the houses in the world – and she said, "You know, you can have any man you want."'

'Oh. OK,' I say, stumped.

'Right! Like the reward for all the bullshit and the discrimination and all my hard work is a cute guy, right? Anyway, I was fifteen and it made my day.'

I take a solo turn around the gallery to recover and notice that Emanuele's mother Gina's at the exhibition.

'Ciao Bidisha,' she says gracefully to me.

'Ciao!' I shout back too loudly and with a too-big, too-childish smile, so that she goggles slightly and quickly looks away.

Tiziana comes up and stands very close to me, as is her habit (which I don't mind).

'We are going to have an aperitif at Harry's Bar. Would you like to come?'

'Famous Harry's Bar? Yes please. I've never been.' I don't even bother to make a show of thinking about it.

Me, Tiziana, Caterina and the silent wall-like Salvatore (who's sticking close to Caterina) walk into the twilit blue, crowded, humid street. The moon's up. I've always wondered about Harry's Bar, which Stef's parents warned me was very expensive and vulgar. We walk in. I like it. There's an instant crush, heat, light, noise and hospitable chaos, waiters in white jackets, silver trays the size of tabletops and little round tables the size of tea-trays, dwarflike curly-armed chairs, people standing crowded around the bar and stuffed into their seats, silver trolleys, side tables dressed in white linen, paintings and etchings of Venice and Giudecca on the walls, everything small, close and tight, neat banquettes against the walls, a ton of silverware and piled napkins and tablecloths and gold light.

Tiziana's greeted as an old friend by the barman, a short, lean, roguish old pixie with a loud voice and an abrupt wry manner. We're standing squared around the bar and everyone has to edge around us, but I like it because we're close to the centre of power, the head bar guy, and I can see everything that's going on in the room. And, unlike everyone else here, I'm with real Venetians. I turn my radar to maximum. Now, who else is drinking at Harry's tonight? American ditzes of the gum-chewing jock variety; a couple of beer-blubbered English couples on a shag holiday; a petite perfect-faced dark-skinned girl with a sidewave of black hair, in an ice blue silk dress, who looks exactly like something out of a Gauguin painting, escorted by a much older guy in a suit. Yes she looks sexy, but does she look like she's having fun? I watch her from time to time and not once do I catch her smiling.

Who else? A group of Middle Eastern women, perhaps in their thirties or late forties, each one in a printed floor length silk dress, softly powdered cocoa skin and black eyeliner, and the jewellery – oh God – fat nuggets of gold, emerald panther-shaped bracelets, silver cuffs, black pearl necklaces, pink pearl earrings... The room is, in addition, lined with royals: tight-faced tense men, young but with red skiing tans, in blue cotton shirts and blue suits, Scandinavian/German business style; skinny women with none of the audacity and dash of Venetian style, and all so wound up, taking sharp little darting glances at everyone. They seem bored and unhappy and underfed. In the corner seat I spy an impeccably preserved pale woman (and she really does look as though she's been preserved, by a professional, in formaldehyde) in her late fifties, long tight face, thin tight mouth, English or American upper crust, blow-dried grey-blonde hair, cream silk suit. She talks (and, it appears, eats) without opening her mouth. Flanked by two men in suits. Actress? Tycoon? Producer? But she doesn't have the confidence of an independently successful person. Is she just – sad question – *some guy's wife*?

'I'm truly badly dressed tonight,' I say to Caterina morosely. 'I've come out wearing my pyjamas.'

In this setting I really feel ashamed of myself in my cheap dusty flip-flops and travelling student bag, as though I haven't shown respect to the invitation by making the effort.

'No, you can do this,' says Caterina firmly in her raspy voice, staring honestly into my face. 'You are young. At our age it's impossible.'

'But I really feel horrible.'

'No. Don't ruin your mood, your time. It is better to make an understatement than to say too much.'

Tiziana talks me around the room, pointing out the Euro-royals behind us:

'He is the Prince of Wherever, with his wife. They come here often. He's very upset because nobody's looking at them. But this is Venice. The Princess of Blah-Blah was here last week with her friend and nobody looked at them twice. And in the corner [the older groomed lady], no, she's not an actress, she is English but she has been living here for ten years. The family name is Radcliffe.'

'A Martini and a whisky sour,' slurs a young English guy who's sitting at the bar with his girlfriend, wearing a white office shirt that's gone floppy with sweat.

'And a whisky sour, thank you sir!' cries the pixie-like barman, grinning around, a half-wink for Tiziana. She rolls her eyes at him coquettishly.

Salvatore has as yet said nothing at all. He stands behind Caterina like a windblock, his arm around her, his hand resting on the bar. I order a Bellini because the bar's famous for them. Prosecco for everyone else (right! I know! I got it wrong). Anyway, my Bellini's good, pithy pink fruit and the fizz of prosecco right at the end. I look at the trays of plentiful, hot, lovely-smelling rich food being carried back and forth behind me.

At the other end of the room are about a dozen flashy American fat-money guys, painfully red-tanned, in expensive but subtly wrong suits, too black, too boxy. Executive producers, I decide. Or showbiz lawyers.

We talk about how little we ate today after the Do Forni meal.

Tiziana: 'Some grapes, some rocket and an apple.'

Caterina: 'Two peaches and a grapefruit juice.'

Me: 'Fatless yoghurt and an apple.'

And Salvatore? Silence... We order meatballs and they arrive hot and gorgeous. There's so much sheer happiness to be had in getting a tissue and wrapping it around a hot, damp, gritty-breadcrumbed meatball, eating with your fingers, a hot gulp of that, then a sip of fruity Bellini. The next round: aha! Bellinis for everyone this time. Caterina has an egg and mayo sandwich coming, 'because I am *strictly* vegetarian,' she says to me in her hoarse way. We're all purring with prosecco and staring around unashamedly. The Architecture Biennale people are very distinctive in appearance, like Count Orlok in *Nosferatu*, always with that mixture of ego, austerity and awkwardness. Chalky skin, jet-black linen, too lumbering to be elegant.

A priest comes in in full black frock and collar, pale pink egg face, sleazy eyes, holding religious books very ostentatiously in his hand. He's greeted as a regular.

'He is English,' Tiziana says to me. We've fallen into the thing of her speaking English and me speaking Italian. 'Before, he was a seaman, and he had a woman...'

'A woman at every port?'

'Yes. And once, he fell in love with a woman and suffered so much that he renounced all women and became a priest.'

'No! Romantic,' I say dryly, thinking, *yes, it was all about himself in the end*. 'A drinking, Harry's Bar-partying priest.'

'His church is in Campo San Vio in Dorsoduro. Every couple he has married has got divorced.'

I watch as the priest orders a Virgin Mary, appropriately enough, in flat Englishy Italian, then goes to drink it on a wooden chair in the cloakroom, fawned over by the coat check girls and loving every minute of it.

'You can take a seat anywhere here,' Tiziana tells me. 'They'll always make you pay for it.'

After eating and drinking, we stumble out. As ever in Venice I experience the phenomenon of not paying for anything: somehow, because Tiziana knows the bar guy and because she is his cherished friend, a long-time customer, almost a relation, she settles the bill, but at a massive discount. Salvatore, Caterina and I are asked to stand outside while all this goes on, so as not to draw attention to the big favour. Salvatore has still said nothing.

Tiziana comes out again and refuses our wan offers of compensation. Our plan is to visit a party in some millionaire's warehouse/playpen in Giudecca. I see a tall Senegalese man in a long printed kaftan approach carrying a big bag. Bloodshot eyes, mild face. He's holding something in his hand. As he gets close he brandishes it at us – a snake! No, a very realistic wooden toy snake, fretted and cut so that it ripples and bends, painted with dark green triangular scales and fitted with a pink rubber tongue. I automatically scowl and snatch myself away – I hate this kind of thing and in London it usually means you're about to be stabbed by a nutcase – but Tiziana is delighted.

'This is a good snake,' she says. I like her calm, slow manner. 'Can I see it?'

'Here,' says the man, handing to her. 'See the craftsmanship. It moves very well.'

'How much is it?'

'For you, thirty euros.'

'Ah, no, I'm sorry. That's no use to me. Take it back.'

The man refuses gently:

'But look at the eyes, look at the design. And it's well made. For you, twenty euros.'

'No, twenty euros, that's no good for me. No good at all.'

'But look at the two beads for the eyes, hold it in your hand, feel the weight of it. You can't deny it's a good thing. OK, for you, ten euros.'

'Ten euros for a wooden snake? It's purely decorative, it's not as though it's something I can use every day.'

'OK, seven euros, seven euros for the snake.'

Thus the deal is done with maximum flowing politeness. I'm too nasty and cold to participate. Before and during all this the man has reached into his bag and offered out what I thought were gnarled old polished conkers, *regalo* – a present. Tiziana took one, he kept offering one to me and stupidly I kept shrugging it away. Now Caterina and Salvatore, who'd been whispering together patiently, come up and want to know what's going on. In her rough-voiced way Caterina likes the snake. The seller gives her another one to look at, this one red, not green, and missing a tongue, but moving just as beautifully. The seller gives Salvatore a *regalo* and Salvatore (who, praise the heavens, is even stiffer than me) doesn't want it and simply hands it to me in unsmiling silence. I turn away and look at it in privacy: it's a fat little smiling Buddha in varnished red wood. I like it.

'A token for good luck in love and work,' says the seller.

Tiziana gives a droll shrug:

'Work, maybe. But love?'

Caterina decides to take the red snake. The seller helps her thread it into a long plastic tube to keep it clean.

'One more present, please,' Tiziana commands, and he gives Caterina something bigger than our Buddhas. We crowd around and hold it up to the streetlight.

'It's an elephant,' I cry.

An elephant sitting on its bottom with its front legs up, its trunk pluming over its head and its ears spread. Perfect for Caterina the animal lover.

'Like Ganesh,' says Caterina to me, 'Ganesh is an elephant.'

I nod and hug my Buddha in my hand. We walk to the vaporetto stop together. Tiziana and I fall into step.

'Are they together?' I say, indicating Salvatore and Caterina.

'They are married. He was married before, but his wife died. There are two children, two daughters, from that. One is thirteen and one is eighteen. But Salvatore and Caterina have been married now for many years. It works because they live between three different places, they are not always together. This is necessary because otherwise marriage is a prison.'

I hadn't thought Caterina and Salvatore could be married, because they're so affectionate with each other (I just saw him stroking her like a dog).

'Now I have to find a boyfriend,' I say. 'Everyone's telling me to.' Courteous coupledom seems the right thing in Venice.

'Ah yes. But this is difficult for a strong woman,' says Tiziana.

'It's been a *long* time.'

'No!' says Tiziana as the truth sinks in. 'This is fine at my age, but at your age... we must solve this problem.'

'I don't know... I always had a lot of work. I'm a bit Catholic.'

'You're not really, are you?' she says, appalled. Interesting social schism: the secular hedonists hate the religious masochists, and it's mutual. Both parties are completely unprepared to read each other's work.

'No, no, not literally,' I reassure her. 'I mean inside.'

'Ah! You mean you have your grandmother on your back. Come on.' She goes behind me and mimes easing a knife out from between my shoulder blades. 'We must get this grandmother off.'

'I'm not even looking for the person of my life. Maybe just a couple of months. Or a week.'

'Ah!' she warns. 'Don't put limits on providence!'

Caterina has given me her snake to carry in my dirty vagrant travellers' bag. Tiziana's been wearing hers around her neck and occasionally whipping it off and waving it at passers-by, who shriek and laugh and joke along. I watch Caterina and Salvatore. Now I see why he's so silent and watchful, protecting her all the time: he's scared she's going to drop dead right in front of his face just like wife number one.

We're all stumbling along playing with our snakes, arriving eventually at the San Zaccaria vaporetto stop of the Riva degli Schiavoni. To my credit I usefully identify the right stop number. The vaporetto arrives and I hop on, but Tiziana's still waiting for Salvatore and Caterina. The barrier slams shut with me on the boat and her on the boarding barge.

'But wait! She's with us!' she cries to the guard, a short, short-haired female with a brusque manner, possibly a prison guard in her spare time.

'Too late!' the guard replies gleefully as the boat moves off.

She's not going to let me off! I sink bank, inebriated, unsure of what to do. I don't even know where I'm meant to get off. The boat is moderately full. I phone Tiziana. She tells me to get off at the next stop, run across to the Zattere side and get another boat to Giudecca. We iron through the black waves across to the other coast – twinkling gold lights, navy-blue sky. I see the round observatory shape of the church of Santa Maria della Salute. I let myself move with the boat until I realise the guard's making her way around checking everyone's ticket. The guard draws closer,

I drift back. Luckily for me a young Japanese couple have made a mistake: the guy has the right ticket, the girl has a ticket but the wrong one. It's obvious from her face that she wasn't trying to cheat and doesn't understand what she's done wrong but the guard reacts with lottery-winner jubilation: 'No? That's the only ticket you have? Then that is a fine,' she says in English. 'Thirty-five euros. Do you want to pay it now?'

I gulp. I don't even know how to buy a vaporetto ticket. I'm next for the chopping block. I send up a prayer, hoping to cash in karmically on all those candle offerings I've made at Frari church. It works: just as the guard's about to hunt for other victims the next stop draws close and she has to attend to opening the gate and calling people on board.

The boat knocks the landing stage, the gate slams open and looking straight but uninterestedly ahead I jump off and scoot straight across the point of the coast, coming out the other side onto Zattere, where the 82's waiting. I get on. Luckily the conductor here doesn't give a toss about his job and chats and jokes with the driver and guard for the whole journey, leaning against the railings at the front of the boat. I get off at Giudecca (the view: big industrial money chic) and see Tiziana, Caterina and Salvatore right there, looking around for me. We realise that we were on the same boat.

'Have you lost my snake?' asks Caterina.

'No, it's here, in my bag,' I say, getting it out and giving it to her.

We start walking to the warehouse where the party's being held.

'I love all animals and I am *strictly* vegetarian,' says Caterina in English, playing with the snake.

'I like *some* animals,' I say.

'I like *all* animals. When I was a child I used to sleep in the bed with all my pets. I like the sensation of their far – fur – on my skin.'

'Ah, yes,' I say. Confirmed! Animalistic type! I congratulate my intuition.

'Have you seen the film *The Mahabharata*?' she asks me.

'No. But I've heard of it, of course.'

'It is five hours long, a beautiful film, we saw it in the open air and by the time it was finished the sun was coming up. Do you remember, Salvatore?'

'Yes, I remember,' mutters Salvatore on the other side of her. Salvatore speaks! He's gliding along like an FBI security vehicle.

'The man has so many tests and adventures and at the end they say to him, well done. We will now let you into heaven. But there is one condition. You must leave your dog. And he says, what? Leave my dog? That is impossible. I would rather be unhappy on earth with my dog than happy without him in heaven. And,' by now Caterina is almost weeping, 'it is the most beautiful ending: God is the dog. After all those adventures, we find out that the dog is God! So beautiful! That is one of my favourite films. You have to see it. *The Mahabharata*.'

We arrive at the warehouse: a cavernous white-walled gallery space, DJ, mixed-age, well-dressed crowd, a free bar with wine and chilled prosecco, a small tree garden with white iron benches and low tables at the end. I have no idea who's hosting the party or what it's for. Tiziana immediately rushes in and starts talking to a million people. I stroll around feeling badly dressed (and I am, blatantly and objectively, the worst-dressed person in the room), looking at the art (a convex canvas! A concave canvas! A pile of rusty nails!) before sauntering over to the food table: perfect little salty things, mini pizzas, mini cakes with cream and cocoa powder and flaky weightless pastry. I make a point of trying everything. I also get two proseccos and deliver one to Tiziana, who introduces me to a tall guy with a friendly face, dark clothes and chic heavy-framed glasses, but I've just stuffed a cake in my mouth. I roll my eyes and shrug in apology.

'Eat, eat,' he exhorts me, laughing, 'we'll return to you when you're finished.'

I do finish, Tiziana reintroduces me and explains what I'm doing in Venice.

'I did the same move,' says the guy to me in Italian, 'London to Venice. After ten years of London.'

'But why?'

'Ugh. London. Too many people, there's no style, it's too commercial, so after ten years I said, *basta*, and I moved here.'

'But isn't it hard, making the change from such a big city to such a small one?'

'Is Venice so small? Eventually everyone and everything comes to Venice...'

Other people join the conversation and I drift away. Tiziana comes over.

'He is a very interesting man,' she says.

'He seems nice.'

'He's Spanish, he lived in Madrid, then London and now Venice. Also New York. He's a very famous pianist.'

'Ah!' I say, unable for some reason to imagine someone so easygoing playing the piano.

I go back to the, ahem, pastry table and find Charmaine, the beautiful American woman from earlier.

'Hiya,' I say cheerfully. 'The food here is *so* good.'

'Is this good food?' she enquires finely.

'Sure. For a party. Why not? It's nice that they got someone in to do it.'

'Have you had a good evening?'

'Yup, we were just in Harry's Bar and had some very nice Bellinis. I was greatly enjoying looking at all the rich people.'

'Oh honey,' she says pityingly, 'they're not really rich.'

'But what about their jewellery?'

'Trust me, that's all they have. I'm in there nearly every night, I know who you're talking about. They're just Americans who're wearing all their money. They're saying, "Look. I have all this," and I'm like, "No honey, you have a Land Rover and a condo in Texas." I was just with the real thing, just now. A Spanish prince.'

'A Spanish *prince*?'

'Right, and he owns, like, six beautiful palazzos in Venice. An ex-pianist, very decent guy.'

'Oh *him*,' I say in recognition. 'I was just talking to him. He's cool.'

'Right, and he doesn't feel the need to dress up and look all that, does he?'

'No...'

I go away, unnerved. Something about the preceding conversation strikes me as a little bit off. It reminds me of these American tourists I overheard one day near Calle del Cristo in my neighbourhood, looking in at some of the ceramics shops. The guy called to his wife in wonder, as we all walked along in single file, 'and this street's the same size as one of the hallways in our house!'

I notice people congregating around the garden doors. I wonder if there's going to be a speech. No – worse – it's performance art. A sixty-year-old man takes two wooden spoons to two overturned saucepans on a dessert trolley. He begins to drum them with no particular rhythm, then stops abruptly and declares the following:

'Rikka tik a tik, thrum tombo tum, rum tooey tum, rik tik tik.'

Then more drumming and more nonsense. I sit in the corner and make astounded notes in my notebook. *Why* is nobody laughing? Ah yes – this is Venice – they're not laughing because they don't care. He finishes and there's a round of indifferent applause.

Caterina and Salvatore leave early, Caterina air-kissing me so as not to smudge her make-up. I go to the end of the warehouse, right up to the doors, and on my way back I bump straight into Emanuele.

'Hey!'

'Hey!'

We kiss naturally on both cheeks.

'When did you get here?' he asks me.

'Like, two hours ago. You?'

'Just now.'

'Just now?'

'Yup, just now!'

I can't think of anything to say so I smile and glide on, but am sickened to find myself feeling happy... I have by now drunk *many* proseccos. But quite soon afterwards I find myself hanging around him a little bit. I ask him when the slug moustache comes off.

'Sunday.'

'*When* on Sunday?' I press.

'In the morning when I brush my teeth.'

All in sweet and easy Italian. Tiziana saves me by dragging me onto the dance floor where the music is a mixture of everything: kitsch disco, a bit of reggae and dance hall. Everyone's dancing, older people, a few younger ones, Tiziana the prettiest on the dance floor. She dances well too. In the middle of the dancing she manages to introduce me to a German historian, a tall, slimmish fifty-something guy with thick, grey, bohemian-cut hair and a faded grey linen suit. We talk about Venice, in English.

'I'm not sure I could really settle here forever,' I say. 'It's a bit claustrophobic for me.'

'Vell, Venice is like a love affair. You go avay but you keep returning. It's alvays there for you.'

His thin-rimmed glasses glint down at me.

'That's a good way of putting it,' I say. Also, I think, a false way of putting it. A love affair is *not* an arrangement where you go and do what you like and then come back and the other person's waiting for you with their mouth open at the other end.

Then comes the award-winning non sequitur of the evening:

'Vell, you have a vunderful face, and I'm sure you have a vunderful body too.'

Oh, why does this always happen to me?

'Yes, I'm very sporty,' I answer, quick as a flash. 'Lovely to meet you, I think I have to go and mingle.'

I hurl myself into the middle of the dance floor and begin dancing with abandon. Emanuele's there. His dancing is fast and kitsch, a sort of salsa tango with lots of quick fast steps, his shirt soaked through with sweat. We all laugh, he doesn't mind. Then I see his girlfriend, tall, pale, slender, perfect-faced, long straight dark hair, clear features, in a black dance dress and black ballet pumps, with two equally poised friends. She and Emanuele whirl together. I dance sometimes with them, sometimes alone.

'I sweat so much, I can't help it,' he grins.

'Forget it. Me too,' I say, plucking my shirt away from my back.

He puts his hand on my waist at the back in a friendly way.

'No, you're not sweaty... but you have more tattoos than just the one on your forearm.'

He's seen the little seahorse at the base of my spine.

'Yes, everywhere. I was really depressed when I got them,' I joke.

'But you're OK now?' he says, concerned.

'Er. Yes. Of course! It wasn't serious.' How exactly did we get into this heavy exchange during the bossa nova?

'Good,' he says tenderly.

I ignore the false sentiment and dance on. Emanuele twirls near me, then leans against the back of one of the sofas and stops to take a break.

'You said you were allergic to alcohol,' he says.

'I am.'

'Yeah right! You're drinking very well tonight.'

'But I'll pay for it tomorrow...'

'But I see that alcohol doesn't go to your head the way it does with some people.'

'No. Tell me something, Emanuele... by the way, I have to say, you're very pretty... how old are you?'

'Guess.'

'No, come on, I can't!'

'Guess!'

'Twenty-eight.'

'No. Lower.'

'Twenty-five?'

'Nope. Try again.'

'Twenty-three.'

'Yes!'

'Twenty-three? My God. You're a baby. Sorry for saying twenty-eight.'

'That's OK,' he says easily. 'It's because of the moustache.'

'You dance very well.'

'No, I know I don't but I like dancing.'

'No, no, you dance beautifully...'

I move away carefully before I started leering too much at the poor boy. I get some (more) food then go to the garden, where I find Tiziana, who makes space for me next to her on the bench. The party's now thinned noticeably.

'How do you dance all night long?' I ask her. 'I'm exhausted.'

'But this is fun,' she grins.

'I know! It's *very* fun...' We observe the party for a few minutes. 'The elegant girl in the black, is that Emanuele's girlfriend?' I casually enquire.

'No, that's his sister. She's thirty. Her name's Anna.'

'Oh! I see... Does he have a girlfriend, just out of interest?'

'He had one. They broke up in July.'

'But July's recent,' I say.

'Yup... but he's a nice boy. Intelligent.'

'Mm. I'm enjoying myself. But it requires a lot of energy.'

'It depends on the size of your...' She makes a pregnant stomach shape.

'Your inner child?'

'Yes! Mine's always pushing to come out.'

'That's why you look so young.'

'It's a question of your mentality. I am fifty-three –'

'Jesus!'

So Stef had been telling the truth. I hadn't quite bought her analysis of Tiziana's life situation as I do feel that Stef, for all her greatness, has a bit of lurking ageism going on.

'Thank you!' cries Tiziana, laughing at my shocked face. 'But you see Gina also, Emanuele's mother. And Caterina. She comes here, she dances... and then I have some friends, they are the same age as me and they act like my grandparents.'

'Thanks for this evening and yesterday evening. You've given me my Venetian life.'

'Oh no, don't be silly...'

'No, it's true, Tiziana...'

'A friend of mine told me that I'm a woman for all occasions, high or low.'

'Now *that's* true!'

We go back out – she plucks a red napkin from a table and does a dance of the seven veils with it – the music is belly dancing stuff so we all shimmy. There are only about seven or ten of us left on the dance floor, and about thirty people watching us. Emanuele, his friends and his sister, who's been friendly to me in a rather cool, graceful way, drift outside to get some air. I eventually also drift out alone and sit away from them out front. I catch the eye of the woman sitting on the bench next to me.

'You were dancing earlier, weren't you?' she says to me. 'I was just saying to my friend, you dance very well.'

There's a pause as I translate what she's said. Then I give a big, gratified, simpering grin, at which the woman looks a little disconcerted.

'Do you speak Italian?' she asks slowly.

'Yes, but I can't believe that I dance well. I feel mortified when I'm dancing,' I bumble.

Emanuele's sister Anna comes up to me and says, 'Come on, one last whirl before they pack up.'

She's like a queen, pulling me along, wiping my face down where I'm flushed. Emanuele and Tiziana come too.

'I know all the old tunes,' I boast to Emanuele.

'The waltz, the rumba? The salsa?'

'No, not the salsa.'

'Shall I ask them to play the cha-cha-cha just for us?'

'No!'

'Too late!'

He runs off and has a word with the DJ. Immediately the air's full of fake bright tropical rhythm. We all whoop and dance around each other. The next half-hour is a haze of movement. Finally the songs slow down and I find myself in a close no-contact sway with Emanuele. I pretend to wipe a tear from my eye at the mournful song.

'Why are you crying? You have nothing to be sad about,' he says in English.

'I'm sad because the evening is ending and the music is so beautiful.'

I accidentally walk into his shoulder and get a faceful of his sweaty shirt.

'*Now* you have something to be sad about,' he says regretfully.

We go slower and slower and occasionally I'm close enough to feel the heat of his neck near my face – but really, who needs this stuff? At the end of the song he sweeps me towards the couches holding my hand up high. A deep actorly bow. We disperse.

It's nearly three in the morning and we're a set of six or so. I have no idea how I'm going to get home. We say our thank yous and goodbyes and drift out. Anna produces a black silk wrap to match her dress.

'Do you have something Emanuele could wear?' she asks Tiziana.

'Ah! Yes.'

And then from *her* bag Tiziana produces a fine saffron-coloured wrap and arranges it around Emanuele's shoulders. I had not realised that a wrap was necessary to be carried, like a concealed weapon, by every woman in Venice. Everyone turns to me, indicating that they'll wait while I put on *my* wrap – but I have none. I indicate this with a hopeless shrug and they sigh sympathetically. The officials of Venice should produce an etiquette guide, sub-headed Food, Clothing, Introductions and Shopping or somesuch for hapless vulgarians like me to memorise before visiting.

We drift out together, go to the water's edge and find... a million-dollar boat containing an American lady in a long red dress and a man in a black linen suit. A cognac advert come to life. From Tiziana's explanatory whispers I find out that the woman's family, wealthy beyond belief, own Cipriani's and that she and the man used to be married but now... operate a water-taxi service together? Surely not, but I ask no questions. We get into the boat, sitting in the open air in the back, Tiziana on my right, yet another linen man standing up to my left. Anna and Emanuele are sitting opposite each other in the cabin inside. You can tell what great friends they are, they both sit forward, lean towards each other and chat away constantly. Anna goes to the front of the boat to talk to the red dress woman.

'Come here,' I say coolly to Emanuele.

He sits right next to me and puts his arm around me. His arm is very warm and very heavy.

'No,' says Tiziana authoritatively. 'Emanuele, give Bidisha some of your pashmina. It's cold.'

It is not cold, it is very hot and humid. But I say nothing.

'Ah, yes — of course — sorry,' says Emanuele fussily. Then there's a lot of business as Tiziana, worried about my health and the likelihood of me catching a chill in this sweltering climate, takes the pashmina and winds it around both of us.

'That's the best way,' she says, sitting back down.

Now Emanuele embraces me with both arms — but still somehow not sleazily — and my entire body becomes warm and heavy and rather interested. But I'm still not relaxed. First, his touch is too heavy, too dominant. It feels suffocating. Second, I have the strange thought that my laptop, folded up and hidden under a tablecloth on the breakfast bar, knows I'm out being embraced in a boat when I should be working.

Venice from a boat at night is so strange, a Murnau horror film: everything black and old and high up, seeming to loom at the corners and bend over you, a feeling not of liberty but of restriction, of never quite being able to see where you are, stuck nose first in the water. It's like looking at the world through a fisheye lens. Every so often Emanuele tightens his arms around me as I sit alertly within them. I get claustrophobic and try to pull the pashmina away.

'What're you doing?' he asks.

'I don't need it, I'm not cold.'

'You do need it,' he coos, 'you'll get ill.'

'I haven't been ill in years,' I grumble.

I lapse back into his arms.

'You embrace me because you don't know me,' I point out.

'Yup!' he agrees readily.

The boat gradually drops people off. The red dress woman steps off, the guy who's been standing up at the back (who seemed a little melancholy to me) gets off, finally Anna, Emanuele, Tiziana and I go. I throw out a thank you and goodbye at the driver, whose face I don't even log. We're in a narrow street near San Marco. Kisses and goodbyes to Anna and Emanuele, who gives me a deep baroque bow, twirling his fingers. I laugh and wave and say I'll call him. Tiziana and I walk back to Campo Santo Stefano, where she lives. I'll go home from there.

'I had a lot of fun today,' I say to her. 'Oh human contact!'

She laughs: 'Before anything happens between two people, love or hate, there first has to be the human relationship, the contact. Everything else can come afterwards.'

I try to give her the gold pashmina, which Emanuele had put on me when we got off the boat, but she insists that I keep it for the walk home. After all that dancing my body feels loose and strong, vibrating mellowly like a cello string. We part and I stroll through the hot extinguished city, empty Campo Santa Margherita, closed shops, silent black church. Shower, glass of water, bed.

Chapter Eleven

The night after these two expeditions I go out again for an opera-ballet thing, arias sung by masked performers and a dance performance in the Scuola di San Giovanni Evangelista, very close to my house. I get there in good time, spot the long queue at the entrance and realise instantly that I've been had. The tickets were a whopping thirty euros. The queue is full of tourists. How can I tell? Because they're so unkempt. Prints with stripes. Black shoes, white socks. Beer guts. Glaring colours. Waders. Slutty dresses. Lederhosen. A short chunky man dressed all in black with an 'I'm intellectual' pair of specs on pushes past me, then backs into me. He loves himself so much that for the whole of the queue his shoulder's nudging me out of the way. Why can't he tell I'm here? Because he's the only person in the room. Silent nervous girlfriend who clings close to him while he graces her with not one word or look.

The guides and ushers are all speaking in English. They grab our tickets and cash 'em in a tin money box. We get inside. The main room is a riot of wooden panelling and big blowsy paintings. There's no stage, just seven music stands set out a few feet away. Then the horror begins.

The lights don't dim. Out comes a woman in a full white mask, eighteenth-century fancy dress and scuffed white plimsolls, holding a one-euro rose from a street vendor. She glides forward and gives the rose to one of the men in the front row, then goes to sit at a harp on the left and does a little trill on it. The other players come in, with cello, violin, oboes, all in fancy dress and wearing masks of different types – a long expensive dodo one, the others little more than eye covers, like club-class sleeping masks. It's obvious from their slightness (and the way they're giggling, fidgeting and nudging each other) that they're students. There's a young lead violinist with a painted-on beard who keeps fiddling with his bracelet. They play away, pieces all recognisable from perfume, airline, car and clothing adverts. Out comes a woman, also in fancy dress, but additionally wigged, powdered and rouged, holding a mask on a stick. She sings in a wiry soprano and she's great but the fake acting – the smiles at the audience, the manipulation of the mask, the sighs of love, the gliding-about – is nauseating. Then she goes away and a man comes in, big, heavy, meaty face with small eyes and mouth, hair in a ponytail, a long fancy frock on. He sings 'Nessun Dorma' and goes up on his tiptoes when he's gunning for a high note. The atmosphere in the audience becomes warm. They like him and shout their congratulations.

Then the pain deepens. Out comes the 'ballet': a girl of sixteen or so, self-conscious and humourless, in a leotard and a home-made polyester overskirt, who jumps and twirls while the musicians play, looking exactly like a five-year-old putting on a birthday show for her parents. Between moves she casts brave, frightened looks at the audience. These three acts take it in turns to keep us 'entertained' for the next two hours. The dancer is good, especially at modern dance, but all in all it's excruciating. At the end both singers come out and do a duet, pretending to fall tenderly into each other's arms before separating and each plucking a man and a woman from the front row to have a quick waltz with. I run off halfway through this, revolted by the con and the spectacle and feeling my thirty euros very sorely.

The next day there's a message on my phone.

'Hi Bidisha, this is Charmaine — we met at the gallery opening? Just calling to check that you have my mobile number and wondering if you'd like to meet tonight for a pizza? I'm at my office near San Marco.'

It's the pretty American lady. I want to go, especially for the pizza element, but not so soon after neglecting my work for three days. I call her back that afternoon and then we enter the weird zone.

'Hi, Charmaine? It's Bidisha.'

'Oh. Hi Bidisha. How're you.' In a voice as flat and cold as a day-old pancake.

'Er. Fine.' There's silence at the other end. 'So! I got your message and I'd love to go for a pizza, but could we do it over the weekend? It's just that I've got a bit of work on —'

'Right. Actually I wanted to talk to you about that. Why don't you just call me again when you've finished your work?'

And basically hangs up. I'm left staring at the phone in confusion: but you called *me*! You invited *me* for a pizza! I'm not running after *you*!

The week goes by in working. Just when I hit another down-spot Tiziana drops by and invites me to a drinks thing at the Metropole. I'm so pleased that I go for a massive three-hour run in the blazing heat before snaffling a cake at Tonolo: a great heavy wedge of chocolate infused with liqueur, very nice if you like that kind of thing. I don't — it lies in my gut like a rubber brick at the bottom of a school swimming pool.

That evening I end up wearing a terrible outfit: jeans, cream silk shirt with a sailor collar showing strangely under a royal purple silk jacket and plain brown lace-up shoes. The colours, shapes, proportions *and* textures are all wrong together, an impressive feat of quantum wrongness. I arrive at the Metropole at the right time, except that the garden is completely empty, apart from some girls in black cocktail dresses, all wearing fantastic hats, and more hats on stands all around. But no guests. Either I'm very early or very late. Is this what Tiziana invited me to? Has she been and gone? Is the party elsewhere?

Then begins the evening of unbelievably rude people. I don't have my phone with me so I go back to the reception where a man is tending the desk. I stand in front of him for about twenty seconds (I know because I'm counting) while he, perfectly aware of me because he saw me approach, plays with some Post-its stuck to his ledger book. He's about fifty years old, with a plump, clean-shaven, dark-tanned face, neat hair, neat lips, neat nails. He eventually lifts his head and offers me an unsmiling Italian 'Good evening.'

In awful and quiet Italian I spill out, 'Hello, I just wondered if there's a message waiting for me. I was supposed to meet my friend here but I'm a little late. Did she leave any word? My name's Bidisha.'

'Are you staying here with us?'

'No. No, I'm not.'

'Is your friend staying here?'

'Ah. No. We were supposed to meet in the garden...'

There's a long pause while he looks me straight in the eyes. His own are narrowed with smiling contempt and 'You are stupid' is the message in them, writ very clear.

'There is no message for you,' he says.

He looks at me a moment longer to make sure I feel it, then bends his head and attends to his ledger again, his lips twitching with amusement as though he's putting together a particularly clever Scrabble word. I wait. He doesn't raise his head again. He knows I'm still standing there. Stung, I return to the garden and begin admiring the hats, which're being showcased by a German company called Hat Office. They're great: soft felt trilbies, some beaded or embellished but generally austere, cupping the head elegantly, some showpieces, one or two arching feathers on a base, a neat little pillbox. Eventually more people drift in. A bunch of super-shit-hot fashion guys arrive: too-white shirts glowing from navy-blue suit jackets worn with jeans, tanned skin, the James Bond yuppie look. Then Charmaine (yes Charmaine) comes in. She stands for a few seconds at the mouth of the party and gives it a very slow, bright, toothy, open-eyed doll smile. She's carrying the little black and white dog. And why is the dog with her? It's a little doggy way of saying *notice me*. Charmaine looks beautiful, in a pale green silk dress trimmed with pink ribbon and flat pale green sandals.

'Hey,' I say in a friendly way.

'Oh hi! How're you?' she says, and she's friendly this time.

'Er, I'm good. A little tired.'

'Yeah, you said you were working a lot.'

'Finishing a bit of writing,' I nod.

'And is that for yourself?'

Ouch!

'No. It's my job. But tell me about you. You said you have an office near San Marco.'

'Well, we don't *have* it, we're renting it. It's shared. We might buy it soon though.'

And still I can't work out what she does for a living. She mentioned something about TV and the BBC at the beginning but I can't make the connection. Producer? Director? Scout? Meanwhile the yappy dog's running around.

'What a beautiful dog,' I lie.

'It's hard work though. Possibly harder than bringing up a kid.'

'Don't have kids, you'd be a terrible mother,' I don't say. I do say, 'I can imagine. Because they don't grow up.'

'I'm sorry, he's never usually like this. It's the hats. Excuse me, I just have to play with him for a second.'

She's brought a little rubber ball with her and begins tossing it around for the dog to catch. I don't want to hang around her so I drift off. More people, more drinks: globes of red wine, flutes of prosecco, the odd orange juice. I can't leave until Tiziana arrives, but she's nowhere to be seen. Everyone begins trying on the hats. Two strange people enter: one is a pale guy, tall with a gut, ugly, very fey like a bashful kid, with long strands of thin bright yellow hair and a sunbleached jellyfish face with pink cheeks, in burgundy jeans and a clinging long-sleeved white T-shirt (clinging, that is, to the gut). He's about thirty-five. The woman with him is fifty-five or so – his mother? No. Grey hair in a plait, sweatshirt, nervous, her hand up to her mouth, following the man around. His lover? His owner? Or his – ah! – his fag hag. The guy meets one of the hat women, they shake hands, his

224

voice is a lisp, 'Jason Harendon' is how he introduces himself, his whole name, as though he's famous (he isn't). He's American. He doesn't introduce the woman, who hovers at his shoulder trying to get in. He tries on a plain grey felt hat, then picks up another, a burgundy trilby with a soft black band.

'But this is for a woman, right?' he says.

'Well,' answers the hat girl cleverly, 'it depends what you're trying to say. This is for the confident man who isn't afraid to show the world his feminine side.'

Now the man-worshipping fag hag can't stand it any more. She bursts out, 'I dread to think what they'll say to us if we wear that in church in New York! If we duck into St Thomas's in that!'

The man ignores her. The woman gives a nervous laugh after she's spoken, puts her hand over her mouth, begins to play with her grey plait and casts imploring glances into his face.

I go under the canopy and try on a white trilby with crystal beads. Charmaine comes over:

'Oh that's a good one on you. That gives me the chills,' she says of my hat.

'You try something,' I say.

She tries on a hat that's so right on her that the entire party grinds to a halt and comes over to congratulate her: a leopard print skull-cap in a 1920s style, moulded to the head in the softest felt, with an undulating edge that fits the nape and ear, trimmed with pink ribbon at the back.

'That looks incredible, you have to get it,' I say. 'It was made for you.'

'It's cool, right? I feel very Eartha Kitt Catwoman.'

Out of nowhere a professional photographer turns up and starts shooting her.

'And you look like that other singer,' says Charmaine to me. 'Who's that girl with the piano?'

'Alicia Keys.'

By now we've gathered an admiring little crowd with our hat-compatible faces.

'Right!' says Charmaine to me. 'Alicia Keys. Now give us a demo. Hit it!'

Everyone looks at me. There's a silence as I become the big sweaty clown-show of the party. I sing one line of an Alicia Keys song in a deliberate drab monotone. The onlookers laugh. I look at Charmaine hatefully and take off the hat. Now the fey American guy – 'Jason Harendon' – comes over with his pet woman.

'These are fun,' he says mildly, his chin down, his belly out, pointing at the hats.

'They're fun, right?' says Charmaine immediately, glomming on to him.

They're like two animals picking up on each other's scent. I marvel at these words – 'fun' – so insipid.

I try on every damn hat in the garden, then take a seat on one of the circular stone benches – the husband bench, where lots of chaps are patiently eating nuts and waiting for their wives. At long last, two hours after the appointed time, I see Tiziana come in with silent Salvatore, Caterina's husband, in tow. She rolls her eyes at me apologetically and calls me over, instantly gets a spoonful of nuts and dumps them in my hand, asks if I've met Salvatore before – I smile a smile of terror into the grey abyss of his face – and starts introducing me to people: witty artist girls, graceful women, a couple of flannel-like older men, then a weird guy I've seen around town a number of times. He has glowing pure white skin, a completely bald head, full lips and clear, heavy-lidded eyes with no eyelashes – a Russian face – dressed like a science fiction doctor in a floor-length cream linen coat, cream silk waistcoat, cream shirt and cricket trousers, a white panama hat, all awful. I was right, the man is Russian – he speaks excellent Italian and good English. He's polite enough. Then I spot the willowy Oscar Wilde guy from the antiques shop in my area, whom I see about twice a day. I look straight at him and he frowns and blanks me. More of their friends come and they close off in an all-male circle of their own, looking at each other eagerly, gathering shoulder to shoulder in front of our faces. Tiziana and I are made to stumble back and suddenly find ourselves literally on the outside of the circle. We give each other a *very* dry look.

'I need a prosecco,' mutters Salvatore into Tiziana's ear. 'I can't find the waitress anywhere.' A few minutes later he mutters into her ear again: 'There's a woman over there who has a basset hound *this* big.'

He shapes his hands into a neat loaf of bread. I've seen the dog – chocolate brown, sweet and soundless, but a very inconvenient shape, too long in the body, it must have such trouble turning corners. We all try on hats and begin to have fun.

Then Tiziana has to go. She's very apologetic: they've been invited to a party at Palazzo Zenobio but it has a strict guest list so she can't invite me. In saying goodbye we've drifted over to where Charmaine is. I hear Charmaine claim an Italian man by saying out of nowhere, 'That's a great jacket on you, that look really suits you.' He is far too beautiful, is gay and has clearly heard it all before. I just can't figure out Charmaine's thing at all. Tiziana unfortunately begins to introduce me to her all over again. Charmaine doesn't break off her conversation but merely extends her hand gently to me as Tiziana's explaining that I'm a very interesting writer/thinker/philosopher, etc. 'I know, she told me,' Charmaine coos. By now I've automatically reached out and am holding gently, damply, onto Charmaine's hand. Charmaine has clearly labelled me a loser and since I'm no use to her, she has no interest in me. I stand there. She turns her doll-eyes full onto Tiziana and says, 'Can you recommend some good restaurants around here? I've just been speaking with some very interesting people, people from New York. We want to go out for a meal.' She means 'Jason Harendon' and his stray pet woman. I try to back away but Tiziana, who's giving Charmaine restaurant tips, has got me by the arm.

Tiziana and Salvatore eventually go to their other party. I leave a little interval so I don't bump into them on the way out. Charmaine's holding forth by the exit and out of politeness I murmur 'Bye, lovely to see you again' as I leave. She stops everything, turns her whole body towards me, gives me a slow, thrilled smile and gazes at me with her big, blankly glistening eyes and teeth.

'Well, have a beautiful evening,' she says to me in excruciating slow-motion insincerity, all honey and cream.

It's still very early and the pizza and junk food places around St Mark's are lively. To top off my night of ill encounters I almost bump into a man coming around a corner. He owns the cafe there and is closing up for the night. He's wearing a white apron. We both freeze. I'm closest to the wall so I flatten myself against it instinctively, expecting him to step aside around me. Then he pulls back and shouts full into my face, 'Yes! I've stopped. I'm not going anywhere. This is where *you* go to the side of *me*.' The force of his hostility, so sudden, pushes me to the side. 'There you go! Well done!' he screams, laughing. I go on, then turn to see him go into his cafe and begin stacking the chairs noisily, wearing a very happy smile on his leathery face.

At the end of that week a small irritating incident leads to a big irritating incident. I go food-shopping and somehow lose a new ten-euro phone credit voucher on my way home. I kick myself, dump my bags and then stride out crossly to look for it. It's dark, early evening, and my neighbourhood's full of people on their way home from work or college. I'm just round the side of Frari church staring at the ground and talking to myself when I hear an exclamation. It's Emanuele, standing close by me, minus the moustache and with a very pretty face – a long defined nose, full lips, high cheekbones, warm brown long-lashed eyes and the standard lazily-growing-out dark brown hair. Dark clothes, dark velvet jacket. He seems delighted to see me.

'Have you lost something?' he asks.

'My phone credit thing.'

'Not a credit card?'

'No.' *Ah yes, you're rich – phone credit is nothing to you*. 'But it was new... never mind, I'm sure someone's taken it by now. How are you?'

'Quite good...' he says with a sigh.

'Why only quite good?'

'I'm tired today.'

We stand there for a few moments, me still annoyed about the phone card, he perfectly at ease and smiling.

'Where are you going?' I ask.

'To meet some friends for a drink in Rialto. Want to come?'

'No, it's OK, I feel a bit of a mess today. I only came out to find this thing.' I haven't showered or even brushed my teeth and only finished work a few hours ago.

'No – why?' he says pleasingly. 'You look fine, come for a drink. The other thing I was going to do tonight is see a play at the Arsenale but I decided just now that I'm not going to do that. I'll have a drink with you instead.'

'Let's take a walk,' I say, wondering how to get out of it. 'Why not the theatre?'

'What d'you think?' he says, undecided.

'I think it could be nice. It's a good season this year, a friend of mine saw two good plays. And one bad one by Pasolini.'

'Pasolini? Are you sure it wasn't *about* Pasolini?'

'No, it was dark and long and neurotic and tormented. It was by Pasolini.' I'm still scanning the cobblestones. 'Why are you tired?'

'I got up at eight-thirty today,' he groans. 'I went to a screen-printing workshop at the design school. But this is the first day I've got up that early all summer.'

He's carrying an army bag with a roll of paper coming out of it. He calls his mum and tells her he's coming to the play, then calls his friends and tells them to meet him at the theatre.

'Are you a design student?' I ask.

'No, I'm just finishing my degree in philosophy.'

We're strolling along and without thinking too much about it I get on the vaporetto and pay five euros to get to Arsenale. We stand close together on the boat – he puts his hands on my shoulders to move me out of the way of the barrier. We talk philosophy. He has to decide what to do his thesis on:

'I've done nothing all summer. Now I have to start working.'

'It's impossible to work in the summertime. Especially in Venice.'

'I'm always outside in the summer,' he agrees.

'What did you do today in the workshop? Show me.'

He shows me the rolls of screen prints he made, flattening them out on top of the luggage hold. The image he made was of a woman's face – beautiful, with longish hair that flicks up at the end, a sweet smile and delicate, pretty features, and what does it look like? I examine the picture and puzzle out the answer... it looks familiar... ah yes... it looks exactly like Gina, his mother. I look at the dozen or so reproductions he's made. Then I look at his face as he gazes at them, and I laugh and laugh. I want to clap him gaily on the back, embrace him and say, 'Tell you what, I'm going home, OK? I'm not your type, you're not mine, let's not waste our time – and I'm not looking for a new friend. In ten years' time you're gonna marry a woman who looks exactly like your mother, and I *know* it'll be a happy union. Why not concentrate on that?'

Emanuele talks me through his pictures.

'You could choose, whether you use the positive or the negative for the finished picture. I did a lot in red, on newspaper, and they looked like communist party propaganda posters. I did ten or twelve of them, everybody was asking me for one... and so here I am, speaking English,' he says, a little surprised.

'You speak it beautifully. You're trilingual.' Italian, French and English.

'And on top of being tired, I'm now really hungry,' he says, switching back to Italian, 'but we only have ten minutes before the play starts. I haven't eaten anything except a sandwich today.'

We get to the deserted fortress-scape of Arsenale and crunch across the gravel.

'This area is very beautiful,' says Emanuele to me. 'Except at the moment, it smells.' True – of sewage – but Arsenale does have the subtle quality of belonging to another planet.

At a crowded cafe outside the theatre we spot a group of older friends including Tiziana. Gina's there too. Emanuele taps his mum on the shoulder and she jumps — why so skittish? Maybe because she hasn't eaten in twenty years and her shoulder might disintegrate under the weight of the tap. She greets me very nicely and tells us to go and get our tickets before they sell out.

'Save me a morsel of bread!' Emanuele calls to her as we run to the box office, where, unable to fib my way to a discount, I pay sixteen euros for a ticket, thus finishing all my money in one go.

There's no way for me to get out of this now, even though I hate plays, I'm broke and unwashed and I want to go home. I have a strange instinctive dislike of Emanuele even though he's done nothing so far to vindicate it.

Back at the cafe we chat with the jovial, bluff owner and Emanuele orders something to eat. Me nothing. The cafe's ugly, noisy, large and interesting. The owner's a bit of a showman, slaps things about and wipes his hands too much. When Emanuele asks if he can have the bill he replies 'Maybe!' From the counter it's possible for me to see into the kitchen. Four Japanese guys in their forties are labouring in a tiny workspace amongst the steam of the dishwasher and grime of the toasters, and a fifth is trying to clean up around them.

'If you want something to eat or drink, order it. Don't worry. Or a *sprizz*. A *sprizz* is good for the spirit,' says Emanuele.

'I can't,' I smile.

'You can — you do. I saw you drink four proseccos at the Giudecca party.'

'Four? Try ten,' I confess.

When his sandwich comes we grab it and hurry into the theatre.

'Here I am,' says Emanuele sweetly, 'speaking English, running *and* eating a sandwich, all at the same time.'

On the way in we bump into his university friends, a beautiful young, fair, clear-skinned boy and girl, like young Caesars, both in their early twenties. The girl is shy with me and I can barely hear her voice when she says hello. When I shake the boy's hand the girl gives me a sharp, insecure, testing look.

Emanuele and I sit elsewhere. The play begins. The play goes on. Years pass. The clichés keep coming. There's a sage in a turban, a femme fatale in red lipstick and black heels, a plucky young girl who takes off her shirt, a young male clown, a randy old man, a woman who's lost her children and will do 'whatever it takes' to get them back. Emanuele is in constant forward-backward, eye-rubbing, watch-checking, face-massaging movement next to me, trying not to fall asleep. Eventually it's over. He asks me ironically if I'm OK. The playwright comes out onto the stage. He's a tall, thin, middle-aged man with red hair and a beard, so pale that he disappears under the lights. Nobody claps.

We drift down and join Emanuele's perfect young friends. They don't talk to me, not a single question or overture, not a smile, and when I speak they glance mockingly at each other and don't respond. They chat loosely amongst themselves and decide to go for another drink. It's clear I'm not invited. On the vaporetto ride to the theatre I was touching Emanuele's shoulder a lot: look at the colour and line of the velvet jacket, where did he get it from? Such an interesting style. Yes, I had a lot of questions about the jacket. Now I walk well clear of them, and fast as usual – politically difficult because they're walking exceptionally slowly. But I don't know what to do. I can't stride off because he invited me. And yet none of them want me to be a part of the group. We walk until we reach the Riva degli Schiavoni and the sea's in front of us. By chance and not, I think, by choice, Emanuele's next to me.

'I run here,' I say, for something to say. Something else I could say: You erased me when your friends arrived.

'From Frari?' he asks.

'Yup.'

'But that must be... five kilometres.'

'A marathon's forty-four. I run here nearly every day.'

'Up to?'

'Sant'Elena. Plus a few times up and down Zattere.'

He falls back in astonishment. We wait for Tiziana and Gina and the others and all drift along the river together. I like the older people, no vibe, no games, no bullshit, of whom Stef told her parents over dinner, 'Bidisha's fallen in with a set of rich old Venetian wankers.' Gina tails off and says goodbye to me nicely.

'Mum, did you eat? Aren't you going to have dinner?' Emanuele asks her.

'Oh! No. I'm fine. I had this little mozzarella thing...'

I spy an anorexic. Tiziana also leaves, loping away towards St Mark's.

'And where are *you* going?' Emanuele asks me pointedly.

'Oh. Um. Accademia,' I say, hoping that's in the opposite direction to where he's going.

'So you're going with Tiziana?' he says even more pointedly.

'What? Oh yes!'

A quick kiss and a ciao to his friends, which they return so feebly that their voices make no sound. I turn around, bump straight back into him, get a mouthful of his jacket (the jacket I love so much), then run on and call Tiziana. We walk along together and finally I relax. Tiziana is very quiet and seems low. We stroll across St Mark's Square.

'I love this place,' I say, 'even if it is all horrible and touristy.'

'No, no,' she assures me gently, 'St Mark's is ours. It's always beautiful, always.'

'And the other thing to mention is that this is the time of the evening that I always feel like having an ice cream.'

'Ah, now *I* could have an ice cream...'

We go to a *gelateria* next to Caffè Quadri and I make a big show of offering Tiziana an ice cream, telling her to choose exactly what she wants, saying it's some small return for the kindness she showed me and then, when we've both ordered, I open my wallet and realise it's completely empty. I'd spent all my money on the play and vaporetto tickets. I instantly lose my temper with myself, feel a blush rise all over my head and walk away furiously, snapping my wallet shut, and of course now Tiziana offers to pay for everything, telling me all the while that this is nothing, I can pay next time, this is a tiny detail and so on and so forth. I do what she says and tell myself to forget it. I have two scoops, hazelnut and chocolate, on a cone. We walk slowly together and turn back for one last look around the square, the arched windows, the sparkling lights and gold-coloured darkness, before turning in towards Accademia.

I ask after little Luca and Tiziana's mum (both are fine). I get the feeling that Tiziana wants to be alone but is too polite to say so. I ask her if she's tired and she says, yes, a little. We look in at the shops – Etro, Ferragamo, Gucci. Tiziana has disdain for Louis Vuitton and I agree, it tries too hard.

'Except,' I say as we pass a knock-off bag seller in the street, 'this flat multicoloured satchel.'

'Now that is pretty,' she says.

Immediately the seller's on us, speaking fast English-Italian:

'How much you wanna pay? Nice ladies. Gimme forty? No? You like bags? How much you wanna pay?'

We notice a stain on the bag and drift away. Tiziana tells me she bought a 'Prada' bag from a hawker about a year ago, uses it every day, it works perfectly and nobody can tell the difference.

We kiss goodbye at Campo Santo Stefano and I drift home feeling as though I've had a good and necessary evening in which I looked my own nothingness full in the face.

Chapter Twelve

I'm exactly halfway through my stay and I've enjoyed my time here. I love the beauty around me. I don't see it merely as a false mask hiding some 'real' crumbling face, nor are the churches nothing more than dusty museums of forgotten relics. The beauty here is real; even a builder's boat loaded with shovels and hammers looks dainty as it bobs stiffly around a corner. An immense and blissful calm has descended since I moved into my studio in the *campiello* and I love living alone. The weekends bring packages of goodies from home so the postman, a friendly, comfortable-looking man in his forties – perhaps a bit simple? – raps on the door and shouts '*Posta!* Miss Bidisha? A package for you! I think it's from your mother!' up at my window. He can be heard doing this for lucky recipients all over San Polo, a sort of mobile personal information service. I've turned out to be good with money, which is something I never expected, having frittered away nearly every penny I made when I was younger. I've discovered the ascetic inner me: frugal of food and finance, disciplined in work and exercise – and clean! Astounding. I certainly set no precedent for it before. I love having no television and find that not only do I not miss it, but that the few films I see outside I experience with greater attention, sensitivity and patience than before. I am never lonely. It is refreshing too to be in a place where people are not afraid of the streets or the darkness and don't live their lives crippled with the imagined terrors that are so common in a larger city. And thanks to the patronage of Stef's family I can see that there is a certain (narrow) stream of Venetian society which, as the cliché goes, is truly serene, civilised, unsleazy, intelligent, polished and composed.

Underneath the cordiality, however, there is a crabbed conservatism which is dismaying in its obviousness, its hypocrisy and in the speed with which Venetians can switch from the former mode to the latter. And so much of the pleasantness of daily life here is linguistic: it's to be found in the easily flowing orders, questions, enquiries, purchases, pleases, thank yous, remonstrations and avowals that form part of any person's rota of quotidian errands and arrangements. These are hard to adopt with any naturalness if you're a stranger, no matter how good your Italian is, especially from someone who so obviously – racially – has no claim to familiarity with Italian culture.

During the cool, pewter grey days of September I come out only to run, trying to beat the sunset, which starts at seven-fifteen. The twilight lasts barely half an hour, then it all goes dark blue and that's that. I'm a familiar San Marco sprinter now. Before, the waiters used to stare interestedly. Now they stare uninterestedly.

It seems that now summer is over the locals have reverted, all on the same day, to their customary creamy colour. I remain thoroughly brown all over and, chillingly, there's a very distinct difference in the way I'm treated once it's shown that I am definitely, obviously non-Italian. One day I visit the cheap everything-shop in Campo Santa Margherita. The lady in front of me in the queue is having a lively, chatty conversation with the woman behind the till. They finish in good spirits and she leaves.

'Hello,' I say to the woman behind the till, not in a strange way. No reply.

'Two forty-seven,' she says when she's processed my items.

I hand her the money.

'Don't give it to me like *that*, put it down on the counter,' she says with a look of disgust.

I comply.

'Let's see if I have the seven...' I begin to say. Venetian shopkeepers like it when you have the right change. The woman ignores me, takes the money I've already laid down and puts the change on the counter.

'Ah! Right. Thanks,' I say, prising the coins up with my nail.

She doesn't reply. I take the bag she's left for me.

'Bye,' I say.

She doesn't reply. There's no one else in the shop. I get the same treatment in the post office, a newsagent's and a chemist in San Polo when I buy some sunblock – the cheerfully flowing conversation before me, the complete silence when it's my turn.

One minor realisation is that I am not going into Gobbetti's again for a while. I walk in one afternoon and before I can open my mouth the auburn-haired woman and her young colleague both shout 'Cappuccino, *deca*' into my face, look at each other and laugh uproariously (and not kindly). Ha ha ha. It appears that I am a little ridiculous for coming in so frequently, always being alone and always ordering the same thing in too blunt a tone. The two other customers in the shop give me a lesson in how to do it: they're friends, and they approach the counter with a cool, sauntering look. The impression is that they have nothing to do later today except a couple of family errands... and this may well be true. They enquire about the different types of coffee they could have.

'Madam,' comes the answer, 'I have the perfect thing for you: a shot of creamy espresso with the lightest scoop of froth, something I'll whip up myself right now, served in a clear beaker so you can see that rich colour the coffee has. And if you're worried for your figure there is absolutely no need, Madam, we use skimmed milk to keep the froth as light as can be.'

That is the way it's done: poetic, assertive, leisurely, utterly charming. One is not supposed to *skulk* the way I do.

Afterwards I go to another *pasticceria* in my neighbourhood, Pasticceria di Bucintole, along one of the dripping-stone, one-person alleyways. There's a high counter, a multiplicity of bite-size desserts, hot chocolates, drinks and coffees on offer.

An utterly unsmiling woman serves me. She's stocky and dark-haired and resembles a cook in a period drama: large face, strong forearms, etc.

'Good day!' I chirp.

'Good day.'

'Could I possibly have a decaffeinated cappuccino?'

'Yes.'

'And...' It's clear that the woman won't help me if I don't know the names of all the cakes and ask what each one contains, so I go with what I can recognise, 'A little piece of tiramisu to go with it?'

'Yes.'

'And could I possibly sit inside?' I peep.

'Yes. Take a seat. I'll bring it to you.'

She does. The tiramisu is moist, bittersweet, a little almondy, and it hits the spot. Altogether it's three euros, very reasonable. When the woman delivers it I smile and say thank you. No response. She goes back behind the counter. Then two older Italian businessmen enter, their heels clicking. The woman looks up, smiles and instantly turns to full, prompt, sunny devotion. One of the men addresses her smartly: me master, you servant. She's deliriously happy to be his servant.

'Now,' snaps the man. 'Two coffees. One, a plain espresso, with a glass of water, very cold. The other, a *caffè macchiato*. And we'll also have some *pastine*. Now tell me, what's this one here?'

'That is a fruit tart,' she replies clearly and confidently and with a certain rich humour, 'containing blueberries, blackberries and strawberries, made fresh today by hand.'

'And this?' He points at something else.

'Zabaglione.'

'And what's that other one there?'

'That is pear and chocolate, sir. A pear and chocolate tart,' she says with a twinkle.

'Ah! I see, I see. Fine. One of these for myself and one of those for my friend. Thank you.'

I sit in the adjoining room writing this down while pretending to peruse the local paper. Occasionally a Venetian businessman comes in, has a lightning-quick espresso, wipes his little lips on a paper napkin, screws the napkin into a ball with one hand, tosses it into the brass bin and marches out again. The waitress gives a private satisfied sigh as each one goes.

On the upside, though, I'm convinced that the girl who works at the quaint cotton shop may have a little fascination with me. I am *most* gratified. I go in there looking for another little present for Mum. The girl's working at a sewing table, stitching seed-pearl beads to the edge of a white tablecloth. She's pale and soft-faced with lovely red-haired Celtic colouring, freckles, intelligent hazel eyes, jeans and jumper, a studious type. When I walk in she gives a little start and I think, 'Again, I've got the protocol wrong.' Then she tells me nicely that if I'd like to take a closer look at anything I should just let her know and she'll bring it down for me. I select a napkin from the display and together we open a box and hunt for one which has my mother's initial embroidered on it. When I'm paying, the girl pauses, looks at me with a mild, slow, bright look and says:

'I've seen you run here a lot. A number of times. Where are you from?'

'I live in Frari,' I say, surprised, 'but I'm from England.'

'But are you a student at the university?' asks the girl.

'No, a writer, but really a tourist,' I reply.

'Because I saw you, I've seen you, and I was just thinking...' says the girl, making a face to express recognition and wonderment. She's looking at me whole-faced, with a question, and very charming, but my Italian runs out and I leave the shop feeling suitably flattered and pink all over.

That night brings a fantastic, streaming, windy, spraying, pale grey rainstorm, wave after wave of it flying off the roofs and corners of the houses in the *campiello*. The sky's full of immense round drops of water tumbling very slowly onto the stone. My windows steam up. The storm continues with its beautiful sound, horse-drawn chariots racing overhead and a whistling flutelike wind. As well as the snapping thunder and the falling rain I hear the dull crack of wooden shutters swinging to and fro in the wind.

The next day is nothing but mild yellow sun, a sated atmosphere and not a raindrop to be seen. Italian shoes clicking on the stone.

I'm sitting at a table outside the white-tableclothed 'old people's cafe' in Campo Santa Margherita, as Ginevra puts it.

A group of French tourists arrives at the cafe, two women in their early fifties (groomed russet hair in tortoiseshell clips, fawn cashmere coats, brown leather boots, good bags, all unshowy and expensive as hell) with two girls of about thirteen, very well behaved, beautiful long fair hair, pale untouched-looking skin, quietly talking amongst themselves. Finally a boy of about sixteen, a thoughtful chubby poet-type, rich and contented, with a long grey thinkers' overcoat and perfectly laundered white shirt, grown-out brown hair, full lips, dark eyes. The boy says he'll order coffees and pastries for everyone and invites the girls to come and help him choose. They pick their way through the other tables and chairs to the dark interior.

The two women are left seated. After some more minute chat one of them gets up to join her children inside. Slowly she goes between the tables and chairs. As she does so she knocks over two chairs with her hip. Instead of catching them as they fall, she turns and watches them impassively. As they hit the ground noisily she says a slow, loud 'Oh la la!' She steps over the chairs and walks into the cafe and is in there a long time. The woman's friend has also seen all this and does nothing about the chairs. She watches them for a while, then looks away and scans the square with a luxurious scenery-enjoying smile. I'm goggling into thin air. After a long while the owner of the cafe comes out and stares in puzzlement at the toppled chairs before stooping stiffly and setting them upright. She's about seventy years old, at least.

October begins with a bright cold snap so severe that even my miserliness can't withstand it and I'm forced to purchase a coat and jumper and some gloves. Tiziana comes over and I pay her my last bit of rent. It rains all night and clears every day, but at eight in the morning for the last two days the high water sirens have sounded – great doomy blitz-wails, *woah-aarggghhh-oooh*, loud enough to be heard in every corner of the city and pop open all the coffins in the floating cemetery. When I first heard them I shot up in panic thinking someone had bombed the city or that I'd done something personally wrong and God was calling me to account. I come out to see the Venetians as chic and unruffled as ever, only with the addition of rubber wellies, but not big green chunky British ones, no. Theirs are subtly coloured and sleekly shaped around the calf and ankle, like riding boots. There are long ramps and tables running along the main streets, like fashion catwalks, conveying people up over the water.

'High water,' the people are saying to each other with a sanguine shrug – *acqua alta*, 'every year.'

San Marco under high water is really something, resembling a sparkling mirrored box with four tiers. In all it looks wonderful but (I must piously remember) it does wreck homes, buildings and businesses.

When the water level goes down a bit I emerge for rations and annoy myself by watching a local resident (although I don't think he's Italian, I think he's English) cheat the supermarket. He's around sixty-five, a shambling watercolourist type, tall, pale and baggy-bodied with a wiry white beard, wearing old linen clothes, espadrilles and a battered panama hat. I'm watching him fill his plastic bag to the brim with expensive black grapes. He places it heavy and open on the computerised scales. Then he puts his hand in and scoops up three-quarters of the grapes, holding them aloft so that they don't register. With the other hand he presses the button that says 'Grapes'. And so what does the scale say? Ah! Only eighty-five cents for all those luxury grapes.

One Friday I go out with Ginevra and Stef to see a pretty bad film on the Lido, *La Vita Che Vorrei*. Stef's in love with the actor from the film. During a drink afterwards at Muro in Campo San Luca later she rhapsodises about him:

'He's so beautiful!'

'What! He is *not*,' Ginevra and I protest. 'He looks like a little boy.'

'But that's beautiful. Although he does walk funny,' Stef admits.

'Yes, he picks his knees up too high,' I say, 'I noticed that too.'

'But!' she shouts over me to rehabilitate his cult. 'You haven't seen him in his greatest role.' She mentions a film. 'It follows three generations of one family. A masterpiece.'

'A travesty,' says Ginevra next to me.

Stef cannot stand being teased and begins to get cross:

'Imagine the virtuosity required of an actor to portray a life over thirty years —'

'We see him in short trousers,' says Ginevra stolidly. 'We see him in long trousers. We see him in an overcoat. Finally we see him with an artificial beard and talcum powder in his hair.'

The middle of October brings a clutch of ruthlessly good-looking Christmas-cold days. I cross the Campo dei Frari and tuck myself into the tiny two-table cafe next to the *gelateria*. I love the coffee here, eighty cents, hot and flavourful. Plus the newspapers, the well-stocked napkin holders and the people-watching opportunities. There is a group of splendid old ladies at the other table, one with an enormous crocodile skin handbag that she parks on my table, big, black and boxy as a London taxi.

The youngish guy who works there looks at me, a bright long glance, as he hands over my macchiato.

'Where are you from?' he asks suddenly.

'Mm?'

'You aren't Italian,' he says.

'No, I'm a Londoner. But my parents are from India.'

'So you're an Indian from London.'

'Yes,' I say, unable to translate 'second generation British Asian'.

'What work do you do in Venice?' asks the guy.

'I'm a tourist... but I'm also a writer, and I have to finish a bit of work. I'm looking for some... peace? Inspiration? Thanks,' I say, taking the coffee.

'Thanks from Venice,' he replies pleasantly.

Afterwards I go for a walk in Campo St M. University term's started and I see students crossing the square with art portfolios and university bags. I've just given myself a fresh haircut and been mocked for it – 'No-hair!' – by some teenaged boys sitting on a bench. There are a few specks of red and yellow in the dry old trees in the middle of the square. In Caffè Causin I watch an intriguing woman. She's about eighty, upright, with a French pleat of buffed white hair, dressed in a rich green suit with a long tapering skirt, a white silk scarf tucked close into her collar, a stiff black trilby, black patent leather shoes and handbag, scarlet lips, with a long black and gold Chinese necklace hanging across her front. Accompanied by a little white terrier who licks my leg. I wonder at first if she's a renowned artist or writer but over the next few weeks I see her day after day, always at the same table, each time in a new elegant outfit, always with the dog, and when she glances up at me, worried in case the dog's bothering me too much, her eyes are full of timidity as though I might hit her.

At some point during this time I try my longest run yet, a full four hours in the middle of the day. It goes well, although I'm sure that I'm jogging more slowly than most people walk. At the end of the run I'm coming tiredly back along the Riva degli Schiavoni. On one of the bridges I'm too weary to pick my foot up enough and trip over the edge of the top step, splattering myself across the bridge on my knees and knuckles. The woman who was coming up the other side — sixties, hard-working, menial face, beige mac, sensible shoes — stops crossly and barks, 'Anything broken?' At first I mishear her and think she's said, 'Are you OK?' so I get up and brush myself down, laughing and saying enthusiastically, 'Yes, yes, I'm fine!' I look youthfully and smilingly into her face and see there a look that chills me. She's rooted to the spot not with concern but with revulsion, her eyes hard and small, frowning deeply, her lip curled in disapproval, her whole face a tightly-gathered purse. Why? Because I'm badly dressed and did an inelegant thing by strewing myself like litter across the floor.

The next day I've been invited for lunch with Stef, Bruno, Gregorio and Lucrezia. I put on my new coat and jumper, crack open a new white shirt and saunter into the cold an hour early, feeling great — people to see, places to go, schedule to keep. There are loads of people around and for once I feel part of the busy little community of Venice. A couple of steps away from my door two guys walk past. Medium-bulky, not slick, not rough, in trainers and fashionable jeans. One puts his mouth to my ear and makes a long, loud, slow, juicy kiss. After four months of this every single day, five or six times a day, I snap, spin around and blurt, 'Oh *fuck off*, for God's sake,' my entire body recoiling. The guy also spins around:

'What's that?' he says in garbled English, squaring up to me. '"Fuck you?"'

And then of course I feel the tremor of fear, because his shoulder tenses and he's ready to hit me. I turn on my heel, don't run, don't stop or look back, only walk out of the *campiello* shaking my head in disgust. How is it that Venice can be so sublime and such a sewer at the same time? How can it love elegance and loathe women? Once outside Frari church I ruthlessly clear my mind because I'd been looking forward to this day and had decided in advance that I'd enjoy it.

I meet everyone and we go to a large Venetians-only restaurant, very hot and steamy, thick with family conversation, full of the smell of gently-cooked meat. The conversation turns to a wedding that Stef went to for a Croatian-Italian friend of hers and how Eastern Europeans have integrated well into Italian culture.

'When we were growing up the Eastern Europeans were always *strange*,' says Lucrezia, wrinkling her nose in distaste, 'not Italian... but when I finally became friends with them, I saw that they spoke a beautiful Italian, completely natural. You can't tell they're not Italian! They integrate perfectly, they live a completely Italian lifestyle.'

'When you've grown up in a country that isn't stable and you know everything could change from one day to the next, it makes you adaptable,' says Stefania. 'People from these countries, you could put them anywhere and they'll be all right.'

'It helps that they're white to look at, so the host culture gets over its first hurdle,' I can't help throwing in.

'No. It is not the colour of their skin,' says Stef edgily, but the conversation moves on.

Later that evening Stef enables me to experience the commodious civility of the Italian private health service. I need a certificate for the marathon and Ginevra has donated me the one-off use of her doctor. Tucked around the corner of Rialto, on my side, is a long, narrow doctors' waiting room, perfumed and gently lit. The building's old wooden columns have been integrated into the architecture of the place, which feels like the lobby of a boutique hotel in jazz age New York.

Stefania comes in and asks the nearest waiting woman who's next in line. A cordial conversation ensues as she ascertains that two doctors are in this evening, and who is waiting for whom. I lurk at her shoulder. I could never live here permanently. I don't have the volubility, can't follow the rules or get into the oddly formal flow of daily exchanges, straight out of a GCSE Italian role-play textbook. We come in and sit down, greeting people left and right. Stefania has a carrier bag containing some smart leather shoes that she's just had re-heeled and the man two seats along moves his coat off the next chair so that she can put her bag on the seat. Unwritten Venetian rule: don't put plastic bags on the floor. I don't know why. I spy the usual chic people, like the lady in cappuccino colours with a slouchy buttery-caramel leather bag, everything – shades, watch, hair slide, shoes – matching. She may be at death's door but I see she can still coordinate her outfit.

'Jesus!' I say, looking around. 'This is a revelation. Look how chic it is.'

'It's very quiet today,' says Stef disappointedly. 'Usually there are some interesting conversations going on. But look at these nice pillars.'

'In England you never speak. You just look straight ahead. You never speak!'

We finally gain entry to the doctor's surgery, which smells of roses and violets. The doctor is an exquisitely pretty, gentle, oval-faced petite woman, soft-skinned and pale with soft brown eyes, fine sable-coloured bobbed hair and pristine white lab coat. She has a wonderful way of talking, very beseeching, laying her hand on her heart as she speaks. She looks at us both with a mild, sweet, questioning expression; Stef immediately goes into her expert patter:

'Good evening, Doctor, we're friends of Ginevra Tealdi, your patient. My English friend here needs a certificate to do the marathon... do you mind if I sit down? Thank you... and we just wondered what it involved.'

The marathon organisers require a respiratory test, urine sample, lung scan and other highly neurotic tortures. Strange. In London they just take your registration fee and sling you in the pen with all the other chumps. The doctor phones a colleague to set up the tests for me and they have a delightfully civilised conversation:

'Good evening, Doctor Giulio? I do hope I'm – no? – ah! I'm fine. Thank you, what a kind enquiry. Now, I have a young girl here who's planning on doing the marathon...'

She notes down my name and gets me to sign a piece of paper to prove that I've been to see her. The paper, I can't help but notice, is custom made with her name inscribed in coppery italics. With many sweet and gentle exhortations she refuses to accept a fee for helping us. She sprinkles fairy dust on us from her fingertips and then flutters us away and we float out.

'A very nice woman,' says Stef faintly.

'A *very* nice woman,' I echo.

We go on to meet Ginevra at Billa, where we buy provisions for that night's dinner (to be made by Ginevra) and get quite hysterical over it, especially when choosing the wine. There are a few other similar groups of young people at the supermarket, all doing the same thing. I feel fresh and free and female and fun.

'You know Ginevra is an excellent cook,' says Stef to me.

'*Are* you?' I ask Ginevra, smiling.

'Yes,' she says bashfully.

'What can you cook?'

'She can make anything,' says Stef, 'like last year she made a famous Roman bread – a piece of bread with risotto inside that I still remember.'

'It became legendary,' Ginevra admits.

'And she had her Sicilian period.'

'I'm still in my Sicilian period,' corrects Ginevra.

'And she had her French period, with a selection of five cheeses.'

It's my job to put the trolley back once we've finished, and I do so. Afterwards I run back to where Ginevra and Stef are waiting on the street.

'Did you get the euro?' Stef asks me.

'What euro?'

'The euro from the trolley.'

'*You get it back?*'

'What?!' Stef and Ginevra shriek.

'Oh my God,' I say faintly. 'I thought the trolley cost one euro...'

The other two find this hilarious.

'Sorry to say it, Bidisha, but you are really a writer,' Stef manages to say.

'I've never used a trolley before,' I admit. 'Not even in England. I can never steer it, and I can never carry all the stuff home afterwards.'

'You've never used a trolley before?' scream the other two.

Laughing terribly I run back inside, rifle through the trolleys and retrieve the bloody coin. At Stef's place I sit in the kitchen while Ginevra works busily.

'If you want me to leave tell me,' I say.

'I am waiting for the... garlic?... to cook. Can you open a bottle of wine – can you?'

'Of course I can!'

'I am sorry if I'm not making conversation. I am concentrating.'

'Of course. Don't apologise.'

'I am totally absorbed. I want to make a good impression.'

Stef comes in.

'*Please* give me something to do,' I beg.

'No,' says Stef. She has strong views on what guests are and are not permitted to do. Ginevra says something to her in Italian.

'OK, you can grate the Parmesan,' says Stef to me grudgingly.

I do so, with zeal.

'Is that not enough or too much?' I say after a while.

'It depends on if the risotto is good or not,' says Ginevra. 'If it is bad, you add the *parmigiano* and it becomes good.'

We lay the table with the heavy pottery set that Ginevra bought Stefania upon her graduation. There's good music in the background, which I'll now always associate with Venice, with the water. It's by Cat Power.

'What's this album called?' I ask Stef.

'Um... Feel Free and, um, Be Brave and, um...'

'Sleep well,' says Ginevra, 'and don't forget to take your medicine.'

I burst out laughing (the album's called *You Are Free*). The risotto's perfect, molten and hot, with asparagus and a touch of cheese. There's also a soft Spanish omelette with courgettes and a good white wine. I'm a pig, as ever when taking advantage of someone else's food talents. Seeing the two of them lighting up at the end of the meal I say, 'If you're both having cigarettes then I'm going to have some more risotto.'

After she's finished her cigarette Ginevra lights another and asks me, 'I'm having another cigarette, would you like some more risotto?'

Shame on me, I take it – but I do clear up afterwards. As we're relaxing around the table later Stef and Ginevra mention a few dozen Italian cultural heroes of song, screen, page and stage, none of whom I've heard of.

'It is a pity that in Europe we know so much about England and American culture,' says Stef.

'But we know so little about your culture,' I finish.

'It is unfortunate.'

'But you are the Empire and we worship you,' Ginevra jokes.

'But to put the nice side of the bad situation, we Italians can say that we are lucky to have knowledge of more than one culture,' says Stef. 'Can I offer you a coffee?'

'Yes, please, if that's OK,' I say.

Stef and Ginevra laugh.

'At the end of the day,' Stef says to Ginevra, 'she is really an English woman.'

Chapter Thirteen

Well, I don't do the marathon. I go to the expo in Margher to pick up all my bits and pieces for it and manage to get ou of providing the health certificate and paying a foreigners' fe by being excessively incompetent, to the point that the olde chap organising the queue grabs my hand, holds it aloft an shouts, 'Hey, everyone, this girl's come from England and can understand a single thing that's going on. Let's all help her successfully bringing the entire expo to a bemused halt. The he turns to me and demands, half-mockingly, 'Is there anythin I can do for you, in this humidity? Would you like some wate Do you speak the Venetian dialect? Would you like to take a sea Would you like a biscuit?' Anyway, the result of this performanc is that everything is fixed in my favour.

I get home, work for the rest of the day, go upstairs and la out my shoes, bib, safety pins, bum bag, sunblock, shorts an socks, do my stretches, go to bed and sleep right through it. I sleep through the runners' buses at Tronchetto, the journey to the start line in Stra, the sunrise, the beginning and middle of the race, the fast finish on the Riva degli Schiavoni, the makeshift bridge between the two slices of coast, the prize-giving, the champions' celebration and the results. Exhausted from my work, training and fun-making I sleep, like a fairytale character, until the middle of the afternoon.

Later on, zombified by my own stupidity, I wander around the nearby streets trying to bury my guilt but keep seeing guys in trainers with medals. They're all the same type: bald, wiry, orange-tanned virile types like upright racing dogs. I go down to the course at exactly the time that I'd be crossing it myself at Zattere, and it's depressing. No crowds, no atmosphere, just thrown-away Gatorade bottles and Venetians going about their business and ignoring the limping runners: 'Look at these daft puffing *stronzi* taking up space when I'm trying to stroll along the waterfront with my Billa groceries.'

The story of my marathon non-starter is received with high hilarity by everyone.

'Now we will not be able to believe anything you say,' teases Ginevra, 'for example I do not believe you have ever done a marathon in London.'

A couple of days later, at the end of October, Emanuele calls – showing a nice contrition, given his behaviour last time. It's just as I'm working downstairs and the phone rings.

'Bidisha?' says a young male voice.

'Yes?'

'Emanuele.'

'Oh my God!' I have no time to be nervous so the conversation proceeds in Italian, even though I ask him how he is about three times. But lucky me, the laugh in his voice when he replies each time shows me that he finds it intoxicating. He proposes an aperitif. I say yes.

We arrange to meet at Toppo, the blue bar a few steps from my front door. I feel unhealthily pleased and force my mind back to my work for the rest of the day. At the appropriate time I take a shower and dress carefully: powder blue jumper, straight jeans and my plain old lace-up shoes (well – I have no other shoes, shirt, jumper or trousers with me), plus the new coat. I stuff a huge Italian dictionary into my bag. I also need some kind of prop to keep my hands busy but can't find anything in the apartment except for a banana, which I take with me. It's dark and there are a lot of people out enjoying a drink. Unfortunately I'm so hungry and nervous that I eat the banana in two big mouthfuls and am holding the skin in my hand when, just as the Frari bell-tower strikes seven, Emanuele crosses the square, darts up the steps and calls hello. Swiftly, naturally and warmly we kiss on both cheeks, then I hold up the banana skin, which I've produced from my side like conjurer, forget all my Italian, indicate the dustbin, run away, dump the banana skin and run back (not winsomely) before he's had a chance to log what I was doing and why.

The Frari bells are still ringing, one of my favourite Venetian sounds, great big circles of noise. Emanuele and I look at each other and smile. Rarely have I met anyone who radiates such simple-mindedness, and I mean that in the best way. Like the poetic young rebel he is, Emanuele's flouted the Venetian don't-wear-black rule.

'Perfectly on time,' he says joyfully.

'You look very elegant,' I say.

'All in black,' he chimes in – black velvet jacket, black cashmere jumper, black jeans – 'and you all in blue.'

We walk into Toppo.

'You find seats, I'll order,' he says gallantly. 'A *sprizz*.'

Oh here we go.

'Water,' I say.

'Water? Not a *sprizz*?' he says, puzzled.

'Yes, water.'

'Coca-Cola?'

'No! Water, water.'

'You're sure?'

'Yes, I'm sure. I've had a long time to think about it.'

We bicker and insist playfully and I shoo him towards the bar. He dances over and orders. The place is crowded, people of all ages but equal elegance chattering, music playing, the deceased blue-lipped owner holding forth behind the bar. Emanuele delivers the drinks, sits down on a chair, me on a banquette, our poses mirroring but not speaking to each other – legs tightly crossed, both tense, separately worried.

'I've brought along my best friend, Mr Dictionary,' I say.

I hold up the dictionary. Emanuele laughs and gives me the thumbs up. I have drunk all the water. He has had two sips of his *sprizz*. I can't think of anything to say.

'I have a lot of questions for you,' I say boldly. 'Research. I may as well use you for my purposes.'

'Questions!' He smiles at me, flattered. 'What questions?'

'Well, let me see. What're you doing at the moment?'

'Studying for my exams,' he says promptly. 'I have four at the end of the year. I'm studying at the library in Campo Santa Maria Formosa. Do you know it? When I'm there it seems to me like the most beautiful library in the world.'

I nod and smile slightly and realise that even though he is perfectly fluent and nice in English, he has a divine, graceful way of speaking in Italian.

'You don't like to study alone?' I ask.

'No, it makes me feel too isolated.'

'Really? I can't concentrate when other people are near me. And you live,' I prompt, and we both say 'with Mum!'

'And after your exams? What'll you do then?'

'I have to write my thesis.'

'And after that?'

'I don't know. I'd like to go to Rome, then to London for a while.'

'If you'd like to stay with us, please do, there's plenty of room.'

'No, no, thank you, but I've got a friend – we've known each other since we were little kids – I can stay with her.'

'And after London?'

'After London!' he repeats, looking exhausted.

'Do you want to be a teacher, a writer, a philosopher?'

'None of those things – well, maybe a professor, with a nice pipe to smoke. But really, I'd like to be a graphic designer, although I don't have the background for it.'

Having secretly wanted to be a designer all my life I approve of this.

'I thought I might study in London,' he says tentatively.

'Absolutely. You should apply. It's the ideal place for you. It's difficult though. If you want to go to St Martin's, the best place.'

'It's difficult?' he repeats worriedly.

'Yes. I mean, it's difficult but if you're talented then it's easy.'

'Ah! I understand.'

Having run out of questions and lacking the ideas, vocabulary and inclination to advance the talk to more reflexive territory, I sit in silence and grind my teeth for quite some time.

'How's the work going?' Emanuele asks me.

'Ah. It's fine. It's OK.'

The truth is, it's going terribly. My instinct is that it'll never come out, at least not in its current form; the harder I work at it the louder my instincts shout against it.

'Have you finished?' asks Emanuele.

'Nearly. I have a bit of checking left to do. And then,' I sigh, 'I'll say it in English: sometimes I think that I haven't done anything interesting at all. I've just stuck on some conversation – not conversation – words, meaningless words...'

'Chat,' he says, understanding immediately.

Again we lapse into silence.

'I can't speak today,' I apologise. 'I've spent too much time indoors.'

Still, we do manage to keep a decent conversation going, fuelled by tremendous goodwill and hard linguistic labour on both sides.

'I've finished my *sprizz*,' he says after a while, with comical alcoholic suggestiveness.

I begin to smile and let myself be beguiled.

'And now?' I say.

'A white wine, but I can't drink if you don't. What could you have?'

'Oh, no... well, OK, a red wine.'

'A red wine! Excellent choice. Stay there, I'll get them.'

I lean back and watch him while he orders. He brings the drinks and we taste them.

'Good wine?' he asks me.

'Very good. And instantly my Italian's better too. We're wearing the same shoes,' I gloomily notice.

'So we are! I have an obsession with shoes. I'm always trying to find ones which don't have big fat soles.'

'Ones which don't look like boats,' I agree. 'I'm always trying to find ones in a masculine style, but for women. It's impossible, you have to get them made.'

'You know what time it is?'

'What time *is* it?' I purr.

'Postali's open by now. We can have another glass there.'

I smile out at him broadly, not at the prospect of another drink but at his easy charm. We get up together and go over to pay. He refuses to let me pay and elbows me out of the way laughingly (and again, as at Do Forni, I notice how physically strong he is). The bar owner watches us with a tight and knowing smile, not indulgent, more of a bored, '*plus ça change...*' rictus.

Outside in the cool unpopulated darkness we walk to Postali, which is almost empty. The grey-haired sexy owner, Roberto, greets us both familiarly. Emanuele sticks with white wine, me with red, a Refosco, and we sit outside in the same attitude, slumped with one elbow on the canal railing, facing each other. Boats knock gently beside us. Our table's directly in front of the door and I feel exposed to it, feng shui-wise, so I put an empty chair in front of it.

'For my imaginary friend,' I explain, toasting the chair.

'And here you are speaking Italian,' he says.

'But I can't speak either in the past or the future. Only the present.'

'But that is an excellent approach.'

'A very Buddhist approach,' I agree.

'Moving through life perpetually in the moment, not overshadowed by memories of the past, not constrained by hopes or anxieties about the future. It's a good way to live.'

We laugh and share a slow, twinkling silence. I tell him I've booked my ticket to go home.

'Isn't it true that you fall in love with a place when you're about to leave it?' he asks.

'Maybe,' I say, circumspect. 'But there's something else. I can't say it in Italian, I'll say it slowly in English: I thought that when I came to Venice, "everything" would happen.'

He nods once, silent.

'I know what you mean. When I went to Paris I thought the same thing,' he says eventually. 'The only thing that happened was that I got robbed in the Marais at five o'clock in the morning. It was at a cashpoint. I got my money out, turned around and immediately there was this guy on me, he held a knife to my throat and told me to give him the money. I said, "Please! Be my guest!" and off he went. I was shaking...'

I sit there, hand clapped to my mouth, eyebrows knotted in empathetic alarm. Robbed at knifepoint in a bad area: the ultimate yuppie nightmare.

'The lesson is not to have any expectations,' sighs Emanuele.

'But that's difficult. How can you not imagine things, if you're going to a new place? ...How's your wine?'

He wrinkles his nose.

'Average. Yours?'

'Average.'

We lapse into a friendly silence again and I begin to rethink what I've just said. I wanted some scenes of grace and this, I realise, is one of them.

'Tell me, Emanuele, do you have a girlfriend?'

An instant sorrow and aggrieved face like a tragedy mask.

'No,' he wails. 'No girlfriend.'

'Why not?'

'Because she left me!' he yelps with no humour whatsoever, just a bitter gulp of a laugh and a stinging stare into the canal.

'Why? Are you a *stronzo*?' I ask, teasingly on the surface but actually seriously.

'No... no, I'm not a *stronzo*,' he says softly.

His body language has changed in a flash and he's now cowering over the table, smiling grimly with his jaw clenched. Both hands deep in his hair, trying to pull it out at the roots. I note these contortions with deep fascination. He continues:

'She left me because she's having a psychological crisis and because she isn't very intelligent... no, I can't say that, it's a lie. She left me because she wanted time away from me...'

'And *when* did she leave you?' I probe, to back up what Tiziana had told me.

'At the beginning of the summer,' he says with a wry smile.

'The ideal time,' I say with equal wryness.

'But relationships are always hard for me,' he confesses. 'I had a few... moments... with friends. But they did not transport me.'

'I know what you mean, but we don't need to mention them, they're not important.'

'No, they're awful... I have a problem with possessiveness.'

'Ah, really? You, or them?'

'Me. I'm possessive. Worst of all, I'm possessive about the past. About events in the other person's history.'

At this I explode quietly in humorous but real indignation.

'Oh *come on*. That is completely unfair and irrational.' I switch into slow English: 'What a good excuse to bully someone, over something they can't change — and which isn't any of your business anyway — I mean really...'

He bows right down and covers his face with his hands.

'I know!' he moans. 'But it's like a demon that possesses me, I can't help it. The obsession!'

'How convenient! "It wasn't me. It was the demon that did it." You *have* to stop.'

'I know! I know! You're right!' he howls. 'And the other thing is, I hate to be in a couple. I can't function that way, always making consideration for the other person, always being seen as part of a duo by other people.'

'I feel the same way,' I say seriously. 'I hate the feeling of being closed in a room with just the other person, it makes me claustrophobic. I like being alone. I like working alone. I like to sleep alone.'

'I like having a double bed, but just for *me*,' he declares.

I smile.

'I've been single for a much longer time than you. And I was basically single for all the years before that too,' I say.

'Are you happy about that?'

'I *am*, actually. My fantasies are much worse, they're about work and travel and fame!'

'*Much* worse!'

'I do miss the kissing, *some*times. But then I did have big metal braces for two whole years after my teens. With elastic bands going from the top to the bottom. And believe me there's no getting over *that*, no matter how interesting a person you are.'

'And was it worth it?'

'For my teeth? Yes I'm very happy with them...'

'You have great teeth...'

'Thank you, everybody says so...'

'And they're so white...'

'I brush them very carefully. And the gums as well. That's the secret.'

'Maybe you don't like life to give you any surprises,' says Emanuele.

'Maybe. But let's leave this discussion.'

'Yes, after two glasses of wine the conversation is always about love,' he says woefully.

'OK, we'll change the subject. I'll tell you something I've noticed and you can tell me why,' I say. 'Venetians are very elegant.'

'Do you think so?'

'Certainly. They have this classic style that I love. Amazing use of colour.'

'It's because Venice is a small place and not a commercial centre. It isn't touched by passing trends and fashions, so the style remains but the fads don't. Although I do have some friends of my own age who dress like they're forty years old! Some of them look like they could be friends of my mother! Honestly, I can't tell them apart. "Mum?" In cities like Rome and Milan the young people all look the same, as though they've stepped out of an MTV video.'

'I prefer the classic style. Classic shapes.'

'Me too,' he says, 'because really I'm an old man. I've been forty since I was eight. And I have old-man values too. I think about my digestion, and I can't lie, I just can't, it makes me feel awful.'

'Me too!' I chime in happily.

'And I like people to call when they say they will. And I respect punctuality. And directness in speech.'

'I noticed. You really *are* a little adult.'

'I told you! I'm a very old man.'

Then something happens which reminds me yet again that I could never be deep friends with Emanuele. Two people walk past, a guy and a girl, and Emanuele, recognising them, shoots to his feet to greet them, instinctively turning his back to me. I'm left staring up at the three of them. I don't 'mind' because I don't consider this to be my real life – my real life is with Stef and Ginevra, and alone. As it turns out I know the guy vaguely because he's an acquaintance of Stef's. The girl is silent by his side and when he mentions that he's been to the doctor's she makes a sorry face, strokes his arm comfortingly and appeals to us for group sympathy for him. He doesn't really react, merely blinks like an emperor. For the duration of the conversation between Emanuele and the guy, which goes on for fifteen minutes, Emanuele ignores me and the guy ignores the girl. When I smile at her she gives me a blankly hostile look.

We finish our wine. This time I insist on paying. We are very jostly, friendly with each other. As I'm paying, Emanuele finds a strange coin in his pocket.

'What is it?' I ask.

'It's a Mexican dollar. There. I give it to you as a present.'
I laugh with delight at the gesture and look at the coin carefully. He joins me and we stand with our heads close together.

'It's a plant. A cactus,' he says.

'Where? Where?'

'Right there... hang on... oh, I've taken it back.'

'No! It's my present!'

I put it in my pocket and later place it carefully under the little wooden Buddha from my Harry's Bar evening. Two Venice mementoes. We walk back towards Frari church.

'The barmen at Postali and Toppo look similar, don't they?' I comment. 'Pale face, grey hair, a little bit like Dracula.'

'They're brothers,' Emanuele jokes.

'But the wine at Postali wasn't great, was it?'

'No, his brother's was better!'

'Shouldn't you be working?' I ask. 'You said you were revising.' We're speaking softly and easily. There's no one around.

'But I am,' he assures me. 'I am with you, but I'm thinking of Karl Popper.'

'Oh, me too. Plato is constantly on my mind.'

'But not really,' he says, playful now. *Yes*, I think sadly, *when nobody else is around to witness your weakness, what a delight you are.* 'When I close a book, that's it. I cease to consider it. But I've left all my stuff at the library.'

As we walk along we bump softly and strongly against each other once. Neither of us particularly notices. Well – I notice. We walk well together, same rhythm, same pace. The alley by the Scuola di San Giovanni Evangelista is dark and empty. We're back on the bridge between Toppo and Frari church and I'm ready to say goodbye. I point out my apartment window and the newspaper hut where Massimo sells his papers.

'So Massimo spoke, and while I was asleep the words drifted up to my room and into my ear, and one day I woke up being able to speak Italian.'

I tell Emanuele about Massimo's insistence on sending everyone to Rialto.

'Maybe he just loves the Rialto Bridge and wants everyone to see it for the benefit of their soul,' he jokes.

'Or maybe he's a *stronzo*.'

'When tourists ask me for help I make certain to give them very clear, detailed instructions, and sometimes I accompany them halfway there.'

'Ah! How nice you are! Oh well.'

I make to turn and leave. We're both on top of the little bridge.

'No! Wait!' says Emanuele. 'Now we're going to Campo Santa Margherita to have some pizza.'

I turn back to him, laughing and positively *full* of red wine. Emanuele's smiling.

'No?' he asks.

'No. Surely not? Are you serious? I have to work.'

'How on earth can you work if you have no food in your stomach? The brain requires sustenance!'

We're stepping around each other laughingly and quite spontaneously reach out, clasp hands and lean back, taking each other's weight. Warm, dry, strong hands. We laugh again and let go.

'OK. I've changed my mind. C'mon. Pizza,' I say.

I set off towards Frari. Emanuele is now humble:

'But are you sure? If you really have to work...'

'No, come on. I do need to eat something.'

In Campo Santa Margherita, unfortunately, I begin to get bored. It's crowded, there's a covers band singing Erasure songs, Emanuele and I dance around minimally. I am now totally sober. While we're eating our slices Emanuele bumps into a couple of friends, one of whom is a wannabe Jim Morrison, but pasty, too tall, too old, too blonde, too pale and too overweight, in cowboy boots and tight beige polyester trousers and so on. And really, this is Venice, pal. Nobody from an LA record company is out scouting here. The guy's friendly and shakes hands with me, then his face changes and he cries out in Italian, 'Ouch! What a pain!' The corner of my square silver thumb ring has pricked him. I apologise and move away. The guy's girlfriend is also with us, vague and silent. Once again I witness a woman being ignored. Eventually we drift away.

We walk back to Accademia together.

'I'll accompany you halfway,' I say with my pathological politeness. 'Good pizza, by the way.'

'I like to eat,' says Emanuele happily. 'Meat. Fish. Sweets. Anything. And I don't do any sports.'

'None?'

'Not for at least a month, anyway. In the summer I swam in the sea every day. But really I'm very much looking forward to getting old, when I can eat all day. I'll have a nice long beard –'

'And a gut,' I point out.

'And a gut. Like Father Christmas.'

'God... how can you do that to yourself? You only have one body, one figure.'

'And you should get the full enjoyment of it!'

'Exactly! So go to the gym. And you know, Father Christmas is a paedophile.'

'No!' cries Emanuele in genuine appalled disbelief, as though I've told him about a terrible crime from that day's newspaper. 'But he's married,' he says, distressed.

'Look,' I retort, 'any guy who breaks into houses and visits children with "a little present" in the middle of the night... and even when he's at home, what about all those little people – I don't know the word –'

'The gnomes. The elves.'

'Right. They're children substitutes. And they're all on his payroll so they can't say anything. And Mrs Christmas –'

'Is ugly?'

'Er, no. Hello? That's not really an excuse. I'll say it in English... I'm sure a lot of paedophiles are married. So people won't suspect them.'

We come to Accademia Bridge. There are few people around. He takes me to the railing side of the broad wooden structure and lays his hands on the banister.

'Last year I walked on this all the way to the top and back down again. I was drunk. One of my sister's friends did it and I wanted to copy them.'

We ascend the bridge laying our hands end to end on the wide rail, looking down at the black water and exclaiming about how deep it is, how high the bridge is, how silly it is to walk along the edge and – eventually – how, having reached the top, it's psychologically easier to go down the other side, although the danger's just the same.

At the bottom of the bridge we vow to see each other again before I leave (me: no intention of this) and then kiss easily on both cheeks. I promise to call him and walk off home. The rest of the night is spent doing no work and having sexual fantasies. And honestly, I'd do marvellously well if I lived in the nineteenth century as an austere but fiery governess, possibly harbouring a religious passion (expressed in thrilling private verse) for the local curate, but too independent really to submit.

The next day a call from Mum puts me into a glowering mood. It seems that a surprise package she sent me ages ago hasn't arrived. It contained a silk shirt, plus other items intended to bring a glow to my soul. Thievery! Thievery is afoot in Venice.

There's only one thing for it: Stefania must fix the problem. She, Ginevra and I go to the central post office. I'd been expecting a great machine factory full of yammering grey machines and whizzing parcels on conveyor belts. What we get is: an ancient building that looks like a monastery, a small high window carved into the stone, protected by rusted black bars. Behind it a lugubrious, phlegmatic man in funeral black, possibly with an oiled moustache, who licks the end of his pencil before carefully inscribing something on a parchment. There's a wealth of almost black mahogany office furniture behind him. There's nobody else in sight. He glares silently at us as we approach. Stef does all the talking.

'And when were you expecting the package?' the man interrogates us. 'And where is it coming from? And who sent it? And how heavy was it? And how was it wrapped? And what did it contain? And was it properly weighed and stamped? And on what date was it sent?'

There's no computer on his desk. In fact no abacus, telephone, monitor, scale or calculatory aid of any kind. Instead, at his leisure, he reaches under the counter and pulls up a large, cobwebbed, leather-bound book, the edges of its tattered pages yellow with age. He thumps it down in front of him, licks his fingertip and slowly begins turning each page. The lines on the pages have gone dark and discoloured with the years. On each one, by hand, in fountain pen, in chronological order, are the details of every package that has landed at the central post office in the last, well, ever. He asks us repeatedly when the package was sent and when we expected it to arrive and we find ourselves widening the parameters each time. The pages flick slowly back and forth; the man's thumb travels down entry after black ink entry.

Eventually, with barely concealed pleasure – with a glow in his eye, that a mortician might have on beholding a new corpse – he says only, 'There is no package.'

His face slams shut like a trapdoor and that's it. No further discussion permissible. I make a mental note to keep an eye out for silk-clad postal workers in the near future.

The thievery theme continues, not amusingly, when later that day I round the corner of the aisle near the supermarket checkout and see a guy with a basket on the floor between his feet. He's standing in front of a sweets display. Jeans, sweatshirt, trainers, bland. His basket has a few things in it. In one movement he swipes a chocolate bar off the shelf and slips it easy as you like into the back pocket of his jeans. I let out a spontaneous 'Huh!' of disbelief. He clocks me and freezes, his hand still on the chocolate, which is half in and half out of his pocket. I take a good slow look inside his basket in complete silence: milk, cheese, normal stuff. So why steal? Then I look straight into the guy's face for about four seconds, doing a spot of calm yogic breathing. His expression clears and he pretends visibly to change his mind about the chocolate – he doesn't want a sweet thing after all, I see him conclude – takes it out of his pocket and begins thoughtfully to read the back of it, 'decides' from the nutritional information provided that it is not for him after all, slips it regretfully back on the shelf and with a wonderfully clear brow starts gazing at the other items on the shelf. I laugh again to myself – give that man an Oscar – and glide away.

Chapter Fourteen

I'm due to leave on 3 November. On the first of the month I finish my work and clear up the apartment. In the Chiesa dei Carmini I light a candle and meanly don't make an offering but send up a prayer – *Dear God, don't make the plane delayed because I don't want Mum to have to wait at Stansted Airport* – looking very pious with my eyes shut. Then I turn around to find that a priest and two nuns have been watching me beadily all the while. I cannot feel too bad about this; I doubt very much that the candle offerings go on bread for the poor. Funny how you never see priests looking hungry or thirsty.

On my last day I zip up my bags and wait for Stef and Tiziana to arrive. They do, Tiziana checks everything's in order and takes my last set of bedclothes to be washed. I've done everything else – try washing, wringing and hanging a duvet cover, pillowcase, double bed sheet and throw by hand, in the shower. We stand around for a moment.

The boat paintings are all back on the walls. I've swept the floor. Folded down the breakfast bar. Cleaned and emptied the fridge.

Tiziana looks sly for a moment, then with a grin she reaches into her bag and pulls out a book of Venetian ghost stories and legends – 'Here's something for you to read in Italian once you're home' – and I whoop and hug her. She's been one of the bright spots in my life in Venice, and she doesn't know it but I'd been looking at that book all summer and refusing to buy it for economic reasons. Here it is, given to me out of nowhere, wrapped beautifully in dark blue thin paper with a gold stamp. I realise I should have got her something too. Stefania, of course, picks up on my feelings and eloquently persuades her to have an aperitif with us at Toppo. This is an object lesson in Italian cajolement and I realise I should have pressed more because whenever I asked Tiziana to have a coffee with me on the days she came to collect rent, she said no and I immediately let it drop.

We finally part at the door of my now empty, clean, bare apartment. Hugs and kisses between all three of us. Privately, once Stef has gone inside, Tiziana turns back and kisses her hand to me. I reciprocate.

Stef and I move my stuff to her house for my final twenty-four hours. That night we go for a meal with her parents to a restaurant called La Colombina. *La colombina*, the dove. The efficient young waiter has, Gregorio and I agree, the kind of face you see etched on the side of an Etruscan vase, a squared oval with a strong, high brow, the nose, lips and chin all wide and bevelled, crisp neatly-cut dark hair, a very professional and knowledgeable chap. His family own the place.

The food's excellent: prosciutto to begin with, then home-made pasta with caviar, roasted vegetables, then hot chocolate goo mousse. Over dinner Lucrezia tells me that the family wealth was gained in the seventeenth century. Her family made Venetian glass beads and one of the older men (her multi-great-grandfather) hit on the idea of exporting them. The famous bejewelled headdresses of Indian elephants were made of Venetian beads.

'No! I thought they were Indian rubies and emeralds,' I exclaim.

'No,' she says firmly. 'Venetian. All Venetian.'

The family pioneered the export of the beads. Thus the craft became known to the world. The lower floors of the palazzo were the workshop, the seat of the family empire.

I sleep very well that night at Stef's place, full of food and listening to the water of the Canal Grande.

My flight's late the next evening so we have the whole day to ourselves, although Stefania leaves early to have a massage:

'The woman says that the masculine left side of my body, which relates to my work and my active life, is fine, but the feminine, emotional right side of my body need to be more relaxed. But I won't say any more about this, Bidisha, because I know that you think it is stupid.'

'I don't think it's stupid – don't you know me even one little bit Stefania? – I just object to her calling the active side masculine and the passive side feminine. And I'm not sure about there being two distinct sides to the body anyway, that's exactly the way to create a problem, not solve one. You know I believe in the unity of mind and body. Why d'you think I do so much sport? It's a Zen thing, I don't do it to stay thin.'

'Bidisha.'

'Yes?'

'Call Emanuele.'

'But why? You take things too seriously. He's not my intimate friend.'

'No, but come on, just for one coffee, it could be nice.'

'Or it could be a huge waste of time.'

'Everything does not have to be an effective use of time. You are free today.'

'I'm not as easy-going as you, Stef.'

'I am not easy-going.'

'Well, you're very tolerant.'

'No. I am not tolerant. Call Emanuele.'

Against all my instincts I venture into the street for a walk and call the young man in question. He is polite and solicitous as ever, but is working in the library and doesn't – as I had known even before I called – sound happy to hear from me. Although by Venetian rules I'm doing the right thing.

'I just called to say goodbye,' I say foolishly. 'My flight's in the evening.'

'Well then, we absolutely have to see each other,' he murmurs smoothly.

Good manners, it seems, have won over his natural inclinations.

'But if you have a lot of work we can say goodbye on the telephone.'

'No, no, we can't do that, that's not good form,' he says in an intimate voice. *Bello* is the word he uses.

We fix to meet at Rosa Salva in Campo San Luca, the *pasticceria* famed for its *limoncello* ice creams, so potent with lemony liqueur that one lick can get you drunk. I have to meet Stef in half an hour and Emanuele has to get back to his studies so we have a very quick coffee together, standing with the crowd. Unfortunately I've run out of all my Italian and exhausted my fund of goodwill towards him generally, so I don't have anything further to say. Emanuele congratulates me on finishing the book. I congratulate him on his jacket. It appears that when I'm around him I can talk about nothing but outerwear. Indeed, he tells me – we really have reached the last dregs of our mutual fascination fund – that he has another similar jacket in a terracotta colour; I tell him I like natural colours. When our twenty minutes is up I give a huge sigh of relief and we walk the short distance to Campo Santo Stefano together. It's warm and bright and everyone's out doing their business.

Stef approaches us, looking loose and definitely massaged, wearing her new shades, smiling and waving. Instantly clocking my emotional rigor mortis she turns the situation around, introduces herself to Emanuele, asks him about his studies and persuades him to come for a coffee with us in Campo St M. And what of his revision? Thoughts of *that* appear to have evaporated from his mind. Thanks to Stefania the conversation carries us over Accademia Bridge into my half of the city and our favourite place, Caffè Rosso. As we sit down and order Stef keeps up a constant stream of intelligent, persuasive talk, establishes that Emanuele was born in Rimini and attempts to discover a few common acquaintances, then gives him advice about how to tackle his thesis (he's nervous but she vows that it won't take an entire year, just four or five months of applied effort). I watch. He is far less charming with her than with me, less witty and forthcoming, in fact he seems almost shy. No, he seems almost complacent. That's the word. In Stef's presence I see the Emanuele I sensed at the very beginning – the nice, pretty rich, smug guy – come out fully. He doesn't joke or ask questions or exclaim or tease. Or laugh winningly. In fact he seems rather obnoxious. She asks him about his domestic situation, his schooling, his plans and so on. I lean back and enjoy my coffee.

'I live with my mum and it's ideal. Me upstairs and her downstairs. The perfect situation. I don't intend to move out. Of course it's because I love my mother but it's also because I'm lazy!' he says exultantly.

'You, I see, are the archetypal Italian male,' Stefania jokes back elegantly, but I give a secret smile in her direction. Stef never jokes for the sake of it, and she always makes her point.

Ginevra calls as we're finishing our coffees; she's on her way to meet us. Emanuele and I kiss on the cheek, he bows deeply to me, I bow back. We'd already exchanged e-mail addresses at Rosa Salva, with the joke, made by me, of 'There you go. Now please never contact me again.' As soon as he's out of sight I stare maliciously at Stef.

'And so what's the verdict Stefania? Tell me.'

'He is very representative of his social class,' she says beadily.

'Ha! I *told* you!'

'But I think you like him...'

'You're too sincere! I do like him. I like them all!'

'But still, it was nice. Ginevra!'

'Ciao,' Ginevra says, coming up. She makes a sad clown face at me. 'Your last day.'

'I know...' I say.

'How do you feel?' she asks me.

'How do *you* feel?'

'*Triste ma intenso.*' Sad but ardent.

'I met Emanuele,' says Stef, beginning to smile.

'Ah! And?' asks Ginevra eagerly.

'He's very elegant. And very young. We had a coffee together. I had to persuade him quite a bit before he said yes. He was being a bit precious.'

At this I bend right back and guffaw to the skies. Emanuele having been disposed of, the three of us spend the rest of the day together: a huge meal at La Cantina, then two glasses of wine at two different places, then I bug everyone by saying we have to visit Gobbetti's and Tonolo because I want to bring back some of the *pastine* I've been rhapsodising about in my e-mails home. While we're in Gobbetti's a large comfortable-looking woman brings in her contribution of cakes for that week: a tray of rich chocolate rollovers, each one on its own tissue paper square. Everyone in the shop glances over and salivates in approval.

In Treviso Airport they make me open my bag and start up my laptop. They grab their way through my possessions wearing kinky skin-tight black gloves but treat my paper bag of miniature cakes with tenderest regard, passing it delicately through the X-ray machine. On the way home I close my eyes and wonder what I'll miss most about Venice. The answer that comes to me instinctively is that I'll miss my friends. More than the view, even more than the religious art, which after all aren't going to change or move. As Tiziana says, everything in life is a human experience, and ever since I left school I'd hankered for the companionship of a set of cool girls with whom I could revert to my customary teen-style silliness. I found that in Venice, away from the bustle and speed of London. With Stef, Ginevra and Tiziana I enjoyed an absolute ease and humorous companionship that took us, if not from museum to church then at least from cafe to bar to restaurant.

When I arrive at Stansted I feel as though I've been beamed down from another planet. The crowds, the cars parked outside, the scale and the *jolie-laide* urban view leave me floundering for a moment as I quickly shrug on the old skin of brittle street-wisdom necessary for city life.

At the end of the Arrivals run I see a beautiful woman staring and smiling at me. I run over and we hug. It's strange to think I haven't seen her in four months – the longest time I've ever been away from home. We spend the next three days sitting talking.

Chapter Fifteen

Over the next six months I get hit hard by a double realisation: first, that the book I wrote won't be coming out, having been rejected by (at the last count) fifty publishers; second, that I had known this all along and went against my own instincts in pursuing it. This happens often in publishing but the resulting career vocation crisis produces a deep tiredness and frustration. I'm quite amused to find myself suffering from the famous yuppie fatigue, in which victims claim to be so tired that they can't even lift a pencil. Reminds me of poor Beth in *Little Women*, so weak that she couldn't pick up her embroidery needle (she died shortly thereafter). Anyway, everything they said about it turns out to be true. Who would have thought moving your arm to turn a page would require so much effort? Slayed by the phantom tiredness I spend afternoons lying in bed groaning spontaneously with misery. I miss Venice sorely: miss the art, miss being alone, miss being in the centre of town, miss having friends, miss the surface elegance. Miss that particular *thing* which Venice has, the morphine addictiveness of its beauty, and keep starting my sentences, lamely, with 'When I lived in Venice...' That city ought not to be seen as a repository for all the losers of the world but I find myself hankering for it over the spring, until one day I dial Stefania's number in desperation. Stefania, by the way, has been very silent over the last six months, doesn't answer her e-mails and sounded mighty distracted the two times I called her. Interestingly, last summer she was suffering exactly the same claustrophobia in Venice that I had felt in London. The next thing I heard, she'd dumped Venice and moved to South America to organise a human rights documentary festival there. Fearless heroine! Ginevra, for her part, has been fully absorbed into the Barone–Ritter dynasty and is now working for Gregorio, translating his academic papers into French.

Gregorio answers the phone and after a bit of chat I ask to speak to Lucrezia.

'Yes,' he says, cheerfully obliging, 'I'll just get her.' There's a shouted echoey conversation in the background and Gregorio returns to the phone. 'Bidisha? Lucrezia is in the, er... well, you can imagine where she is! How much time... let me calculate... if you call back in five minutes. Ah, no, ten minutes. Certainly not less...'

And within a week of that, in mid-May, I'm on my way back to Venice in a very fatigued and fed-up state. I'd e-mailed Lucrezia and asked if I might come and visit, staying in Stefania's apartment during the Art Biennale, adding countless grovelling riders saying that if it was inconvenient then of course I wouldn't come, all in flowing obsequious prose. Lucrezia said that I could stay for as many months as I wanted but I decided one was enough because I didn't want to impose. There was originally a bit of skirmishing over the arrangements because Lucrezia, although she put it most mildly, wanted me to pay rent. As she told my mother over the phone, 'The cost is eight hundred euros per month at a reduced rate, which is very reasonable.' This demand was sharply and embarrassedly retracted after Stef banned her mother from taking money from me on account of me being her best friend.

The early morning flight's packed with families and a few art/fashion people. Already there's a buzz about the Biennale, which I've been looking forward to for a year after having scrambled to get free passes to the opening. There are some trendy twenty-something Italian guys on the flight too and as we're waiting in the departure lounge at Stansted they amuse themselves by sizing up every woman who walks by. I am dismissed with a decisive 'Yuck! No *way*' but others receive more attentive analyses: 'Ugh, that one's so ugly, so masculine... That one looks like a bitch... Have you seen how skinny that one is?... But what about... oh my God... Oh sweet Mary... look, look... Oh... What a babe! What a hotty!... Kill me, I'm dying!'

Just after take-off I get up and put my rucksack in the overhead locker. I've forgotten to zip up the front pocket and as I give it a shove my sunglasses case and lip balm fall out sharply. I pick the things up and put them back in. Ten minutes later I hear a nervous English man three rows back saying to the stewardess very intensely:

'A young lady was putting her bag up there and suddenly about three items came *flying out* in *that* direction.'

I – the 'young lady' in question – stand up once more and take a good look at the man. He's in his late forties, handsome, I suppose, in a Home Counties antiques dealer way, sunburnt with flyaway hair and a quality jumper. He's pointing helpfully in the direction in which my 'items' flew. The air stewardess, an Italian six-foot Amazon goddess, is standing by his seat giving him about two per cent of her attention. Quite visible in a thought bubble above her head is the phrase 'Silly English man. I will ignore him.'

'And I picked them all up,' I say to the man calmly and loudly.

'Oh, it was you, was it?' he says quite nicely, very vaguely, and with dawning embarrassment.

It seems that even he does not know why exactly he was recounting the flying-items anecdote to the stewardess, who stares at him silently in undisguised pity before walking away without a second glance.

But the episode is not over.

'Oh, you got them all, did you?' says the man's wife to me now, twinkling at me from between the seats. She's a comfortable artistic type who possibly has her own pottery workshop at the end of the garden. There's something about the wry conspiratorial smile that makes me think that she's well aware of what a buffoon her husband is. We pass this awareness between us like an interesting item at a bookshop.

When we arrive at Treviso Airport I notice something unfortunate about the security guards' behaviour. The guards are all much older, short men in grey military-looking uniforms with badges, medals and pins galore. They're standing one on each side of the exit, watching people as they leave. They stop every single black person and open up their bags. I'm waiting far back in the extremely long passport queue, look up to see one young black man being checked. Look up three minutes later and it's another young black man. And so on.

At the customs and security exit before the luggage reclaim I find myself a couple of metres behind a black woman in her early thirties, well-dressed, very tall and handsome with a shoulder bag and a little wheelie case, like all the other passengers. I watch the customs guy to see what he'll do. Quick as a flash he leaps into the queue and begins stepping close behind the woman, almost nicking her ankles with the edge of his boots, and he shouts loudly into her ear, 'Bag check! Bag check! C'mon, c'mon, don't waste my time, you know what's coming.' I'm horrified. I see the woman turn slowly, frowning slightly as she is harangued by the man, whose eyes are sparkling. His tone is that of a prison guard with an already-condemned criminal: you know what you've done so don't give me any fuss. As he talks he slaps one hand against the other to hasten her along, then gets his walkie-talkie out and begins passing it from hand to hand in anticipation. The other guards surround the table as she hoists her wheelie case onto it.

'Quick, quick,' the main man snaps at her while they all grin at each other, shuffling in anticipation, 'open it up, we don't have all day.'

At the vaporetto ticket booth at Piazzale Roma, I heave my backpack along the line.

'Hello, could I have a single ticket to Ca' d'Oro please?'

'No.'

The guy looks at me and gives a deliberately bland idiot grin.

'OK, fine, thank you very much,' I say, and drag my bags out of the queue.

I ask another official who says only, in English, 'Try walk.'

Eventually I log that because of some public event called the Volgalunga there are no vaporetti crossing the Canal Grande so

I shoulder my backpack and creep along the very slow trudging lane from Ferrovia towards Rialto. I find I still know the way to Stef's place. Dying under my bags, I press the apartment buzzer from the ground floor and crawl up all the marble stairs.

The door's open and Stef's parents' white marble apartment is full of hollering and light and the warm smells of garlic, basil, fennel, olive oil, good wine. There's a crowd of people, it seems, on the stone balcony, which is flooded with bright clear morning light. Lucrezia comes forward, her angel-white face very tight and beautiful, chiselled. We kiss.

'Bidisha! How are you?'

I smile in relief at seeing a friendly face and say 'Exhausted!' But it's clear that her attentions are elsewhere; she's entertaining her friends and goes straight back to them. I dump all my bags on the floor, go to wash my hands – a kiss and a greeting from Gregorio on the way – then join everyone on the balcony. There are two women and one man, all in their mid-fifties, ripe, sanguine and scholarly. There's a newspaper full of alphabetical lists open on the table.

'You have arrived at the right time for the race!' says Lucrezia to me.

'The huh?'

'The Long Row, the *Volgalunga*,' she says impatiently, and points downwards.

I look down: the sparkling ice blue canal is filled with rowing boats of all types, canoes, kayaks, fishing boats, gondolas, some flying flags, some prettily painted, some rowed solo, some in teams. Lucrezia, Gregorio and friends are shouting encouragement, looking up the provenance of boats they like or flags they don't recognise.

'What's that yellow boat? Someone look it up. Number two nine six.'

'Two nine six... Rotterdam.'

'Ah! Bravo Rotterdam – come on – bravo!'

'Look at that man in his tub. He must be eighty-seven. At least,' says Lucrezia. Then something catches her eye, a fast black boat. 'They're all women! Come on! *Brave!*'

Thumping the walls of the balcony, we urge our heroines on. My head's swimming with tiredness, light, self-consciousness, hunger and the instinctive feeling that I am not amongst friends, I'm being grudgingly put up with because of an order from Stef.

Lucrezia points out the boats who've already reached the finish and are now leisurely swinging back in the opposite direction, keeping close to the banks so as not to impede the other racers. Gregorio offers me a plump mozzarella and tomato tart and I'm so starving and weary (and had, to be frank, expected something of the sort) that I take it without the slightest hesitation. Then comes the immediate shadow-thought, when the first bite of the tart's already in my mouth, that it would have been more correct to demur a few times instead of grabbing it as though I'd been waiting all along.

I'm just settling into the far corner of the balcony, feeling as stiff and posed as a tin soldier, and melting like one in the heat, when I hear in Italian, 'Are we leaving then?' from Lucrezia and her friends, and before I know it the glasses are drained, the newspaper folded up, bags and sunglasses grabbed and donned. Lucrezia says hastily to me, 'We're going to the Something Bridge to watch the end of the race,' then turns on her heel and heads towards the door.

Gregorio gives me the keys to the upstairs apartment and asks me if I'm coming to see the race. I smile, apologise, bow, crouch, simper and begin to say, 'Ah, no, thank you, I'd better clean myself up and unpack –' and haven't even finished before they're all bundling out and going down the stairs and I'm standing on the landing with my bags. I hear Gregorio whisper to Lucrezia, 'Bidisha's staying here' and Lucrezia shrugs and makes a noise to mean 'Whatever' and then I'm alone.

I go upstairs, locking up carefully, and walk around Stef's lovely apartment. Something I hadn't thought about in my keenness to come back here was how barren Venice would be without her. Ginevra's also away for the next week or so, holidaying with her parents. I wash my face and, seeing that the bed has a sheet but no duvet, lie on the daybed in the living room after finding a rather stinky green blanket somewhere. Because I haven't slept the night before it only takes a few seconds before I'm in a perfect sleep, until the buzzer goes, very shrill like a scream, and I lumber up with my hair stuck flat to one side of my face. I open the door and they'll all there, peering in. Lucrezia, Gregorio, assorted friends.

'Oh, sorry, hi, please, come in,' I say thickly, before realising that I've hit the wrong note. I shouldn't ask Stef's parents to come in to their own palazzo.

There's a frozen pause.

'Are we *invited*?' says Lucrezia with a stinging smile. I give an embarrassed laugh and go through the whole 'Sorry, yes, no, please, I'm so humble, of course I know this is all a loan, a wonderful loan' performance, and so they all come in and the friends are shown around the apartment, with me following dazedly after them. Lucrezia sees that I've been sleeping on the daybed, under the dog blanket (I'd wondered what those black soft hairs were). She frowns and turns sharply.

'The bedroom is *here*,' she says, pointing to Stef's bedroom. O
course I know where the bedroom is, but it has no covers or quil
or anything on it. I laugh in humiliation, feeling like a peasan
who's been discovered kipping behind a neighbour's haystack
'You need a quilt and a quilt cover. I'll bring them for you,' sh
goes on. As they leave, Lucrezia turns to me and says, 'We ar
going out for dinner. Do you want to come?' with such a fla
unreadable face that I can't tell what she wants me to reply, i
she wants me to go or not, so I say, 'Ah! No, thank you, I shoul
really wash and unpack and rest.' And she says, very dry, a phras
I'll come to dread over the next week: 'As you like.' Intended,
think, to mean 'Whatever you want' but really coming off as
slighting 'Suit yourself.' I retreat, laughing foolishly.

I'm left to myself for the next five hours or so. I can see th
Frari campanile and rooftop from my window and just abou
hear it ringing the hours and half-hours. The quilt doesn
materialise and I'm scared of being caught beneath the doggie
blanket again.

I sit at the desk in the living room and look out through the hig
window. Total silence. The TV and CD player don't work. I'v
brought *The Golden Notebook* and *The Well of Loneliness* with m
to read but I can't focus because I've been awake for about thirty
five hours and my head's spinning. At 8.20 p.m. the sky above th
Canal Grande goes milky grey-blue, then the colour drops dow
through the whole city, right to the ground, and soaks into th
stone. It's fully dark by nine-thirty. The darkness in this part o
the city is a distinct black, matte like cartridge paper. Boats pass
The water's high and makes a muscular plunging sound.

At 10 p.m. Lucrezia opens up the studio next to Stef's fla
(where she works and where there are spare rooms and studio
and then knocks on my door. She's brought a duvet and cover

Lucrezia – why didn't I notice it before? – has a way of observing me, as if she's peering over the edge of a cliff, at the bottom of which lies a cold, black, watery grave. At everything I say she takes a couple of tottering steps back and holds out her hands as though against an icy blast from the Siberian peninsula.

'Do you know how to –?' she says, gesticulating towards the bedroom.

Do I know how to put the cover on the duvet.

'Yes, yes,' I laugh, but she thinks I'm laughing her off and she goes away and starts checking her e-mail with the dog at her feet.

A few moments later I come and lean in her doorway at an intimate distance of about fifteen feet.

'I'm sorry about before, I unpacked and then I just...' I slap my hands together dully and loll my head.

'Collapse?' she supplies.

'Exactly!' – and it comes out in one big gulp of friendliness.

We bid each other goodnight and, after having found and added two (human) blankets and one throw to the thin duvet, I put on my socks, shawl, tracksuit bottoms, T-shirt and zip-up top, put the hood up, tie the cords tight under my chin and fall asleep.

The next day I go down with my presents for the family: a Liberty leather-bound guest book, Penhaligon's room spray, Prestat chocolates. Just some fun kitsch things, which I know Stef's parents have a fondness for. They'd looked pathetic sitting on the floor in their smart purple bag the previous day, especially since Lucrezia's attention wasn't on me long enough for me to give them to her.

I ring the bell and Gregorio opens it.

'Ah! Biddy!' he says, but there's a question in his voice. 'Come in...'

'Hello! It's OK, I just wanted to give you this.'

I dangle the bag coyly in front of me. He takes it and looks deep inside.

'What is it?' he asks sweetly.

'Just a present for the house. It's nothing really. I also wanted to know if you'd both like to have an aperitif later,' I say.

'Yes,' he replies naturally, with a smile, 'Lucrezia gets back at eight-thirty so we'll come up and buzz your buzzer then.'

I bow and back away and creep down the stairs to go out. That evening the buzzer goes at the right time and the three of us walk out into cool, quiet, dark Northern Cannaregio. Gregorio chatters away in his usual good mood but Lucrezia is distinctly brittle and silent. She walks far ahead of us with her hands crossed tightly over her bag. At the top of the bridge she turns and asks Gregorio in English:

'Where are we going?'

'This new place,' he replies, 'just over there. Look at the windows. Very welcoming, I think. I saw it the other day.'

Lucrezia points out three new luxury hotels around the Fondamenta della Misericordia:

'So now even our area is being taken over. Let's hope they fail... and you know the newest wave of tourists are the Chinese.' A look of sudden nausea passes across her features. 'And there are billions of them to begin with, but so, if the rich are in the top one per cent, that is still a *lot* of people. The other problem with the tourism here is that people tend to return to Venice. They see it once and they always want to come back.'

Again, as so many times last summer, I am led to one of the secret Venice places, nameless, absent from the guidebooks, dark warm, cosy but sleek, with only Venetians inside, and expert staff. The young guy behind the counter greets us and the usual genteel dialogue ensues:

'We'll have a white wine,' says Gregorio, '– no, a prosecco, something light and dry, *very* dry, with some air and fruitiness to it.'

Much debate and application of thought from the bar owner. He eventually selects one – a perfect choice, it turns out. Much complimenting from the parents. I plump for a red wine and the quickly-hidden frown of surprise on the faces of them and the bar guy tell me that I've missed the protocol of pre-dinner drinks. A long discussion ensues.

'I need something light,' I say.

'What have you got that's from the north, from the more arid regions?' Stef's parents ask the bar guy.

'We have a few which are like that,' says the bar guy. 'The soil's less rich and so the wine is less steeped, less heady.'

'What's this one like?' say the parents, pointing to a name written on the chalkboard.

'Flowery, a little sweet, good for whetting the appetite.'

'And *this* one?'

'More direct, less playful, very crisp.'

'And what's this? *I granelli*, is it called? That's from the north isn't it?'

'Yes. The grains, in English. It's made by monks.'

Nothing is being sold hard, the wine guy's eye rests on me or Lucrezia or Gregorio with unsleazy, respectful, knowledgeable candour. We take our glasses (tall and thin for the prosecco, big-bottomed for the red) and sit at a booth table. The place has large plain windows on two sides, no decoration save a thin strip of worked iron grille at the very top.

'These windows, I think, are very fine indeed,' says Lucrezia in English.

I watch them opposite me, both turned and leaning in towards each other, knees pointing inwards, like keen new friends. Gregorio's arm is stretched across the back of the seat and almost touching Lucrezia's shoulder; her hands are clasped in front of her on the table and yet held forward to him. They don't ask me anything. Every so often Lucrezia throws me a look of sudden irritation. I am getting on her nerves. What have I done wrong? I shouldn't have invited myself over, even though she said one hundred times that I could stay and I'd thought that if she didn't want me she'd find a way of saying so.

Gregorio mentions Ginevra's brilliant translation into French of some ancient document.

'And it was difficult, it had lots of bits in italics, and bold, with a lot of medical terms, with asterisks, and one section referring to another section far away...'

'A very good piece of work,' Lucrezia chimes in

'But can this really be her career?' I ask. 'Taking work from you? She has so much more to offer.'

Lucrezia shrugs:

'She does not want to work.'

'Out of laziness?'

'No,' she retorts, 'I think it is a life choice. She doesn't think she wants to work. She only wants to read books.'

'She could have done a PhD,' I say. 'Every time I see her I try and push her into it.'

'She says her tutors didn't encourage her,' Lucrezia answers, her annoyance growing.

Conversation dies and we look around. Because I'm taking favours from them I only want to speak when they introduc a topic in case they think I'm getting above myself. Lucrezia follows my gaze and tells me a couple of stories about the square church whose very flat front we can spy from our window:

'During the annual church ceremony for St Marina, patron saint of health, everyone takes a candle to San Marco. Not everyone cares about religion, but everyone cares about their own health, so of course every year they light a candle and attend. But some old ladies are too delicate to go all the way to San Marco so they go to this church here.'

She tells me that Marina is a very common name in Venice and recounts the tale of that saint's canonisation. It concerns a nobleman, his daughter and a Venetian monastery. It was a very difficult time in the history of Venice, as well as being a difficult time in the history of this particular family. The family had a clever, energetic, resourceful daughter called Marina, who was unfortunately surrounded by lascivious, poor, unsuitable suitors. For political reasons the family was in peril, so together they hatched a plan which unfolded as follows:

One day the father was seen publicly wearing an aggrieved frown.

'Why are you so troubled, my friend?' asked one of his neighbours.

'I'm very worried about my *son*, Marino,' said the nobleman craftily, with a deep sigh.

'But why? What has young Marino done?'

'Nothing! Not a thing. He is full of virtue. But I am afraid for his life. I wonder, is there any monastery you know of nearby, where we can put him for safe keeping?'

And so it was organised. Known as a boy to everyone but her family, Marina became a monk, Marino, and flourished at the monastery in an atmosphere of piety and learning. One day some years later a young servant girl who worked in the monastery kitchens fell pregnant by (it was generally rumoured) the abbot himself, a man of notorious lusts. Unable on pain of slander and scandal to point the finger at the real culprit the servant girl instead pointed it at the youngest monk, that is to say – oh cruel world! – at Marino. Upon which 'he' was ejected from that place for good, and shame and foul infamy followed his name.

Things got even worse for Marina after that. Her family had fled the city and she wandered like a beggar, with no profession, no home and no honour and almost perished, unable to survive. She was eventually found some miles away, starving, betrayed and on the brink of death. There was just enough time for her to crawl back to the monastery door, knock on it and die before she was brought in, disrobed, discovered to be a woman, privately forgiven, officially absolved and publicly made a saint.

After a tiny bit more chit-chat Lucrezia drains her glass (I'm still trying to finish mine) and looks pointedly at Gregorio.

'Are we leaving now?' she says to him abruptly.

'Um? Ah! Yes, yes...' says he, and has the grace to look embarrassed.

They both look at me and reach with telling slowness for their wallets. Having already decided that I was going to pay for this drink I raise my eyebrows at them and trill, 'No! It's my treat,' and I can tell by their unsurprised vindicated nods and very mild thank-yous that I was expected to do exactly this. So now, feeling as though I've just had my politeness-passport stamped, I pay up. It's only seven euros for four drinks (the parents had one glass of prosecco each, then shared a second, and I had one glass of wine). Makes you realise how criminal the tourist price jack-ups are. We get up and Lucrezia marches us back 'home' quick-smart.

I'm still not getting quite what I need to from this evening, which is to reset the scoreboard and start again on the right foot. At the door of their apartment there is a ceremonial moment. Aware that I owe them *something* (blood? Hard cash? But they already refused it! Why this unwillingness to talk about money? Especially when that is what they secretly want), I pause.

'Would you like to eat dinner with us,' asks Lucrezia flatly, making it clear that she is being impelled by social obligation, not personal desire.

I look into her face for a clue.

'I don't know, I... don't want to interrupt,' I hesitate.

'You are not interrupting, but it is [the lethal code words] as you like.'

'No, no, I'll – er – I'll join you.'

This, at long last, entirely by accident, appears to be the right answer. Then Lucrezia says to Gregorio in Italian as we go in, 'Bidisha wants to stay for dinner,' and once again I'm struck by the grudge in her voice. Gregorio, sensing that something has displeased Lucrezia, is very tense and doesn't know what on earth to do. We go into the great apartment and Lucrezia gets dinner together while Gregorio crouches on the floor and plays with the dog.

'Can I help? Can I do anything?' I ask him.

He looks befuddled for five, then six seconds, until an expression of sudden inspiration brightens his face:

'Ask Lucrezia!'

Lucrezia, irritated, declines my help. She sets the table with cloth place mats, cloth napkins, big plates, shallow stew bowls, red wine and two types of water. Gregorio sits down, takes one look at his napkin holder and pretends to be repelled, dropping it from his hands as though it's covered in venom. I look at it, then laugh: the silver oval is engraved with the word 'Lucrezia' in curly script.

'Horrible!' Gregorio shudders as he swaps them around. I admire the slants and curls of the engraved 'Gregorio'. 'In Italy this is a very common wedding gift.'

The meal: a tomato and mozzarella tart, shared; a delicious pastry and anchovy twist, shared; a spicy wintry venison stew; a light green salad with sweet balsamic vinegar and four different types of cheese. Red wine to accompany the mains, white very sweet wine with the cheese. Plates cleared away between every course. Strange how they're considered to be dirty when they clearly aren't and yet these are people who wear their shoes indoors when the streets of Venice are quite literally caked in dog shit.

'I have a funny story that happened to me today,' says Gregorio in English. 'I was in Tronchetto. I was with the dog. And I put the muzzle on the dog to go on the vaporetto, and a woman came up to me: "Excuse me! Excuse me! Is it absolutely necessary to put a muzzle on the dog to use the vaporetto?" And I looked past her and I saw that she and her friends had a big dog with them too. "Yes, it is mandatory," I said, and she...' He clasps his hands together. 'She said, "Please, we have no muzzle. Would there be any way that I can buy your dog's muzzle? We are in certain need." And I said, "But really, I have not any need of your money and also, I am afraid, I searched for a long time for this muzzle, it has an excellent shape and it fits my dog perfectly." And the woman said, "Please! Name your price. We must get onto the vaporetto." And then I had an idea. I said, "I cannot sell you anything, but if you come with me I have my spare muzzle in the car, and I can lend that to you, and when you have used it you may return it to Piero, the man who works at the car park and who is a great friend of dogs. I give you my name – Barone – and he will keep it for me." And the woman thought about it and went back to her friends and said to one of her male friends, "Go with him to his car," just in case, you know, I...'

We all laugh while he makes a ghoulish face and mimes holding a knife and swinging it down lustily.

'So now will come the test: do they return the muzzle?' says Lucrezia.

'I did not want money, but I did think, "How can I help them?"' says Gregorio. 'And the way in which the woman asked me –'

'These people think they can buy anything,' Lucrezia jumps in in Italian.

'No, I did not understand it that way,' says Gregorio, puzzled.

'You took it to mean here's someone who's willing to do whatever is required to solve the problem,' I say.

'Exactly! I admired her. Her attitude was, what can we do to obtain a muzzle?' says Gregorio.

'Are you thinking that this is something they do all the time? With various different items?' I ask Lucrezia.

'No, maybe just with muzzles,' she says. 'And at home I imagine they have an enormous pile of other people's muzzles.' To Gregorio she says, 'The woman, what was she like? Was she Italian?'

'No. German, or a Dane. Very tall, with fair hair.'

'What language did you speak? Italian?'

'No, English. And the friend with her, he was a Latin, I think.'

'A Latin? How could you tell?'

'His features,' says Gregorio cryptically.

'But, look,' Lucrezia presses, 'was he...' She glances carefully at me and then switches to Italian: 'Was he dark and swarthy?'

I keep my eyes on my plate. Gregorio, embarrassed, nods and looks away, then changes the subject. As we're finishing our dinner, Lucrezia leans over to me and says nudgingly:

'You tried to escape but in the end you could not.'

'Oh, I *knew* I was supposed to say yes to dinner yesterday!' I burst out, annoyed at myself.

She gives a small smile. To signal that dinner's over she sits back in her seat, sighs and says, 'Well!'

'Thank you so much, that was wonderful,' I say truthfully.

'Thank you for the book and the fragrance and the chocolates,' she says, but in such a way, and with such a laugh and such a smile that I instantly feel ridiculous. 'Now you can go upstairs and sleep,' she dismisses me.

So I go upstairs. Venice is silent, black water, black buildings opposite, white candelabra lights on the canal side. I watch and wait and eventually the gods oblige me with some drama: hissing jet-black rain falling with a beautiful sound, muted piano keys on the roof, an uninterrupted exhalation like stroked paper as it falls into the canal. Afterwards everything is black and soaked and spent.

In the days that follow I visit shows of paintings, of costumes, of statute books, great offices, furniture and musical instruments and prints and maps and knick-knacks. In northern Cannaregio there are almost no tourists, just sun and strange Salvador Dali proportions: a vast blue sky, a few arches and alleys and wide bridges that mislead the eye and open into a dead end of infinite tinted space. Empty boats tied and tilting on the water. Walking along the *fondamente* I look in at the houses, low-lying, some partly open-sided, airy like barns, quiet but not abandoned, empty but not deserted, merely snoozing peacefully. In the church of the Madonna dell'Orto I find some hilarious marble busts, all the great men bursting with character – sometimes literally. The bust of Alousius Catareus, done by Alvise Contarini in the mid-seventeenth century, for example, is so eye-poppingly fat that the marble itself looks like it's straining and might explode in a great deluge of suet and meringue. At the Chiesa di Sant'Alvise I find an absolute gem, an artwork full of power and joy and confidence: sumptuous small square panels by Lazzaro Bastiani (1449–1512) – not as flat as the usual style of the period; crisp, but not stilted; pure chemical colours, blood red, tincture blue, flaring wipe-clean white, and in the background a marbled still sea and smoky mountains. It's a shame that this church is so out of the way and so plain from the outside, few tourists must find it. There are some sturdy white marble statues of St Dominic, Mary plus Jesus and St Therese by Giovanni Maria Morlaiter. Also a winsome Annunciation by the school of Bonifacio de'Pitati, the Angel Gabriel grinning his head off and positively leaping in through Mary's window with his arm aloft as though he's just scored a goal. A churchwoman – a nun? – comes out and begins clearing the altar for the Mass, putting out new candles. She's small, about seventy or more, very slender, very fit, moving quickly and efficiently. Grey hair curled close around her head, a sharply sunken visage like the face on a Roman coin, a steady hand as she lights the candles.

I visit the museums, feel alienated by all the dead Venetian politicians, club-makers, theologians, schemers and patrons. The only memorable women in the culture are usually half-mythical and always sexual, just meat: colourful poetry-spouting hookers;

canny political hookers who drafted judicial decrees in their spare time; errant nympho nuns who were really undercover hookers; pragmatic hookers who colluded with the government; trendy hookers who inspired mainstream fashion. There are countless paintings of women: women naked, women sleeping, women bathing or doing their hair, women powdering their noses, women laughing, women despondent, women perplexed, sprites, sirens, fairies, naiads, romantically perishing women, women taking tea. The images pretend to be tributes but were created at a time when the doors were resolutely locked against real female artists. Sometimes this city does seem like a giant graveyard, a shrine to dead 'great men' in which everyone else – most other cultures and races and all women, even Italian ones – must step with all due reverence.

One morning I awaken to find a key in an old envelope with my name scrawled on the front shoved under the door. I have no idea what the key is for, it doesn't fit any of the locks in here. The question does cross my mind, lightly, on day six or so, that surely Stefania's parents should be making a *tiny* bit more effort with me? Just enough to qualify as basic decency? If I say hello to Lucrezia she jumps up and her eyes bulge as if I'm about to mug her. This is followed by an eloquent look of utter loathing. I've also offered to accompany her while walking the dog (our old custom last year) twice, and was turned down flat both times. At one point I bump into her at the main door downstairs and tell her spontaneously that she looks very elegant (it's true: a short Chanel-style jacket with a black orchid corsage) and she scowls wretchedly before making herself say thank you. I know it's not my place to make comments about my friend's mother's looks but it just slipped out.

'I have something to tell you, very important,' she says in
nglish. Finally! A breakthrough! But no: 'You are not to put
nything solid down the kitchen sink. Not even tea leaves. Only
ater.'

I, thank goodness, am guiltless in this respect. I manage to take
e opportunity to ask, smiling hesitantly,

'The key I found under the door? What's... it for?'

'It's the other key to your old apartment. Sorry, we have not
turned it to Tiziana yet. So I give it back to you.'

Which means, now you have to phone Tiziana and give it
ack to her yourself. Fine, fine, all fine. Wanting to get away and
ink, I go down to the Riva degli Schiavoni and walk between
e public gardens and St Mark's Square. Half the gardens have
een cordoned off as the pavilions are prepared for the Biennale.
see a pale English woman petting her boyfriend like a monkey,
cking invisible bits of dust off him as he stands reading a map.
oth wear small smiles, hers servile, his luxuriant. I also see plenty
f sets of Italian parents wheeling around kids who're clearly
d enough to walk. The children sit in their pushchairs with
eir legs nonchalantly crossed like presiding judges, positively
pping their toes at the weariness of it all. Clue, mums and dads:
it's got enough muscle development to cross its legs, it's strong
ough to walk.

And much later, finally – *finally* – it dawns on me that Lucrezia
Gregorio, I realise, is a sort of zero quantity here) does not want
e here, has decided to pretend that I do not exist and would
refer it if I did the same. They feel no special fondness towards
e. The dinners and outings they invited me to were simply
hat is done in polite society for the friend of one's child.

The Biennale's in about ten days' time so I decide to return
ome in the interim to let Lucrezia and Gregorio have a break

from me. I book a ticket back to London for the following day,
plus a ticket to return to Venice for five days of the Biennale, to
arrive the night before it starts. That way I can limit and break up
the favour I take from Stef's parents. I note down all my plans,
flight details and return times to relay to Lucrezia but neither she
nor Gregorio are at home that night. Sensing a bit of oncoming
humiliation I go down every half hour to knock on their door
but nothing.

The next day's my last day and they're still not around. I pack all
my things and wait for the weekly maid who comes in to handle
the family filth. She's a nice woman, perhaps in her late thirties, in
a slogan T-shirt and jeans. We said hello the previous week and I
saw her look at me fleetingly, bright and curious. Today I go into
the utility room to ask if I could leave her my keys and note. She
says I can, comes close, asks me where I'm from and tells me how
good-looking I am... it's only later, thinking it over and parsing
her grammar, that I realise she mistook me for a boy.

I shoulder my backpack and trudge to Piazzale Roma, from
where I can get the bus to the airport. I've been phoning and
phoning Lucrezia to no avail until, when I'm standing in line
about to get on board, I finally get through.

'Bidisha! How are you?'

'I'm fine. I'm very sorry to disturb you on a work day. I'm
calling because I have to return to London for a few days for
work.'

There's a long, delighted pause and then, very slowly and
gradually, I realise that I can actually *hear* Lucrezia smiling.
Instantly, smoothly, the sun comes out over Venice and I feel
a wave of love and pleasure flood into me through the phone.
When she speaks again her voice is utterly changed and is now
the sly, urbane voice of the woman I knew last summer.

'It's not *bad* news, I hope?' she asks, very concerned.

'No, not at all. But it does mean I have to be back in London for a week, or thereabouts. If it's all right with you, I thought I might just return for five days or so, to see the Biennale.'

'Of course,' she says, all warmth and charity, and the words pour over me like oil, 'just let us know when you are returning. Send me an e-mail.'

'Actually, I've left a note with all the details on it. I've already booked the tickets to return. But I'll e-mail too. One problem, my mum's already sent my Biennale tickets on to me at your address.'

'But that is fine,' she reassures me, 'we will receive them and keep them for you. You can collect them when you come again.'

And so we conclude our conversation gratefully, warmly, lovingly. I intend to spend the next ten days seething at home, then get back here, get Ginevra and see the Biennale I've been looking forward to for a year.

Chapter Sixteen

But it doesn't happen quite like that. While I'm cooling my heels in London I e-mail Lucrezia twice, using the most respectful words, letting her know that I'm returning for the Biennale opening weekend as planned and agreed, flight and times confirmed, and will that be all right, and if it isn't all right could she please just let me know — and have my passes arrived? Because my mother sent them quite a while ago and the post from London to Venice only takes two days. I know Lucrezia checks her e-mail every day but receive no reply until very late the night before I'm due to leave London. The words on that e-mail are:

Dear Bidisha, we are full until Sunday. After that you can come when you like. Let us know your plans. Ciao, Lucrezia.

This is unfortunate because my passes are only valid until Sunday and not beyond — as she knows. Still, to maintain form, and tortured as ever by that inability to be rude, I write back and say:

> Dear Lucrezia, thank you so much but I won't inconvenience you with any more Venice guests. I'll find a hotel. Best wishes and see you soon.

I find an e-mail confirmation of my passes, which I hope will get me in, hit the phone and manage to fix last-minute reservations with the Alla Salute da Cici and La Calcina hotels in Zattere. I'll go back and forth between them (and back and forth between different rooms in them) for six days. I pledge all of my savings, £800, for the stay.

I arrive in Venice in the late afternoon, unpack and sleep. In the pretty walled garden at Alla Salute da Cici the next morning I see several couples — all British, we must have bought the same guidebook — coming down and eating breakfast in silence. Solidly middlebrow middle class, no angst, not intelligentsia, not coarse, just plangent. In a freak coincidence the men all look *exactly* the same: bald (all six of them) with raw, plain faces. I watch the couples. Of course there's no particular reason why they should be talking enthusiastically to each other at eight in the morning, especially after, say, twenty years of marriage — but then why not? One couple: the husband looks straight ahead and eats like a robot. The wife, sitting adjacent to him, casts him big anxious eyes as she eats. I saw this at the airport too, the man sitting square in his seat, legs heavily apart, not looking at the woman, who was curled around him in an uncomfortable pose, facing him, legs crossed, hip out, shoulder jammed against the seat-back, eyes fixed on his face, doing her concubine duty.

The pigeon population in St Mark's Square seems to have multiplied over the last month. It's now a dingy boiling grey mass that breaks and reforms like mercury. And finally, I get a price-break at Caffè Causin. After I've asked the price of three scoops of ice cream (four euros), baulked at it and then requested two scoops (three euros), the waiter delivers it and murmurs in my ear, 'I'll leave it at two euros, not three. Two euros is a good price.' I burst open a pleased laugh and become his faithful friend forever. In the public gardens the pavilions are ready, the gallery spaces have been prepared and Venice is noticeably stuffed with art whores from all over the world, although shit-hot London/New York styling looks ridiculous next to Venetian chic. I watch the Very Cool Guys cross Campo St M dozens of times on my first day: tall, long-legged, lightly stubbled, wearing shades, designer jeans, designer blazers with a T-shirt underneath, a piece of discreet chunky silver jewellery and maybe a satchel or a record bag to prove that they're always working, brainstorming, thinking and creating rather than, say, just on holiday like 'the masses'. To narrow it down even further, non-Venetian Italians are tackier, flashier, more hard-boiled than the Venetians: big butch medallion men, tiny gym-toned, sun-glazed women.

I call Ginevra, who kicks herself into gear and escorts me around all of Venice, up and down into every corner, every museum, bar, gallery and cultural place of interest. I feel so bad about all the effort she's making that we begin each day with the same telephone dialogue:

'Do you want to go out?' she will ask.

'No. I mean I do, but I don't want to impose myself on you,' I'll coyly reply.

'You are not imposing yourself on me.'

'I *am* free today...'

'Right! I am free too! I am free for you.'

'And it is a *bit* boring in my hotel room. And depressing. I *would* ke to have some fun...'

'OK! So! We meet and we make some fun.'

And off I bashfully go. One afternoon we're sitting at Gelateria Jico in Zattere, watching the water.

'I saw Stef's father the other week,' says Ginevra.

'Oh?'

'He said you left. He mentioned your note.'

'He mentioned it. What d'you mean he mentioned it?'

'"Oh, Bidisha left. She left a note." Not in a horrible way.'

'Hmm. Now I see how silly that note makes me look. But there vas no other way, I had to get out of there and all the other flights vere too expensive. It's just chance that Stef's parents were away hat night. I told them exactly when I was coming back and they gnored it. I just don't understand it.'

'And he said you did something to the furniture. I mean, he vasn't angry... He said, "It's a funny thing, she moved all the urniture to the sides and left a big space in the middle. What was he doing in the space? Having tango lessons?"'

'No! What?' I splutter. 'How old are they? And it's a huge room you couldn't even see the proportions the way it was before. Vhat was that stupid red chair doing right in the middle?'

Ginevra is now spluttering too:

'That chair is a design classic! That cost thousands of euros.'

'Why is it so big? It looks like a giant strawberry. And who eeds a TV zone and a study zone, Stef doesn't even watch TV. mean, if it was a really beautiful desk, and really huge, I *might* eave it in the middle of the room, but...'

'I'm never going to a furniture shop with you. And I'm never going to ask your advice about design.'

'Stefania's parents are vile people,' I burst out.

'Gregorio is OK...'

'He's OK because he has a nice nature. But what does he do? Nothing. All the money comes from Lucrezia's side. Some other woman does all the really disgusting work. But I see how they're a good match in the sense that he warms Lucrezia up.'

I remember at that last dinner at La Colombina, Stef, who was working on *The Merchant of Venice*, was talking about how old and yet how beautiful Jeremy Irons is (an appreciation I share), when Lucrezia leant over to me and, stroking Gregorio's arm lovingly, simpered, 'I have to say, I still like handsome men in their sixties.'

I tell Ginevra about it and we have a cautious conversation before getting into the full complaint-fest.

'She is always a businesswoman, Lucrezia,' she says.

'But I'm not a customer, I'm a friend of her daughter's. And there's business and there's rudeness. And cruelty. And malice.'

'I always have this problem with Lucrezia, even after all these years. We must stop... we can't say the bad thing about Lucrezia... we can think it but we can't say it, it's rude,' Ginevra gibbers.

'Oh, Ginevra, why the hell won't you come and work in London, you speak totally perfect idiomatic English.'

'What?! Where did this comment come from?'

'You just said "rude" and earlier today you said "hidden" and "dig" and "crackle". And yesterday you said I should do something to "soften and soothe" my blisters.'

'I got that from a L'Oréal moisturiser bottle. All the names of cosmetic products here are in French or English so you have to know what they mean.'

'So? Come and work for L'Oréal in London.'

I move to La Calcina and enjoy my first breakfast in the pretty front room, overlooking the water. I was lucky to find two hotels in my favourite part of the city. Minutes go by as I stare out of the window at the hot, misty, silver air around the sea. There's an engraved stone slab on the outside wall of La Calcina that refers to John Ruskin, even though he only stayed here for a few months. The in-room blurb about the hotel name-checks one-time visitors Bortolo Gianelli, Antonio Zona, Ippolito Caffi, Henry de Regnier, Rainer Maria Rilke, Giuseppe Berto and many others. Is it that no great women ever passed through this hotel, or that no one bothered to remember them? The room's shaded an elegant grey, with good quality antique-seeming furniture, a balcony, a wet room, beams on the ceiling, the splash and sway of thick water and the cry of seagulls close by.

I spend the morning lying on a precariously swaying piece of floating concrete like a barge that's been tethered to the wooden landing stage at the end of the Zattere coast. I think rowers use it to get into their kayaks because floating alongside me there's a long, low wooden boat with 'Rowing School' written on the side. I put on my shades, stick my scarf under my head and stare into the sky, letting the water rock me. A huge cruise ship passes, called the *Aida*. There are hundreds of tiny people standing out on their cabin balconies. The boat is a brilliant plastic white, new, shaped like a domestic iron and twice the height of Venice and Giudecca, which look and feel like ancient ruins by comparison.

The Giardini have been transformed by coffee stands, crowded pavilions, crunching gravel, gossip, eyes, ambition, posturing, visuals, deal-making, opinions, forced vivacity, forced nonchalance and twittering voices. And radically varying art.

Ginevra comments to me (and I hear many people commenting between themselves) that nothing in art really surprises us any more. Everything looks like a weak but still-identifiable echo of something that came before, desperate to make an impression and yet so manic and impure, exciting in its corruption. Even its ironic detachment is of the defensive, wounded kind. The more they set out to shock, the more flaccid they seem. Not that the hipsters seem to have noticed: the vibe around Gilbert and George, who have never featured a woman in their work and whose quotes about women in interviews are always derogatory, is hysterical. Random fan-women in kitten heels cluster around them; male art students, TV producers and journalists edge close, baying compliments. Gilbert and George themselves are loving every minute of it. Everyone is staring at everyone else in the desperate hope that something interesting is about to happen.

There are two major upsides for me though: first, Ginevra never loses her temper and always has a map, timetables, water, sunblock and money to hand; second, this year's directorship of the Art Biennale's been given to two women so there are more female artists in the selection than usual, plus the great American artist Barbara Kruger is receiving the Lifetime Achievement Award. It's the first time any woman has been asked to direct the Art Biennale in its hundred and four years of existence (maybe they thought they'd appoint two at the same time to get themselves off the hook for the next century), and yet one of the headlines of a major interview is 'Long Live Women!' – that exclamation mark *really* kills me – as though the Biennale had a long history of being pro-woman when in fact the opposite is the case; there have been almost no female directors of the Music, Art, Film and Architecture Biennales. In another article the journalist begins sneeringly, 'Seeing as the Biennale is largely

male this year...' when in fact only thirty-three per cent of the
elected artists are women.

And it is impossible, when you notice one thing, not to notice
all the others. One of the exhibits on display is a slick-looking
world map and a list of all the countries that haven't been invited
to submit work: Nigeria, Uganda, India... the list goes on. It's
long.

'All the non-white ones,' I say aloud, wonderingly, after reading
the list, and there's a murmur of agreement around me. So here
we are, keeping the male white Western capitalist hegemony
going. Three cheers for art! That bastion for rebels! Challenging
the status quo with every jingle of our money bag.

One other upside of the various Biennali in Venice is that they
give the local police something to do. The great crime of the
week occurs when some miscreant nicks a bottle of champers
(and, it is rumoured, two whole glasses) from one of the pavilions
and exits stage left pursued by irate officers. Ginevra mutters to
me darkly as they go, 'In Italy we have a saying: "We are ruled
by the police."'

Ginevra and I have a great time at the Biennale and treat it like
our own personal curiosity shop, enjoying the buzz of so many
people gathered together just to indulge in mass art-fandom. In
an event like this, even the weaker artworks contribute to the
overall positive sense of a visual jamboree, a clashing 3D collage
of video, installation, painting and performance. It doesn't
matter if it's 'good' or not: we barely have the energy to debate
the question or the money to buy the postcards in the gift shop,
let alone speculate on the collection like actual art collectors.
What matters is that it's interesting, alive.

The politicised New York art collective The Guerrilla Girls
have a brilliant exhibition right at the entrance of the main

warehouse space. They've submitted a series of huge, wall-wid
posters in kitsch Warhol colours like B-movie adverts from th
Nixon era, facts and figures written out in a 'Martians Attac
Earth!' font:

In 1895, 2.4 % of the artists at the Venice Biennale were women
In 1995, a hundred years later, the figure was 9 %

The posters are full of these bold and bitter info-bites. It's
powerful wake-up call, especially when so many visitors to th
Biennale are women... a dozen of whom are standing appalled i
front of these works, their eyes glumly tracing the words. There a
other posters giving statistics about how many women have (tran
haven't) been nominated for Oscars and other arts prizes and ho
women artists are completely absent from the major museums o
Venice itself. There's nothing really to say about all this, impossib
to express the sense of galling, rank injustice, confront the hat
that keeps us out. Only The Guerrilla Girls could portray thes
hard facts with such gusto, rage, not self-hate.

On Sunday evening, squeezing the last dregs out of our Biennal
passes, we explore pavilion after pavilion looking at all th
inauguration times and wanting to be fed. There's free Illy coffe
to be had in the public gardens, Israel offers strawberries and win
and Argentina offers fat olives and prosecco. We then try the churc
of La Pietà on the Riva degli Schiavoni for the Morocco openin
What joy: long tables have been set up in an L shape, along whic
are sumptuous platters, baked spinach and molten cheese in sof
thin pastry, skewers of tropical fruits, flat toasted almonds, stuffe
green olives, slivers of pink prosciutto, biscuits made of crumblin
light almonds and coated in fine caster sugar, excellent prosecc
and red wine. Ginevra and I press ourselves into the crowd, whic

fierce. With her height and grace and my stumpy flexibility we
execute a dual manoeuvre, filling the plate up at the end of the row
(her) before passing it over the heads of the other people to the low
round table at the end to stock up on drinks and sweets (me).

'We're a good team!' we remark to each other once reunited
to gorge ourselves in the corner of the church entrance. Twenty
minutes of blissful eating and gratified food-related comments
follow. We love art more than ever.

'This serves as dinner,' says Ginevra.

'Mm. Definitely. Good food.'

'I like *this* thing. I think I have the recipe for it.'

'Ah! Is it hard to make?'

'Not at all, it is only a question of getting the *best* almonds.
But why don't they make the windowsills in these churches flat
instead of slanted? Where are you supposed to put your drink?'

'I've got good use out of you this week,' I tell Ginevra in
satisfaction. 'God, my feet really hurt. I want to show them to
you but they're really disgusting.'

'Please! Show me your blisters, I'm like a doctor... Ah!
Fascinating.'

And so, after a last look at the art (stonking great abstract
canvases full of ripped, fiery streaks like larval earth), we depart
high, happy and almost holding hands, rehashing our nimbleness
over the food, my agility in procuring glasses, hers in catching
the eye of the waiter and our joint luck in bagging the best spot
by the church stairs.

We discuss the parental duo.

'When I asked Stef if Gregorio does anything in the house Stef
said he cooks meat very well, but I haven't seen him do anything
of the sort,' I say. 'It was Lucrezia who cooked the meat.'

'Gregorio's duty is to be nice.'

'That is hardly a difficult task if he's nice by nature.'

'OK, his task is to act as a... foreign affairs minister... to keep the peace...'

I laugh: 'Yes, to act as a sort of buffer between the family and the outside world. If I'd asked Lucrezia if she wanted that aperitif that first night, she would've said no. I was lucky to get Gregorio.'

'But at the same time they can be so loving, so generous. They keep giving me work.'

'Yes, they're getting good use out of you too. And they were very decent to me last year, because I was so good to Stefania when she was in London. They're like a family in a Henry James novel.'

'I think it's only that Lucrezia doesn't know how to behave with people. I think you should call them...' says Ginevra.

'What? Are you joking? I'm not going to do that.'

'Not for them. For yourself.'

To change the subject I tell Ginevra about the racist security guards at Treviso Airport and she shrugs, unsurprised, and says 'Yes, of course. All of Italy is like this.' Walking along Zattere one afternoon on my first day of this trip I heard the middle-aged couple behind me mimicking the Chinese-accented Italian of the young couple who run the new coffee bar in Dorsoduro. In San Polo, near my old apartment, I heard two kids mocking the Indian accents of the waiters at the Sri Ganesh restaurant in the same way. Their parents chuckled along.

'Has there never been a left-wing government?' I ask.

'Yes. The one before this one. And it was good.'

'So what happened?'

'The problem in Italy is that we are split fifty-fifty between left and right. And there are a lot of people who just don't know and don't vote at every election, only when they feel like it. Unfortunately the people who don't care are right-wing by nature and that is the way they vote when they can be bothered.'

I mention the possibility of travelling to the south after this, to research another book. She tells me the properties there can be cheap, but I should check carefully and see them for myself 'because they might be next to a steelworks, or a wind farm, or a sewage plant'. Dear Ginevra. She also tells me to watch out for tiny traditional villages with one cafe 'full of men, only men, who do literally nothing except play cards and stare at you in silence for half an hour if you go in'. And if I become pregnant by a local boy the best thing is to leave town in the middle of the night without telling anyone, as the alternative is being lynched from my bedroom window.

The next day Ginevra takes me to a restaurant round the back of St Mark's. It's dark and empty, no tourists, no visible menu, pictures by local artists on the walls. The place is ruled by a woman called Mellia, ancient, pale, white-haired, reticent and efficient, not easily drawn, not quick on her feet but clearly – *clearly* – the long-reigning monarch of the locale. Ginevra and I are given a bowl of simple good pasta ('A little sticky,' Ginevra opines, 'because it has been sitting in the pot too long'), rough red wine and plain salad. As we have our lunch the family who owns the restaurant sits down to have theirs, Mellia holding forth and declaring various things in clear, adamant tones, the rest of the family nodding, 'Damn right!', 'Hear hear!' and 'Yup! Isn't that always the way?' Ginevra and I finish our meal and meekly wait for them to finish too before proposing payment. Ginevra goes to the bathroom and comes back laughing: painted on the bathroom door in a flowing hand are the words *Qui si entra dolenti e si esce... leggeri!* Translation? 'Here you enter suffering and leave feeling... lighter!'

On my last full day in Venice we go to the Lido to see a film. It's dusk and the place is deserted. We walk alongside the locked beach that I went to with Stefania and Bruno last year. A sinister sight, the closed cabanas, the dark clotted sand and cold dark water, padlocked gates, high railings and abandoned view. Stef knows a woman who was raped on this beach one night many years ago.

We get lost, Ginevra refuses on a point of Venetian pride to ask for directions from a passer-by (and in any case, there are none) and so we end up walking from one end of the island to another. As we're about to cross a street I notice a car approach and turn close to us with suspicious slowness. I see the guy inside lean over and peer at the street sign we're standing under. Strangely, the radio in the car's blaring out the Village People song 'YMCA'. It's so loud that it must be agony for him to listen to. The car almost stops. I glance at it again, frowning. There's something wrong here. The man inside (alone, pale, stocky, plain large face with small bland features, about forty) is straining forward, leaning on the steering wheel and staring across the passenger seat straight at us. I frown and murmur 'Strange car' to Ginevra, who's looking around trying to get her bearings. We walk away. I don't hear which direction the car goes in.

We find the cinema, buy our tickets and are waiting outside to kill time and enjoy the air before the film starts. There's almost no one around. Soon I hear 'YMCA' again, distant and then very loud. This time it's unmistakable: the car approaches at, well, crawling pace, cruises by the kerb and almost sputters to a halt. The guy leans across, rolls his window down and slowly, clearly, deliberately gives me the eye. He looks perplexed, as though he's never done this before. Ginevra's got her back to the street and is reading a film listings poster. Suddenly realisation dawns on me. I nudge Ginevra.

'Number one, that car's been following us. Number two, he thinks I'm a boy. Number three, he thinks I'm a rent boy,' I sigh.

Ginevra laughs it off: 'If men here want that they go to Mestre!'

But I don't get these things wrong, and I've been mistaken for a rent boy before. I can't help wondering: could transsexual prostitution be a viable way out of my career slump? 'YMCA' is still playing — it's a tape, not the radio, I realise, and there's just that one song on it — so loud that the street's shaking and we can barely hear each other speak. I shake my head minutely at the staring man and make a get-lost gesture. He looks at me imploringly. I shake my head again. Blushing and not knowing quite where to look, he turns off the music and peels away.

After the film we return to Venice proper and decide on one last drink at Caffè Rosso. It's dark, stormy, past midnight. As we're walking the Toletta/Campo San Barnaba/Campo Santa Margherita route we become aware that there's a voluble drunk guy behind us. I glance back: tall, trendy, handsome in a sluggish way, about thirty or so, full muscles and heavy all over with drink, laughing blearily to himself. Ginevra and I look at each other warily. We pass a phone box at which a skinny, much older Japanese man is making a call, his jeans and cheap cord jacket hanging off him. We hear a sudden laugh of glee behind us: the drunk man has leapt up and kicked the Japanese guy's phone out of his hands and is hammering the sides of the phone cubicle with his fists. He then lunges in and wrenches the Japanese guy out.

The victim spins weightlessly across the street, hits the far wall, yelps 'Help' in a strangely calm voice – the attack's happened too quickly for panic to set in – and walks away fast, ahead of us, his shoulders hunched with fear. He can't run because it'll provoke the attacker, whose laughter we hear behind us.

Ginevra and I are breathing hard. We also can't run. The bully's blackmail: tolerate the little violence or you'll get the big violence. Eventually the drunk guy stumbles off down a side street.

'That happens a lot,' says Ginevra eventually.

'Drunk guys looking for trouble?'

'No. Well yes. But also, attacks on the Chinese and Japanese who live here. And on Sri Lankans. It's not reported in the paper because they are afraid to go to the police – the police are just the same. But let us say, this isn't the first time I have seen this.'

At Caffè Rosso I sip a sour eye-popper of a red wine. After all these days in constant company Ginevra and I are still not bored with each other, mainly because she's so accommodating.

Now that my trip's drawing to a close I still haven't managed to square my ambivalence about Venice. Maybe that's what makes the place so compelling: it covers the entire spectrum of human behaviour from sublime gentility to blatant hate, pressure-cooked and agelessly preserved in a tiny, perfect isle. Despite having seen the reality of Venice I am still beguiled by the cliché. You could say that Venetian culture is deeply sexist, racist, mercenary, bourgeois, hypocritical and pretentious; yet for some reason its beauty isn't compromised by its ugliness. A cynic might even say that Venice is best experienced with deliberate shallowness. Protected by money, constrained by time, maybe the right method is the one that real Venetians have most contempt for.

rent a hotel room and stay for a week or two. Do all the touristy things, don't delve too deep beneath the surface or read people's faces or voices too accurately. Too much perspicacity will reveal some uncomfortable truths about Venetian life.

What's so striking for me is that the city seems to change its nature according to who I'm with and what I'm doing: mellow and family-orientated on one day, youthful and culturally vibrant on another evening, sleazy and crude some other night. While learning valuable lessons about the easy-going rhythm of 'the Italian way', I've also glimpsed a coldness that lies close beneath the sophistication of this famously stylish place. I've uncovered a city in which exquisite art and a strong family ethos exist hand in hand with a thriving daily routine, picturesque market scenes and characterful dogs; in which I have been charmed by my new friends' sanguine temperament but repelled by the narrow-mindedness I've witnessed and the constant, violating harassment. I didn't fall in love but I did get within literal sniffing distance of a real live Italian boy; didn't do the marathon but witnessed countless beautiful sunsets on my runs. I'll never forget the saturated waiting blue haze of the sea. I finished the book and though the lesson was a hard one to take, it prompted a revolution in my career, a dark and cathartic realisation of where I'm going as a writer. It's a neat reversal, and a nice gift from the fates, that the heavy, monolithic work of fiction I went here to perfect once and for all wound up being dismantled and overhauled in subsequent years. Meanwhile it's this, a distillation of the diaries I scribbled effortlessly in all my Il Prato notebooks, which ends up being published. I found some brilliant girlfriends and along the way I learned to 'be less rigid', in the oft-repeated words of Stef and Ginevra – a revolutionary change for someone as stiff as me. For various reasons I'd been low in London but now I feel calm, less prone to the dark side, one step closer to The Path or The Way or whatever it is that my vocation wants me to do. And I encountered, still in their original places, not ripped out for a distant museum, some of the most beautiful art I've ever seen – my first and deepest passion. No other city could give me that.

The next morning I wake up at five, collect my bags and take the vaporetto to Piazzale Roma. There's no one else on the boat or the streets and the sun hasn't risen yet. Everything – sky, water, mist, buildings – is a soft blue-grey and there's no sound except for the vaporetto engine grating as it turns. The journey doesn't take long but because of the endless stretch of water on one side and the silent, mistily concealed buildings on the other it resembles an Ancient Greek allegorical dreamscape, a scene the pensive returning hero might travel through after wrestling his demons. Hundreds of years ago, travellers on this route saw and felt much the same thing. Venice hasn't changed, and that is both its worst crime and its greatest attraction.